Praise for
Quit Your Day Job!

"While there are always a few charmed souls, most career-bent writers are destined to struggle. Jim Denney has been there, done that. Read his book and save yourself much of the anguish."

—James N. Frey, author of *How to Write a Damn Good Novel*

"Wow! Jim Denney has written the definitive primer on freelance writing. If you think the writer's life is for you, you must read *Quit Your Day Job.*"

—Angela Hunt, author of *The Canopy*

"I've been writing for a living for well over a decade, and still I found a treasure trove of nuggets, tips and inspiration in Jim Denney's book. *Quit Your Day Job* is an essential resource for the serious writer—the one who truly wants to make a living at it and is willing to work hard. Follow Jim Denney's suggestions and you will be well on your way to making the dream a reality."

—James Scott Bell, award winning novelist and *Writers Digest* contributing editor.

"Jim Denney has written a book that every writer and every aspiring writer should own. Extremely well-organized, up-to-date information with helpful lists, guidelines, a glossary, and extensive index, yet it reads more like a novel than a how-to book. Denney's anecdotes are full of humor, wisdom, and insight a writer can take to the bank."

—Deborah Raney, award-winning author of *A Scarlet Cord* and *Beneath a Southern Sky*

Quit Your Day Job!

*How to sleep late, do what you enjoy,
and make a ton of money as a writer*

Jim Denney

Sanger, California

Printed in the United States of America
Published by Quill Driver Books/Word Dancer Press, Inc.
1831 Industrial Way #101
Sanger, California 93657
559-876-2170 • 1-800-497-4909 • FAX 559-876-2180
QuillDriverBooks.com
Info@QuillDriverBooks.com

Quill Driver Books titles may be purchased in quantity at special discounts for educational, fund-raising, business, or promotional use. Please contact Special Markets, Quill Driver Books/Word Dancer Press, Inc. at the above address or at 1-800-497-4909.

Quill Driver Books/Word Dancer Press, Inc. project cadre:
Doris Hall, Susan Klassen, John David Marion, Cheree McCloud,
Pam McCully, Stephen Blake Mettee, Brigitte Phillips, Linda Kay Weber

First Printing

To order another copy of this book, please call
1-800-497-4909

To
Ray Bradbury and Harlan Ellison.
Their stories awakened in me
the dream of being a writer.

Library of Congress Cataloging-in-Publication Data
Denney, James D.
Quit your day job : how to sleep late, do what you enjoy, and make a ton of money as a writer / by Jim Denney.
p. cm.
ISBN 1-884956-04-11.
Authorship--Vocational guidance.
I. Title.PN153 .D46 2002808'.02'023--dc21

2002008622

Contents

ACKNOWLEDGMENTS

I want to thank the writers and other experts who generously shared their insights with me, filling the gaps in my knowledge with their wisdom and experience:

Piers Anthony	Dennis E. Hensley
James Scott Bell	Vicki Hinze
Leonard Bishop	Angela Elwell Hunt
David Brin	Kelly James-Enger
Robert Darden	Ros Jay
Bert Decker	Dave Lambert
Dru Scott Decker	Deborah Raney
Beatrice Gormley	Robert J. Sawyer
Robin Lee Hatcher	Janelle Schneider

I especially want to thank my publisher at Quill Driver Books, Stephen Blake Mettee for his belief in this book. I am continually amazed at the time and energy he selflessly devotes to encouraging and developing writers through the William Saroyan Writers Conference and in so many other ways. Steve genuinely loves writers, he understands their struggles and aspirations, and he wants to see them succeed.

Thanks also to Steve's hard-working team at Quill Driver Books, especially David Marion and Brigitte Phillips, who have both been so supportive to me.

Finally, thanks to my wife Debbie, daughter Bethany, and son Ryan, who have been alongside me throughout my writing career. They are my encouragers and my inspiration.

A Holy Calling

"If a young writer can refrain from writing, he shouldn't hesitate to do so."
*Poet-dramatist **André Gide***

"If you *can* be discouraged, you *will* be discouraged. Quit now and you'll save a lot of time."
*Novelist **David Gerrold***

I WAS NINE YEARS OLD when I wrote my first short story as a class assignment. It was a three-page suspense story about an innocent man escaping from prison. My teacher read it to the class. Later that same school year, I wrote a story about a rocket ship crashing on Mars—and at that point I *knew* I wanted to write for a living.

At age eleven, all I wanted for Christmas was a toy printing press I had seen on TV. I had big plans. I would write my own books, set them up in type, staple them together, and become an eleven-year-old author-publisher. On Christmas morning, there it was—my own printing press, made of red and yellow plastic, with a bag of rubber letters you positioned by hand. Problem was, there was only enough type for five or six sentences (in ALL CAPS yet). I could scarcely set one complete thought in rubber type before I was out of E's and O's.

My favorite haunt was the public library. I even loved the *smell* of the library. Some would say it's a musty odor, a whiff of old vellum and bindery glue. But to me, it's the scent of adventure, discovery, and endless pleasures on long summer afternoons between the fifth and sixth grades.

I've always loved the feel of a book in my hands. The weight of a book is the substance of an author's thoughts pressing against your flesh. Old books are the best—books printed by the antique letterpress method, from type cast in hot metal on Linotype machines. Run your fingers over the page and you can feel the indentations made by the metal letters as they pressed the ink into the paper. Those books always held a holy fascination for me. They were filled with words so important and so powerful they were cast in metal and assembled on the page in soldierly rows.

I started writing for pay as soon as I left college. Throughout my twenties and early thirties, I pursued my craft as a sideline on evenings and weekends, writing for magazines and newsletters. By age thirty-six, I had six published books to my credit. When people asked me what I did for a living, I would hesitate, then say, "I have a graphic arts business—typesetting, illustrating, advertising—"

Notice, I did *not* say, "I'm a writer." Even after six published books, I didn't see myself as a writer, but as someone who wanted to be a writer *someday*.

But that was the year I was forced to either become a writer or let go of the dream. It was 1989, and I saw that our graphic arts business would soon be put out of business by emerging desktop publishing technology. My choices were clear: I could either jump into writing with both feet, or I could take a day job in an ad agency somewhere. I had already been self-employed for ten years, so the insecurity of self-employment didn't trouble my sleep. But I also had a wife, two small children, and a mortgage, so I knew it wasn't going to be easy.

While pondering my decision, I called a couple of writers I knew. Both had been freelancing for more than ten years, so I asked their advice. The first one, Al, had over thirty books to his credit, both as a ghostwriter and a sole author. He had no encouragement to offer me. "You called me just as I'm quitting the freelance life and going in-house as an editor," he said. "I'm still writing on the side, but I need a steady paycheck. I just can't take the uncertainty anymore. You want my advice? Don't even *think* of full-time writing unless you have at least a year's worth of living expenses saved up. Better yet, two years' worth."

The second writer I called was Bob, a veteran freelancer with over five million copies of his various titles in print. Despite his success, he wrote in his spare time, evenings and weekends, and he urged me to do the same. "Don't quit your day job," he told me. "Write in your spare time and make sure you have a regular paycheck." Not much encouragement there either.

Around the same time, I exchanged e-mails with an award-winning science fiction writer. "You're going full time?" he wrote. "Hope you have a high tolerance for insecurity." He told me that the bank had taken back his house during his second year as a full-time writer—but he wished me luck nonetheless.

Each of those writers had given me sound advice which could be summarized as, *Don't even think about writing for a living.* They had been there. They knew. I knew they were right—but I didn't follow their advice. I couldn't. I had come to the realization that I *had* to write. So I did. Fourteen years later, I'm still here, still pounding out books for a living—and I haven't missed a house payment yet.

But it hasn't been easy.

Right up front, I want to give you the same advice those other writers gave me when I first set out on this journey: If you can live without being a writer, if you can be happy and satisfied doing something else for a living—*then do something else.* I mean that sincerely. Don't quit your day job if you can do anything else with your life and still be happy. You shouldn't write for a living unless you simply can't do anything *but* write.

Since I was a boy, I have known that I *have to* write. If you're nodding your head, if you know what I'm talking about, if you, too, *have to* write, then this book will speed you on your journey.

WHY WRITE?

If you are a civil servant at the Federal Trade Commission or the White House—as I was before I became a freelance writer—you can sit at your desk and shoot the breeze with your boss and get paid. You can take sick days and get paid. The momentum of the organization takes up the slack of individuals. Income is to a large extent severed from output.

Freelance writers get paid absolutely zero if they do not produce. (They often get paid zero even if they *do* produce.) They stand no chance of paying the mortgage and feeding the kids if they have not ground out the pages to sell.

Benjamin J. Stein
Wall Street Journal, *April 3, 1989*

Do you have to be a little crazy to want to write for a living? Humorist-publisher Bennett Cerf thought so. "Samuel Taylor Coleridge was a drug addict," he once observed. "Edgar Allan Poe was an alcoholic. Christopher Marlowe was killed by a man he was trying to stab. Alexander Pope took money to keep a woman's name out of a satire, then wrote the piece so that she could still be recognized. The poet Thomas Chatterton killed himself. Lord Byron was accused of incest. Do you still want to a writer? And if so, why?"

Why indeed? Think about it: Why *do* you want to be a writer?

Do you want to get rich? Do you want to become famous? Okay, it could happen. Don't bet the farm on it, but it's possible. If you're smart, tough, tenacious, hard working, and talented, you can make a comfortable living as a writer. If you have a touch of genius or if you are just plain lucky, you can win the literary lottery and become the next J. K. Rowling or Stephen King (genius category) or the next James Redfield (author of the tripe best-seller, *The Celestine Prophecy*—he's crazy-lucky).

Personally, I don't write for riches or fame. True, I want to make a good living for myself and my family, and I've achieved that (more or less). If I go on to write a million-seller, all the better. But that's not why I write.

So why would anyone want to become a full-time writer? I can only think of three valid reasons:

(1) *You have something important to say*—and you are willing to spend the rest of your life saying it.

(2) *You are in love with the adventure of writing.* To you, a blank computer screen is an entire universe waiting to be explored—a window on love and hate, reality and fantasy, drama and comedy, good and evil, God and humanity, the nobility of death and the meaning of life. You know that writing is nothing less than the transfer of meaning, emotion, and imagination from one soul to another through the power of the printed page—and you know there is no better way to live than living to write.

(3) *You can't keep from writing.* For you, writing is an itch you've got to scratch, a hunger you've got to feed, a life you've got to live. In fact, you don't truly feel you are living *unless* you are writing.

Those are powerful motivations—and you'll need them. You'll need every ounce of motivation you can muster to persevere through the self-doubt, the rejection, and the lean times that are part of every writer's life. You may be enormously talented, brimming with dazzling ideas, and loaded with charm and enthusiasm—but that's not enough to make you a successful writer.

Talent alone doesn't make you a writer. Ideas don't. Perseverance helps—a lot of perseverance. Add to that some luck, timing, a connection or two, and your odds of surviving as a working writer start to look a little less dismal. But if you *really* want to make a living as a full-time writer, the one thing you need, above all else, is a *plan*. You've got to have a deliberate, carefully thought-out strategy for getting published, and you should work that strategy every day of your life. In this book, you'll find a roadmap to that plan.

Natalie Goldberg's *Writing Down the Bones* is a book of exercises and advice for would-be writers—a touchy-feely writer's workshop between soft covers. I have mixed emotions about that book, because it contains some good advice, some not-so-good advice, and some advice that, if you follow it, will probably ruin you as a writer. The worst piece of advice comes at the end of the book, where Goldberg quotes her Zen instructor:

> Katagiri Roshi once told me, "That's very nice if they want to publish you, but don't pay too much attention to it. It will toss you away. Just continue to write."[1]

My friend, you not only must pay attention to getting published, you must be *focused* on it, *obsessed* with it, *fanatical* about it. If anything will "toss you away," it is writing without a deliberate plan for getting published. Writing for a living requires the discipline of writing daily with the *express intention* of selling what you write.

True, you won't sell everything you write. Even the best and most accomplished writers get rejected. Ray Bradbury once said, "I get rejection slips every week of my life. I've published thirty-five stories in *Playboy* magazine, but in recent years they've rejected eight short stories. And *The New Yorker* rejects every time I submit."[2]

Even though much of what you write will never be published, publication *should* be the goal of *everything* you write. When you write with the intent to be published, you force yourself to think like an editor, an agent, a reader. You learn something about your craft that you could never learn any other way. When you write for publication, you know that every idea, every paragraph, every sentence will be given a critical evaluation. You know your work will be judged on how well you entertain, inform, enlighten, inspire, and enthrall. This knowledge imposes a discipline and concentration on your work that generates improvement, learning—and paychecks.

There is only one way you will ever be able to write for a living: You must write words that people will pay money to read. If you do that, you'll make a living as a writer. If you don't, you won't—simple as that. The money you make as a writer represents more than just the ability to pay the mortgage and buy groceries. It is the writer's strongest and finest affirmation. It is tangible proof that someone thinks your words are worth purchasing and paying attention to.

There is nothing crass or ignoble about trading your writing for money. Your words *are* your stock in trade. Doctors sell their medical knowledge for money, lawyers sell their legal knowledge for money, and you sell words. If they are good words—well-chosen, skillfully crafted, filled with ideas and energy—the world will buy them. You prove your own craftsmanship by writing saleable words. It's a great feeling to receive a check for a publisher's advance, but it's an even greater feeling to receive a royalty check, because that means that it is not just the publisher who likes your words; the public is willing to pay money to read them.

It is that feeling that enables you to say, boldly and unabashedly, "I am a writer."

LIVING ON GRUB STREET

There is no more disgruntled pilgrim on Grub Street than an author of a freshly published book. The labor is over but the torment has just begun, as the newborn creature is wrenched untimely from the nest. "Mind-children," Mary McCarthy named the author's progeny. "Product," the industry calls them, or "stock," as in "signing stock" at a bookstore "drop in."

Carol Brightman (Sweet Chaos, Fat Trip)
New York Times, *March 7, 1999*

In the Moorfields section of London is a street now called Milton

Street. But before 1830, it had another name: Grub Street. Famed as a hub for impoverished literary hacks, Grub Street was once described by Dr. Samuel Johnson as "much inhabited by writers of small histories, dictionaries, and temporary poems." Dr. Johnson should know. After quitting his poorly paid job as a schoolmaster, he served a stint as a Grub Street hack himself, before rising to literary prominence in the mid-eighteenth century.

Today, Grub Street is a metaphor describing all of us in this honorable but underpaid community of working writers. By "working writer," I mean a person who is a full-time, freelance writer by trade. A "working writer," as I use the term, is *not* someone who has a job with a newspaper or magazine, and draws a paycheck every two weeks. I'm not disparaging such people, because they certainly do work and they certainly do write. But as I define the term "working writer," I've got to draw the line somewhere, and that's where I draw it. By my definition, a working writer is one who gets paid by the piece or by the contract, who draws no salary or benefits, and who is completely self-employed.

> "My friend, you not only must pay attention to getting published, you must be *focused* on it, *obsessed* with it, *fanatical* about it."

I'm a Grub Streeter myself—cheerfully and proudly so. I am a working writer, a freelance wordsmith, and a good one. Writing is my day job, and I wouldn't have it any other way.

One thing I've noticed as a writer is that, when people find out what I do for a living, they often say, "I always wanted to be a writer," or, "I bet I could write a book if I put my mind to it." The people who tell you such things might be pizza delivery guys or doctors or astronauts, yet they all admire writers and they all have a secret wish that they could write. They all think they could do what you do if they had the time or the opportunity or if their lives were different somehow.

But you know what? I've never met a writer anywhere who wanted to be anything other than a writer. Take any person who says, "I am a writer," and I don't care how penniless he is, how long it has been since his last paycheck, how much he struggles with self-doubt, writer's block, and unreasonable deadlines—he does not, even for a moment, consider changing jobs. Why? Because writing is not a job. It's a mission. It's a calling. It's more essential to your soul than a career. It is not just your profession—it's your *identity*.

A computer programmer can go to seminary and become a preacher. A schoolteacher can tender her resignation and become an exotic dancer. But can a writer give up writing and become something else? Unheard of! Writing is not what you do, it's who you are! If you are a writer, there is nothing else to be.

If you know in your bones what I'm talking about, if you know that you *have* to be a writer, then *you must write*. You only get one life, and the life you've been given is made up of a finite number of heartbeats. Between your first heartbeat and your last is a brief span of time in which you are permitted to write your books and speak your piece. When your time is up, they will put you in a box and throw you in a hole to make room for the next writer waiting in line on Grub Street.

Now is your time, my friend. If you're going to write your books, you'd better get at it.

"But," you ask, "what about my age? Am I too young to be a full-time writer? Am I too old?" Whatever age you are, *right now* is the time to go for it. If you are young—say, in your twenties—you have the advantage of having fewer debts and responsibilities to tie you down and restrict your options. If you are in your forties or beyond, then you have a whole different set of advantages, including a wealth of experience and accumulated wisdom.

Science-fiction writer David Brin is the author of such books as *Earth*, *Kiln People*, and *The Postman* (which was made into a motion picture starring Kevin Costner). Brin earned a Ph.D. in space physics at UC San Diego and held positions with the Jet Propulsion Laboratory in Pasadena and NASA's Specialized Center of Research and Training (NSCORT-Exobiology) before he turned to writing science fiction. He gained an enormous amount of life experience before turning to full-time writing.

"Writing is a worthy calling," Brin told me, "but it was not my first choice as a profession. I wanted to be a scientist, foremost, and I became one through hard work. I also had this hobby—writing—that provided a lot of satisfaction. I always figured that I'd write a few stories a year, and a novel every few years, while mainly working to become the best scientist and teacher I could be. But it turned out that I'm much better at making up vivid stories than I ever was at discovering new truths as a scientist. At least, that's what people say—and they sure pay me better to write novels than they ever did to do science!"

So, there's no such thing as being too old to turn to writing as a career? "Of course not," Brin says. "The best writers I know did something else for many years first. They lived life and did useful things and interesting things, before presuming to preach and write about the human experience."

The net-net: Whether you're young or old, don't let age hold you back. If you are young and unencumbered, you have little to lose by giving it a shot. And, if you are older and more experienced, you have a lot to offer the world as a full-time writer. Either way, *now* is your time. What are you waiting for?

SLEEP LATE, DO WHAT YOU ENJOY, MAKE A TON OF MONEY

It's common for laymen to regard writers as self-indulgent, rather indolent people who like to sleep late, work in their pajamas, and earn their living in fits and starts. Writers don't have their taxes withheld, which makes them almost un-American.

Novelist **Francine Matthews** (Jane Austen *mystery series and* The Secret Agent)

Every weekend writer dreams of turning part-time scribbling into a lucrative career. This book is your roadmap to that dream, written by someone who has been living it for years. I'm not going to throw any hype or hyperbole at you. I'm going to give it to you straight: This "dream" can be a nightmare at times—but if it were easy, any schmo could do it.

But you're not any schmo, or you wouldn't still be reading. You've got the grit and perseverance to push through the lean times, the struggles, the doubts. I've written this book for you because you want it straight, no chaser—a candid, no-nonsense exposé of the daily grind of the writer's life, with all the potholes and pitfalls clearly marked. In these next few chapters, you'll learn the secrets of building a writing career amid the harsh realities of the publishing business. Here are just a few of those realities:

• **Writing is hard work.** Writing for a living is about meeting unreasonable deadlines, waiting weeks or months to get paid, and pounding out your daily allotment of verbiage whether you feel inspired or not. To anyone who thinks writers spend their mornings sipping lattés at Cafe Nervosa, their evenings at cocktail parties, hobnobbing with the literati, and writing only when the spirit moves them, I say, "Don't quit your day job."

• **Rejection is the norm.** Writers dream of acceptance— yet the daily reality of the writer's life is rejection. It's nothing personal. Rejection just *is*. To survive, you learn to screen it out and keep moving forward. If you can't stand rejection, find another line of work. But if you can stay focused and optimistic, believing in yourself even after a hundred rejections, then you've got what it takes to make it.

• **Your bills must be paid on a monthly basis; your paycheck is not.** The bank wants your mortgage payment on the first of the month, even though you haven't gotten a paycheck in five months. When you get a check from a publisher, you have to make it last four, five, six months until your next check. What do you do when the money doesn't stretch that far? Now *that's* when you discover how creative you *really* are.

• **Taxes eat you alive.** Just when you think you've managed to make ends meet, Uncle Sam comes along, grabs you by the scruff of the neck, and demands his cut. Did you set Uncle Sam's vig aside so you can pay your quarterlies? Or do you owe him the entire chunk, plus interest and penalties, on April 15? Remember, you are self-employed now, so you must pay not just the employee's portion of the Social Security and Medicare tax, but the employer's portion as well. Welcome to the wonderful world of the self-employed.

• **You pay for everything out of your own pocket.** Another one of the joys of being self-employed is that you have the privilege of paying for your own health insurance, pension plan, and all those other good things your employer used to do for you. There's no union. There are no paid vacations, holidays, or sick leave.

You may read all that and think, "Yeah, yeah, yeah, I know writing is a tough racket. But I'm good, and I'll make a living at it, no problem."

Look, you may *think* you know how hard it is to write for a living, but friend, until you've done it, you haven't a clue. Think I'm blowing smoke? Well, maybe you'll believe it if you hear it from Harlan Ellison (author of *Angry Candy* and *Slippage*):

I make a decent living—Stephen King could buy and sell me a million times over, and he deserves it, he's a good guy, and that's fine—but I'm still more successful than most writers. I make a better-than-average living. I'm considered in the first percentile of moneymaking writers in the country. That's only because there's so little money to be made that being in the first percentile doesn't mean squat. Nonetheless, I have had to loan out vast amounts of money to my friends who are writers, because they're all starving. We've got about 85 grand out in loans, and we know we're never gonna see it again, but it's okay—you should never loan money unless you're prepared never to get it back. But I look around at my friends, at writers I admire and have admired for decades, and I see them drowning![3]

> "When you get a check from a publisher, you have to make it last four, five, six months until your next check. What do you do when the money doesn't stretch that far? Now *that's* when you discover how creative you *really* are."

Don't get me wrong—for all the drawbacks and pitfalls, I still believe that the writer's life is the best life of all. You never have to wear a watch, much less a suit and tie. You don't have to carry a cell phone. Your daily commute is a stroll down the hall. You can take off to be at your kids' ball games without asking the boss. You can set your own hours, work a night shift if you want. You can write in your pajamas, your underwear, or your birthday suit if you like (I'm partial to blue jeans and a T-shirt). When you are a writer, you really can sleep late, do what you enjoy, and yes, you *can* make a ton of money.

And you know what the best part of it is? You never have to retire!

No one is every going to give you a gold watch and put you out to pasture. People in ordinary jobs can't wait for retirement; writers can't imagine why anyone would want to stop working. I don't know about you, but I intend to keep writing until they find me slumped over my keyboard at age 102, with the words "The End" glimmering on my computer screen. Crime writer Mickey Spillane (*I, The Jury*) put it this way: "If you're a singer, you lose your voice. A baseball player loses his arm. A writer gets more knowledge, and if he's good, the older he gets, the better he writes."

> "Writers dream of acceptance—yet the daily reality of the writer's life is rejection. It's nothing personal. Rejection just *is*."

Robert Darden is a writer whose books range from business (*Secret Recipe: Why KFC Is Still Cooking After 50 Years*) to religious (*I, Jesus*) to the outrageously funny (*On the Eighth Day God Laughed*). "The advantages of being a freelance writer," Darden told me, "are the freedom and the power—which are the same thing. If I want to do a travel article in the middle of the fall, I can. If the *National Enquirer* calls for a story, and they have, and I don't feel right about it, I can say no— and I have. Even though I only get to eat what I kill, I'm still working for myself to a great degree. Plus I'm here when the kids get home from school. There are no benefits, no retirement plan, no security, no guarantees—but in my mind, the advantages of being a writer far outweigh the disadvantages."

Business writer Ros Jay (*Winning Minds: The Ultimate Book of Inspirational Business Leaders*) also defines the advantages of full-time writing in terms of freedom: "The plus points for me are working for myself and not on someone else's payroll, freedom over the amount of work I take on, freedom to work the hours I choose, and freedom to take time off if I need to—even if I have to make it up elsewhere."

Freedom! Yes, there is no life more free than the life of a freelance writer! But I'll bet that neither Robert Darden nor Ros Jay stopped to weigh the practical advantages and disadvantages of the writing life before they took that plunge. I know for a fact that Jim Denney didn't. And, I'm betting you didn't either.

Sometimes the need to write becomes so strong that you resent the time you spend *not* writing—and in particular, you resent your day job. That's the feeling described by romantic suspense writer Vicki Hinze, author of *Duplicity* (St. Martin's, 1999) and *Lady Liberty* (Bantam, 2001). I asked her when she knew it was time to take the plunge into full-time writing. "When I began resenting my day job," she replied, "feeling that it was taking time away from what I *really* wanted to do—write. I took a 'go for it because you love it and the money will come' leap of faith and just did it. A ton of hard work and a touch of luck later, it paid off. There have been a lot of exciting moments since then. The first sale was probably the most exciting—but, truthfully, it's only marginally more so than the second through the fourteenth."

As writers, we can't be satisfied if we are not doing what we were meant to do. "As a writer," says Hinze, "you have the opportunity to touch lives, to open doors in minds that had been closed. That's a powerful life's work for any human being. When you do what you were meant to do in life, you're content and at ease with yourself."

No one decides to write because the hours are good, and no one decides *not* to write because there's no dental plan. The drive to write springs from the need to fulfill our highest purpose, to make a difference in the world, to achieve something meaningful and even noble. If you are truly a *writer*, nothing can keep you from writing. You *write*, regardless of cost, hardships, or obstacles—end of story.

"I would not know how to advise a man how to write," C. S. Lewis once observed. "It is a matter of talent and interest. I believe he must be strongly moved if he is to become a writer. Writing is like a 'lust,' or like 'scratching when you itch.' Writing comes as a result of a very strong impulse, and when it does come, I for one must get it out."[4]

I've always had that itch. You've got it, too. So we write, you and I. We absolutely *have* to write, just like we have to eat and drink and breathe. It's in the blood. It's in the soul.

If you approach writing for a living as a *job*, you'll be miserable—guaranteed. The sputtering cash flow, lack of benefits, and bouts of anxiety and insecurity will kill your spirit and leave you convinced that writing is the worst job on the planet.

But if you approach writing as a *holy calling*, you will be happy every day of your writing life, whether the money is there or not, whether the bills are paid or not, whether you are ahead of deadline or hopelessly snowed under. When writing is not just a job but a *calling*, nothing else matters but the excellence of the work, the beauty of the words, the power of the ideas. You can block out anxiety, pressure, self-doubt, insecurity, and bill collectors, because you are following your holy calling, you are creating your holy writ, you are working holy miracles through the dance of your fingertips upon the keyboard. You are doing what you were born to do.

You know what I'm talking about. That's why you bought this book. That's why you're still reading. So go ahead. Turn the page.

Hold on tight, my friend. Your life is about to change.

Taking the Leap

A professional writer is an amateur who didn't quit.
Richard Bach, *author of* Jonathan Livingston Seagull

I've come to the conclusion that if you do what you *love* to do and *must* do in the world, the Universe will send you a living—*but it's a damned slim living!*
Writer-editor Judith Merrill

IF I HAD IT TO DO ALL OVER AGAIN, here's how I would launch my writing career: I would start out while I'm young, single, and debt-free. I'd rent myself a tiny garret in the city, or maybe an outbuilding on some farm. I'd live on rice and beans, and sell my blood to buy postage stamps and typing paper. I'd live on the cheap until I got established, and I'd write my brains out every day. Finally, I'd produce a string of best-sellers and live happily ever after.

The dream of "overnight success" sustains most of us here on Grub Street. We pound out our stories and books on an assembly line, satisfied with the fact that we are making a living doing what we love. But in the back of our minds is the story of the writer who had that incredible breakthrough, when every word, every keystroke turned to gold! The dream of sudden success keeps us going through the tough times, the impossible deadlines, the innumerable rejections of this business. The dream reminds us that there is no limit to what a working writer can achieve, no ceiling to our aspirations. If we can dream it, we just might make it happen.

One of the most dramatic breakthrough stories is that of

Joanne Kathleen Rowling. J. K. Rowling is, of course, the author of *Harry Potter and the Sorcerer's Stone* (Scholastic Books, 1998). After completing a degree in French at Exeter University, Rowling wrote part-time while working as a researcher for Amnesty International. The result: two unpublished novels and a trunk full of unpublished stories. Then, during a 1990 train trip from Manchester to London, she was suddenly seized by the idea of an orphan boy with magical powers. As the train carried her along, the storyline and characters took shape. Stepping off the train at King's Cross Station, she had a fully formed outline of an international best-seller in her mind.

Tragically, the year Harry Potter was conceived was also a year of tremendous loss for Jo Rowling. In 1990, Rowling lost her job, her home was burglarized, and her mother died of multiple sclerosis. In 1992, Rowling moved to Portugal where she taught English as a second language. She married a TV journalist in Portugal, but the marriage soon fell apart and Rowling took her four-month-old daughter Jessica and settled in Edinburgh, Scotland.

Rowling spent a year on public assistance while looking for a teaching job. Every day, she left her unheated flat, took Jessica to a café, ordered a cup of coffee, and wrote out the adventures of Harry Potter in longhand. Once she had Harry's story typed up, she submitted it to a number of British publishers, where it met a stone wall of rejection. She had landed a teaching position by the time the book sold to Bloomsbury Children's Books of London, and she continued teaching after the book sold (the $4,000 advance didn't justify quitting her day job).

Harry Potter and the Sorcerer's Stone was greeted with almost instant success in Great Britain (the British edition was titled *Harry Potter and the Philosopher's Stone*). Then Scholastic purchased the American rights for over $100,000—the kind of advance that makes all things possible. Rowling quit her teaching job, became a full-time writer, and produced a chain of sequels: *Harry Potter and the Chamber of Secrets*, *Harry Potter and the Prisoner of Azkaban*, *Harry Potter and the Goblet of Fire*, and *Harry Potter and the Order of the Phoenix*. When *Azkaban* was released in late 1999, Jo Rowling owned the three top slots on the *New York Times* best-seller list. Today there are 200 million Harry Potter books in print.

An overnight sensation? Absolutely. An overnight success? Hardly. It took Jo Rowling seven years to guide Harry from conception to publication—seven years of scribbling by hand in cafés, submitting and being rejected, enduring destitution and sacrifice. Rowling's "overnight success" was years in the making—but the payoff was incalculable.

It could happen to you.

Are you ready to reach for that goal? Are you ready to focus on that dream and pursue it for all you're worth? If you are, then there is no limit to the successes and rewards that may be waiting for you.

I've prepared a checklist—ten crucial questions about your life, your habits, and your emotional makeup. If you can honestly answer "Yes" to each of these questions, then you can truly say, "I'm ready to go for the dream. I'm ready to quit my day job and write for a living."

Here's the checklist:

• **Do you have sufficient savings or other sources of income to carry you through the lean times?** When I went into full-time writing, my answer to this question was "No." I survived—barely. I want you to approach your writing career more intelligently than I approached mine.

Your financial safety net could come in any number of shapes and sizes: savings and investments, an early retirement incentive from your present employer, a working spouse who will lovingly support your dream, a gift from a generous benefactor. Some writers scrimp and save for a year or two and sock away a year's worth of living expenses, then plunge into full-time writing for a year. You have to do what works for you. Just make sure you have an adequate safety net in place before you take the plunge.

• **Can you handle stress and financial insecurity?** Be brutally honest. Ask yourself, "Can I handle the insecurity of writing full time?" If the answer to that question is "No," well, that's okay, you can still write part-time.

Fact is, some people are actually *more* productive when they have *less* free time to write. They know that the anxiety and insecurity of the working writer's life would only dry up their creative juices, so they hang onto the regular paycheck and the 401(k). Some find that having a restricted amount of writing time actually makes them more focused and creative during the limited time they do have. Give them a full day to write and they'd just procrastinate. So they write evenings and weekends, or on the commuter train—and it works for them.

But I didn't write this book for those people. I wrote it for people who really want to write for a living—that is, for people who can tolerate the uncertainties of a writer's life. "You have to have a pretty high threshold for financial insecurity," says novelist Lawrence Block. "If a regular paycheck is emotionally essential to you, perhaps you'd be well advised to stay with a regular job."[1] If you know in your heart that you can handle the insecurity, then you have one of the crucial ingredients of a full-time writer.

Of course, during the early years of your writing career, while you are getting established, there are things you can do to reduce your level of insecurity and anxiety: Budget ruthlessly. Live frugally. Build up savings and investments. Pay off high-interest debt, such as credit cards and finance companies. Shop smart for food, clothing, and entertainment. When a big check comes in, use it to eliminate debt. Make sure that check will carry you through the next few weeks or months until the next check arrives. That takes discipline and maturity.

Bestselling novelist Robert J. Sawyer (*Calculating God* and *The Terminal Experiment;* website at www.sfwriter.com) has demonstrated a high tolerance for uncertainty throughout his adult life. "The last full-time job I had," he says, "was when I was twenty-three, in 1983, working at a university; I've been a full-time writer ever since. My advice is if you can't meet your monthly expenses for at least six months, and preferably a year, just on savings with no additional income, it's probably too early to safely go full time. But, then again, it all depends on how comfortable with risk you are. If you've got kids, or a spouse still in school, you've got to be fiscally conservative. If you don't have kids, then you can afford to take more chances and go full time earlier."

• **Do you write at least an hour a day, every day?** Until you're ready to take the plunge, you should "test-drive" a writing career. You do that by writing as much as you can, mornings, evenings, and weekends. In the process, you will develop the discipline that will serve you well in a full-time career.

How can you call yourself a writer if you are not writing *at least* an hour a day in your spare time? Frankly, two hours a day or more would show you really mean business. "Don't you dare complain that you don't have the time to write," says Robert J. Sawyer. "Real writers *buy* the time, if they can't get it any other way. Take Toronto's Terence M. Green, a high school English teacher. His third novel, *Shadow of Ashland*, just came out from Tor. Terry takes every fifth year off from teaching without pay so that he can write; most writers I know have made similar sacrifices for their art."[2]

If you can't *find* time to write, *make* time. Get up an hour earlier or go to bed an hour later. If you're not writing an hour a day—*bare minimum*—you haven't developed the discipline and focus to write full time.

• **Are you submitting what you write on a regular basis?** In other words, are you actively and aggressively trying to sell what you write? Many people put a lot of hours into their writing, but they never seem to produce a finished product and take it to market. They obsessively write and rewrite and re-rewrite, but they never manage to get that story, article, query, or book proposal off to a publisher. If you aren't submitting, then you aren't selling. And if you aren't selling, you can't make a living as a writer.

> "How can you call yourself a writer if you are not writing *at least* an hour a day in your spare time? Frankly, two hours a day or more would show you really mean business."

Kelly James-Enger is a writing coach and a full-time freelance writer who has written on health, fitness, relationships, and business for many top magazines. Her website (www.kellyjamesenger.com) features a wealth of information and ideas for people who want to write. She saved up six months' worth of living expenses, then quit her day job as a lawyer to write full time. With her first round of submissions, she used what she calls the "saturation bombing" approach. "I pitched every magazine I could think of with any idea that seemed appropriate. While this led to lots of queries, I wasn't getting many assignments."

Kelly decided to try a more focused approach. "I realized it would be more effective to concentrate my efforts on a handful of magazines," she says. "Instead of trying to query dozens of magazines, I targeted five or six and focused on cracking them. Once I did so, I started getting more assignments." The first markets she cracked were *Fit*, *Fitness*, and *Bridal Guide*. After selling to each one once, she proceeded to build on those relationships—and her targeted strategy worked. Within a year, she had sold three pieces to *Bridal Guide*, five to *Fit*, and six to *Fitness*.

"I expanded into business writing, mostly brochures and articles for local companies," she adds, "and also began teaching magazine writing classes. I continued writing bridal stories and fitness pieces, but also began focusing on women's health and nutrition. By specializing in these areas, I've cracked magazines like *Woman's Day*, *Family Circle*, *Self*, *Marie Claire*, and *Shape*. I've also developed a network of experts in most of the areas I write about, which is invaluable when pitching and researching stories." The lesson of Kelly James-Enger's experience as a magazine writer: Use a focused, targeted approach with a goal of cracking markets and building relationships with editors. Find your niche, develop it, nurture it, and own it.

What about multiple submissions? Is it okay to submit the same material to several publishers at once? I put this question to Dave Lambert, an editor at Zondervan and the author of a wide range of books, from children's books like *Trouble Times Ten* to the inspirational biography, *Oswald Chambers*.

"Multiple submissions are a common practice today," he told me, "though some publishers still don't accept them. So make sure the house you approach accepts multiple submissions. It's a hair-pulling experience for an editor to shepherd a book for weeks through the acquisitions process, get approval, and make an offer on a book he thought was exclusively his—only to find that the author has just signed with another house. It colors the editor's attitude toward that author from then on. That kind of ill-feeling can be avoided by explaining in the cover letter that you're submitting to other houses as well. If you get a bite from one house, be sure to let the others know."

• **Do you have at least two different editors or publishers that regularly give you assignments or buy your work?** When I went full time, I had good, steady working relationships with three book editors and one magazine editor, plus I wrote advertising copy on the side. I had a full schedule. I was very busy. And I still struggled. Why? Because my cash flow sputtered a lot. That's normal. Book publishers pay slowly—and they were my biggest source of income. Magazines paid more quickly, but the checks tended to be small—in the $200 to $600 range.

To achieve anything resembling a steady cash flow, I found that you must have a number of "repeat customers" who regularly, continually accept your work. You have to keep a steady stream of work in the pipeline at all times.

Ros Jay, a freelance writer in England, maintains a steady flow of work by diversifying. She even writes under two distinct bylines. As Ros Jay, she has produced a series of successful business books, including *The Ultimate Book of Business Creativity* and *ExpressExec: Time Management.* And under the name of Roni Jay, she is the author of more "soft-edged" books such as *Gardens of the Spirit, Herbal Wisdom,* and the ultimate cat-lover's book, *The Kingdom of the Cat.* She told me that, from the time she quit her day job as a PR manager, she made sure she had a number of clients who would buy her writing on a steady basis.

> "Instead of trying to query dozens of magazines, I targeted five or six and focused on cracking them. Once I did so, I started getting more assignments."

She began by doing freelance copywriting for a couple of previous employers. "One of my luckiest skills," she says, "is that I work very fast." When one of her previous employers offered her two days' pay for a writing project she could knock out in three hours (while working at home, no less!) she knew she had found her niche. Within a few days of turning freelance, she had three clients. Using her PR skills, she quickly lined up more clients, and soon had her schedule filled with corporate newsletters and magazines, sales materials, annual reports, press releases, and the like. Before long, a book publisher contacted her to edit a book; a few months later, the same publisher asked her to write a book—they had a title but needed an author.

"After that," she recalls, "I found myself writing more and more books, and less of everything else, except that I still write and edit corporate magazines—online as well as print. It pays well, gives me some variety, and helps keep me in touch with the business world I write about in many of my books." Ros Jay's success as a writer is built upon diversification—writing both books and magazine pieces, writing diverse kinds of books for various publishers, and even writing under two different names, each byline serving as a "trademark" for a different "product line."

• **Have you built a reputation as a writer who delivers a quality product on deadline?** One reason I felt confident to go full time in 1989 was that I had six published books to my credit, and I had editors (several book editors and one magazine editor) coming to me, offering me assignments. I had gained a reputation for meeting deadlines, and the quality of my work had made a favorable impression. Over the years, I've often heard editors complain about writers who can't meet deadlines or complete assignments. When you prove yourself dependable and competent, you stand head and shoulders above most of your peers—and you become sought-after by editors.

"A deadline is negative inspiration," observes novelist Rita Mae Brown (*Venus Envy* and *Loose Lips*). "Still, it's better than no inspiration at all." Many writers resent deadlines. Some, in fact, have such a fierce, unreasoning hatred of deadlines that they procrastinate and even sabotage their deadlines. In the process, they sabotage their careers.

I see deadlines as an ally to good writing, because they help to dislodge bad habits, such as obsessive perfectionism. Deadlines also help me to pace and discipline my writing. I set my own mini-deadlines (say, a chapter every three days), and this helps me move steadily and confidently toward the drop-dead date in my contract.

Missed deadlines are the quickest way to tarnish your reputation as a writer. If you see that you're not going to meet your deadline, contact your editor and explain the situation, so he or she can plan around it. An occasional delay of a week or two will probably be forgiven, especially if you keep good communication going with your editor. But a serial offender quickly becomes viewed as unreliable—and undesirable. The more dependable you are, the more work you'll get.

Here are some suggestions for enhancing your reputation for dependability: Chart your upcoming deadlines on a big wall calendar, preferably one that allows you to see the entire year at a glance. Build a time-cushion into your schedule, allowing a few extra weeks between projects—just in case a project takes longer than planned. Set a personal goal of completing your project a week or two early—imagine the reputation you'll achieve if you consistently deliver your assignments ahead of schedule! Reward yourself for delivering early—take a day off with a good book, take in a good movie or a play, or have dinner at your favorite restaurant. Whatever it takes, make sure you build a reputation as a writer who consistently delivers on-time—if not sooner.

• Are you making serious money as a writer? By "serious money," I don't mean you have to be rich (though a seven-figure advance would certainly be a clue that you've hit the big leagues). Rather, I mean that you should be submitting your work to well-paying markets and experiencing a high degree of acceptance. A high level of acceptance from editors suggests three things about you:

(1) You know how to write well enough that editors want to publish what you write; you have demonstrated a high degree of professionalism and excellence in your work.

(2) You know the markets well enough to target your submissions effectively.

(3) You have established enough connections with editors that you are known and appreciated, and your work is welcomed and given a favorable reading.

Robin Lee Hatcher is the Christy Award-winning inspirational author of *Firstborn* and *Ribbon of Years* and a past president of Romance Writers of America. With more than five million books in print, Robin has been published by HarperCollins, Avon, Silhouette, Zondervan, WaterBrook, and various other houses. She recently told me how she made the move from part-timer to full-time novelist.

"I wrote my first nine published novels," she said, "while working a full-time job and, for much of that time, being a single mom. I wrote evenings and weekends. I got whopping advances of around $2,000, although I made pretty good royalties on the back end if I didn't mind waiting a long time to get them—eked out over many years."

Robin wisely understood that she was not yet making serious money—but she was on the brink of doing so. "When I hired my agent in the summer of 1989," she said, "I told her that if she could get me an advance up front that would equal one year's salary, then I would give notice and quit my job to write full time. Given my advances at that time, I thought there was a snowball's chance that she would ever get them to make such an offer.

"Well, she did it. Once the check cleared, I took the plunge. I had one year to prove myself before I had to go out and find another job. That was thirteen years—and thirty-one books—ago."

Does "serious money" guarantee a sense of security? No way. "I was terrified at first," Robin recalls. "But then I remembered that, back in the 1980s, I lost three jobs in a row to the recession. Nothing is guaranteed except God."

Piers Anthony—inventor of strange fantasy worlds and a lover of puns—has had a long-running career as a writer. His most popular series, about the magical world of Xanth, began with *A Spell for Chameleon* (Del Rey, 1977) and continues twenty-five volumes later with such recent titles as *The Dastard*, *Xone of Contention*, and *Swell Foop*. To date, he has had well over a hundred novels published, currently writes three novels a year, and has had twenty-one titles on the *New York Times* best-seller list in the space of a single decade.

> "Missed deadlines are the quickest way to tarnish your reputation as a writer. If you see that you're not going to meet your deadline, contact your editor and explain the situation, so he or she can plan around it."

Born in England, Piers Anthony became a U.S. citizen while serving in the Army in 1958. He held fifteen different jobs ("the hodgepodge of employments typical of writers," he says), from an aide in a mental hospital to a technical writer for an electronics firm. In 1962, his wife agreed to go to work to allow Piers to stay home and write full time—on one condition: If Piers didn't sell anything after a year of writing, he would quit writing and get a full-time job. During that year, he sold two short stories, earning a grand total of $160. He took a position as an English teacher for three years, then "retired" once more when he lost his job. This time, instead of short stories, he concentrated on the longer format of the novel. His first novel, *Cthon*, was published in 1967—and he's been a successful novelist ever since.

I asked Piers what preparations he made for a full-time writing career. His answer: None. His jump to full-time writing, he said, "was set up by the worst day of my life, when I lost my job, my wife lost our third baby stillborn, and a doctor told me my depression was all in my head and that it would pass when I saw that my problems weren't real. The idiot! But without a job, and without a child, I was free to gamble on trying to become a writer while my wife worked to support us. Out of those ashes came my career—in time."

When Piers Anthony took his second shot at writing for a living, he was in a desperation mode, with his back against the wall. But he approached his goals in a more strategic fashion the second time around by concentrating on a more profitable form of writing (novels instead of stories). His novel, *Cthon*, was accepted by the fourth house he submitted it to (only three rejections—not bad!), and it went on to be nominated for both the Hugo and Nebula awards.

Bottom line: To build a writing career, you must think strategically, and you must think "serious money."

• **Have you built the habits, attitudes, and professionalism that a working writer must have to succeed?** Do you have an organized and well-equipped writing workplace? Do you maintain accurate records of income and expenses for business and tax purposes? Do you carefully track manuscript submissions and reports? Do have efficient working routines in place, so that you don't have to "reinvent the wheel" every time you start a new project? Do you have a copy of *Writer's Market*, *The American Directory of Writer's Guidelines*, the latest *Writer's Digest* and *Publishers Weekly*, and other indispensable writer's tools next to your computer for ready reference? If the answer is "Yes," then it's clear that you are serious about your work, you approach it with a professional attitude, and you make an effort to keep up with changes in the industry.

Nonfiction writer Ros Jay describes the essential traits a person needs in order to be successful as a writer: "The ability to work alone most of the time; self-discipline; good time-management skills; the ability to market yourself and your ideas; a recognition that it's a job like any other and not a glamorous or soft option; an understanding that if you can't deliver to the standard required by the deadline stated you won't keep in work for long. None of these, of course, takes into account whether or not you have any talent for writing—but I think these traits are more important than talent."

Absolutely true. I have actually met a surprising number of unpublished writers who are probably a good deal more talented than I am—but they'll never get published. When I've asked them about their disciplines and habits, they've told me they have none. They write only when "inspired." When I've suggested that they need a daily writing routine, they adamantly resist my advice. They have their idealized image of "the writing life" and they don't want the realities of hard work, focus, discipline, and persistence to mess that up.

Writing is a job—a tough and demanding job. You can't succeed as a writer until you understand and accept that fact.

• **Does your mate support your plan to become a working writer?**
The support of your mate is crucial for three reasons:

(1) He or she is going to be along for this rollercoaster ride. Your mate should be made aware of the sacrifice involved, because he or she will be paying the price just as much as you will.

(2) Your mate's emotional support and faith in you will be a big factor in whether or not your plan succeeds.

(3) Your mate may have to go to work or work longer hours in order to provide financial support during the early years of your writing career.

In *On Writing: A Memoir of the Craft*, Stephen King writes this tribute to his wife Tabitha:

> My wife made a crucial difference.... If she had suggested that the time I spent writing stories on the front porch of our rented house on Pond Street or in the laundry room of our rented trailer on Klatt Road in Hermon was wasted time, I think a lot of the heart would have gone out of me. Tabby never voiced a single doubt, however. Her support was a constant, one of the few good things I could take as a given. And whenever I see a first novel dedicated to a wife (or a husband), I smile and think, *There's someone who knows.* Writing is a lonely job. Having someone who believes in you makes a lot of difference.[2]

Absolutely true. I know I couldn't have achieved what I have without the generous support, encouragement, and optimism of my wife, Debbie.

Ros Jay and her writer husband, Rich, also know. Their partnership enables them to be not only full-time writers but full-time parents as well. Ros told me, "I have two small children, aged four and two, and another on the way. We have a baby-sitter who comes to us for four hours in the middle of each weekday. Other than that, my husband, also a freelance writer, looks after the children either in the morning before she arrives, or in the afternoon. I do whichever 'shift' he doesn't. This means we each work six to seven hours a day, and we get to spend about two hours with the children, plus looking after them together before 9 A.M. and after 6 P.M., and at weekends. How many other jobs would enable us to do that?

"What's more, I can take a few months off around the birth of each child—although there are always a few proofs, proposals, and whatever to be done to keep my mind active. And Rich can take a couple of months off too. Again, few jobs afford this kind of flexibility.

> "To build a writing career, you must think strategically, and you must think 'serious money.'"

"It must be said, however, that any time we take off reduces our earnings. And that's the main disadvantage to the writing life—unpredictable earnings. But this goes both ways: A sudden royalty windfall feels as good as a slump in earnings feels bad. Asked to choose between a secure, steady income versus all that freedom, I'll take the freedom."

• **Do you have the emotional temperament to handle the frustrations and annoyances of being a self-employed writer?** Can you be cordial and courteous to an editor who is curt and abrasive? Can you accept rejection without becoming defeated and discouraged? Can you take criticism of your work professionally—not personally?

On one occasion, early in my career, I turned in a book manuscript that I considered very good. I had a lot of bills, and I needed the back end of the advance. I was praying the editor would accept the book on the spot and write me a check by return mail. No such luck. Instead, the editor flew to California and we had a meeting about what was wrong with the book and how to fix it. Though it was a friendly meeting, it was a long, draining, day-long marathon. The net-net: The editor wanted me to cut two chapters because they didn't fit the theme of the rest of the book—just trash 'em. Two other chapters needed heavy rewriting. And I needed to write two new chapters to replace the ones we trashed. The editor wanted the revised manuscript in six weeks.

I was discouraged, to say the least. But I had to admit it: The editor was right. The changes were needed. So I went home and made all the changes as requested—in *three* weeks, not six. The result: It was a good book—so good that half a dozen magazines ran excerpts from it.

You have to accept criticism of your work in a professional way. You have to look at it objectively and recognize that criticism of your work is not criticism of you. Almost every book, story, or article can be improved by a good editor. Part of being a pro is knowing how to accept criticism, implement it, and make the work as good as it can be.

I once had a phone conversation with an agent, and he asked what books I had done. I mentioned having produced five books for a certain editor who had a reputation for being difficult. At the mention of the editor's name, the agent whistled and said, "You've done five books for her? You're a survivor!"

Well, yes. I am a survivor. Every writer is a survivor, one way or another. Writing is a tough racket. If you're not a survivor, you're a casualty. Survivors are those who have developed the emotional temperament to withstand rejection, criticism, frustration, and pressure.

ARE YOU READY TO TAKE THE PLUNGE?

So that's the checklist—ten questions. How many check marks, how many "yes" answers did you have? A perfect, honest ten out of ten is a good sign. But even if you answer "yes" to all ten questions, it doesn't mean that success is assured. It simply means you have a shot at making it—a *serious* shot, as good a shot as any other writer who is toiling on Grub Street.

And what if you answer "no" to *even one* of these questions? Not a problem. Just use this checklist as a guide to the changes you need to make in your life, so that six months or a year from now, you'll be ready to take that plunge.

Until the day you can answer "yes" to all of those questions, keep writing, adding to your credits, building relationships with editors, and learning your craft. Then, when you're ready to make that leap and write for a living, odds are you'll make it.

It's a Living

Amazon.com: When did you first consider yourself a writer?

Judith Briles: A well-known columnist used one of my ideas that I shared with him over dinner in his nationally syndicated column. When I saw it, I told myself, "If you don't start using your own ideas, others will continue to steal them." My first book was written eight months later and published in 1981. My latest book is number eighteen.

Judith Briles, Ph.D., author of Woman to Woman *and* When God Says No, *interview on Amazon.com*

IT HAD TAKEN ME THE BETTER PART OF A WEEK to write the book proposal, but it was worth it. It was a celebrity autobiography, and I was promised a cover credit. Two publishers had bid on it, and though the offers were lower than I'd hoped, they were substantial offers.

Instead of an up-front fee for writing the proposal, the celebrity's agent had promised me a percentage of the advance and royalties, with a minimum of $25,000 from the publisher's advance. But when the offer came in, the agent phoned me, trying to get me to do the book for less—

A *lot* less.

"Look, Mr. Denney," he said. "When I said you would get twenty-five thousand to write this book, that was based on clearing at least a hundred thousand for my client. As you know, the publisher's total offer was only a hundred thousand—and my commission and your fee have to come out of that."

"You told me you were *hoping* to clear a hundred thousand for the author," I replied. "I told you clearly what my minimum price would be, and you never said I might have to take less if the publisher's offer was too low."

"I'm quite sure I did," the agent said smoothly. "I'm sorry if you misunderstood."

"I *didn't* misunderstand," I said. "But let's move on. How much were you thinking I should be paid?"

"Under the circumstances, I think twelve thousand would be very generous."

I took a deep breath and counted to ten.

"That's absurd," I said at last. "I can't do it for that."

"I understand your position," said the agent. "We'll just have to get another writer. I'm sorry we couldn't do business, but—"

"Just a moment," I said. "That proposal is my intellectual property. I researched it. I wrote it. I came up with the title. The book was sold on the basis of that proposal. I expect to be paid for my interest in it."

There was a long pause at the agent's end of the line. Perhaps it was *his* turn to count to ten. I waited.

"Mr. Denney," he said, "how many hours do you have invested? Ten? Fifteen?" The actual figure was closer to fifty—but it was none of his business.

"I don't charge by the hour," I said.

"Well," he said, "let's say I send you a check right now for a hundred dollars. I think that should cover it."

Was the guy *trying* to insult me?

"I won't accept anything less than two thousand," I said. It was a reasonable number and he knew it.

He exhaled a long, drawn-out sigh. "I'll get back to you," he said. End of conversation. In fact, that was the last conversation I ever had with that agent. But it wasn't the end of the book.

A few days later, I got a call from the acquisition editor at the publishing house that had accepted the book. She told me I was going to be paid $25,000 to write the book, and wanted my address so she could send me the contract. I was astounded. I asked if the agent had okayed that amount for me. She told me the agent had approved the following split— $60K to the author, $25K to me, and $15K for the agent's commission.

And that was that. I got what I was originally promised. Though the negotiations got off to a rocky start, the process of writing the book turned out to be a thoroughly enjoyable experience.

You never know.

The point of the story is this: Writing is a business. You have to approach it in a businesslike way. You have to set your price and stick to it. You have to protect your own interests. You have to hold people to their promises. You can't make a living by letting people walk on your face.

In this chapter we'll look at the all-important (and often-overlooked) business side of writing.

THE BUSINESS OF WRITING

It continues to astonish me what a widespread and enduring fantasy Being a Writer is for the population at large. It's a rare day when I don't encounter some misguided chap who expresses the desire to trade places with me. And it's on those not-so-rare days when everything goes wrong, when the words won't come but the rejections fly thick and fast, when the bank account's gone dry again and editors don't even bother lying about the check's being in the mail, that otherwise sane folks tell me how much they envy me.

Lawrence Block, Telling Lies for Fun and Profit

I broke into this business as a collaborative writer—what some would call a "ghostwriter." In other words, I helped other people write their books, usually by interviewing them, then transcribing the interviews and turning those conversations into books. Collaborative writing was a good way to practice my craft while making a living. In the process, I had the privilege of working with some extraordinary people in various fields, from entrepreneurs to psychologists to entertainers to NFL Hall of Famers. It's been fun—and quite an education. Here are a few nuggets of wisdom I've acquired while freelancing for the past fourteen years:

• **Writing is serious business; approach it in a businesslike way.** Sure, writing is an art—but it is also an act of commerce. The art of writing has to do with language skills, imagination, creativity, and craft. The business of writing has to do with understanding contracts, negotiating deals, scheduling projects, dealing with editors and collaborators, marketing and tracking manuscripts, and managing cash flow. A successful working writer treats writing as a serious business, not a hobby.

• **Rely on professional advice.** Make sure you have an accountant in your corner to help you set up your bookkeeping system and alert you to all the tax advantages that are available. Good financial advice doesn't cost—it pays. You don't need an agent at first, but you should have an attorney read all your contracts—not a general practitioner, but someone who specializes in contract law. This does not relieve you of the responsibility to read and understand the contracts yourself. You should know everything you are agreeing to when you sign on the dotted line.

• **Stay cool under pressure.** Writing requires intense mental concentration. Pressures are distractions, and distractions are corrosive forces that can stop the flow of your writing. Marital and family strife are deadly to your inspiration. Phone calls from creditors make it hard to put two coherent thoughts together. Deadline pressure can make you freeze like a deer in the halogen highbeams.

Understand, I'm not telling you to *eliminate* pressures and distractions from your life. It can't be done. The problems and pressures of life are inevitable, so you must learn to *cope*. One of the best survival skills a writer has is the ability to remain cool under pressure. To be successful, you have to function at your peak whether the bills are paid or not. There may come times when you are under intense deadline pressure and intense financial pressure at the same time—way too much work and no money at all. It will seem massively unfair and unreasonable—but you still have to finish the work in order to collect your next check. Money or no money, stress or no stress, you've got to write.

My most important asset in the early days of my freelance career was a *sense of perspective*. I looked at things this way: Okay, there's no money—so what's the worst that can happen? I put off some bills and make my apologies to a few creditors. The check will eventually get here. Meanwhile, I can still write, I still have my health and my family, and life goes on. On the scale of bad things that can happen to a person, a little short-term financial stress just doesn't even budge the scale.

When creditors call, stay cool, calm, and cordial. Never act stressed, angry, or desperate. Just tell them, "I'm self-employed, and I should be getting a big check in a couple weeks. As soon as it comes in, I'll turn a check right around. I'm sorry you had to call, but I really appreciate your patience." Or better yet, don't wait for creditors to call. Instead, call them and tell them you'll be a little late, but the money is coming. You'll be amazed at how patient creditors will be when you call them before they have to call you.

• **During bad times, avoid self-pity.** Unless you somehow manage to write a best-seller right out of the box (and I'm not sneering at that—it has been done), accept the fact that it takes time, patience, and persistence to build your career and achieve your goals. That's not unfair. That's just the way it is. What's more, that's the way it should be. If writing were easy, everybody would be doing it.

At times, you may be tempted to look with envy upon your workaday friends with their secure jobs and regular paychecks. You'll be tempted to feel sorry for yourself. Don't. You have a lot of things going for you that they don't have:

(1) *Unlimited upside potential.* Sure, the money is lean and the checks are slow at first. But your friends, the nine-to-fivers, top out at a certain level. They reach a point where they are making as much as they can make, and they can't advance any higher. A talented, focused, determined writer has unlimited upside potential. If you can write as well as Stephen King, Tom Clancy, or J. K. Rowling, you can become a one-person publishing empire and deforest half of Saskatchewan with your brilliant words. And why shouldn't you?

(2) *You're doing what you love.* How many of your friends can say that? Most of the people you know are just marking time until retirement. Few are doing what they really love to do. If your friends won the lottery today, most of them would quit their jobs tomorrow. But if you won the lottery, would you stop writing? No way! Sudden wealth would just give you more freedom to write what you want.

(3) *You are a writer.* You aren't mowing lawns or delivering pizza. You aren't cold-calling on disinterested prospects. You don't have to wear a pager to the opera, be on call at all hours of the night, or answer to a mean-tempered, autocratic boss. That's not to disparage the people who do those jobs, because all honest work is honorable. But you have something better than a job. You have something nobler than a career. You have a *calling.* You have a purpose in life. You are a writer.

• **Think like an editor.** If you want to write books, then ask yourself, "What sells?" Become acquainted with trends, best-sellers, and niche markets. Spend time in bookstores, checking out the racks and the displays, figuring out what sells. Read the trade journals, like *Publishers*

Weekly. Know what editors are looking for, and make it your business to deliver it.

I continually encounter people who want to write a book about their own life or the life of someone close to them. Unfortunately, such books rarely get published. Your grandfather may have been a fascinating man who led an interesting life, but the truth is, if your grandfather didn't win a war, a Super Bowl, or an Academy Award, it's going to be tough finding a publisher for your grandfather's life story. Nonfiction book publishing today is celebrity-driven, event-driven, and publicity-driven. Competition is fierce. If you want to sell your book, you've got to think commercially.

Magazine publishing is another thing altogether. There are thousands of magazines filling hundreds of niches. Even the story of your grandfather's adventures as a ringmaster with a traveling flea circus—if the story is well written with just the right slant—will sell to one or more of those magazines. You just have to do your homework and familiarize yourself with the markets. That means you must research potential markets in *Writer's Market* and on the Internet. If a magazine's guidelines don't appear in *The American Directory of Writer's Guidelines* and it doesn't post them on its website, then invest in some stamps and ask for them (send an SASE). Most important of all, *read the magazine*. Get to know its content, focus, readership, editorial personality, and slant. Study the contents page—and study the actual content.

Select a few publications you'd like to write for, then make it your goal to crack that market and keep selling articles there. After you conquer one publication, use your credits to impress editors at other publications, so you can continue to conquer new and even better-paying markets.

• **Sell now, write later.** This is the only sensible way to sell nonfiction, whether article-length or book-length. When you want to sell article-length nonfiction to magazines, you first write and submit a query letter. A query is a short (preferably one page) letter designed to grab an editor's attention, describe the content and slant of your article, lay out your credentials to write the article, and "bait the hook" so that the editor *must* see more! Propose only one article per query—make sure your query is sharply focused, not scattershot. Your query should sound confident and professional and should be carefully proofread and spell-checked before it goes out. It should be as fun to read as your finished article is going to be. Don't forget to enclose an SASE.

Nonfiction books are sold by first writing a book proposal. A proposal is more extensive and lengthy than a query letter, but serves the same function: Grab the editor's attention, describe the content of the book, demonstrate your qualifications, and bait the hook. Winning proposals I have written have ranged from two pages to over seventy-five pages. The average proposal consists of a number of essential components:

(1) *The hook.* Write a "grabber" of an opening or introduction that makes the editor want to keep reading. Your proposal is one of a stack of proposals that are skimmed rather quickly, and you are up against some tough competition. Your proposal should make a strong, compelling, gotta-read-it point, and should do so as concisely as possible.

(2) *Description.* Write a brief, memorable synopsis or overview of the entire book. Include such details as content, intended audience, length of the finished book, projected delivery date, and other special features.

(3) *Marketing and spin-offs.* If possible, include the names of prominent people who will write the forward and/or jacket endorsements. Better yet, get a couple of endorsements ahead of time. Talk about how you plan to help promote the book. Could the book spin off ancillary products, such as sequels, audiobooks, or videos? Mention those possibilities, too.

(4) *Your qualifications.* What expertise or experience do you have to lend credibility to this book? And, don't forget to include your credits.

(5) *Chapter-by-chapter outline.* Describe each chapter in three or four paragraphs. When the editor has finished reading your chapter outline, he or she should have a feeling of what it will be like to read the finished book.

(6) *Sample chapters.* Include one or two sample chapters. The best approach is to include Chapters 1 and 2. If you skip Chapter 2 in favor of, say, Chapter 12, the editor is likely to wonder, "Why didn't the author give me Chapter 2? Is that a weak chapter?" After you have built up a track record as a dependable writer, you probably won't have to include sample chapters anymore.

For a complete discussion of the structure of winning book proposals, read *The Fast Track Course on How to Write a Nonfiction Book Pro-*

posal by my friend, Stephen Blake Mettee (Quill Driver Books, 2002). Steve knows the publishing business from both sides, as a writer and an editor-publisher. His book tells you everything you need to know about book proposals, presented clearly and concisely.

It is suicide to write an entire nonfiction book "on spec"—that is, on speculation, in the hope of making an eventual sale. You can't make a living writing on spec. You have to sell your ideas first, then write them.

I recently had conversations with two unpublished writers who are working on nonfiction books. Both told me, in essence, "I don't want to write a proposal. I want to write a finished book first, then sell it. I'm afraid that if I write a proposal first, the publisher will say, 'We like your general idea, but we want you to do it our way, not your way.' If I write the whole book first, I'll be in control—they'll *have* to publish the book as I wrote it."

> "Your proposal should make a strong, compelling, gotta-read-it point, and should do so as concisely as possible."

That's delusional thinking. Whether you sell your book as a proposal or a complete manuscript, you can count on one thing: You will probably make some compromises before it is published. Your book will be edited, and you will likely be asked to do revisions and maybe even a major rewrite. And that's a good thing. Every time one of my books has gone through editing, it has emerged clearer and stronger—and that includes the book you are reading right now.

If you write nonfiction, it is the height of foolishness to write an entire manuscript first, then try to peddle it. You could spend anywhere from a few months to a few years producing a 300-page manuscript on spec. Once done, you could spend *years* trying to find a publisher. If you don't find a publisher, all that time is lost—and your book ends up in a trunk in the attic. You can't make a living writing books nobody buys. The smart, successful writer *always* sells the book first, then writes it—not the other way around.

"What about novels?" you ask. "Can I sell a novel to a publisher on the basis of a couple chapters and an outline?" Occasionally, but rarely—at least until you are established. Typically, an editor will want to see the first three or four chapters of your novel to start with—just to see if your book gets off to a good start (if it doesn't start with a bang, no one will stick around for the ending). If those first chapters capture the editor's attention, he or she will ask you to send the entire manuscript. That means, of course, that you must have a complete manuscript ready to send at the time you submit those sample chapters.

Editors are reluctant to purchase novels on the basis of a proposal, because a proposal only proves you know how to get started. Novels that start well often fall apart somewhere in the middle. Novelist F. Paul Wilson (*Nightkill*, *Conspiracies*, and the *Repairman Jack* series) put it this way: "You get off to a strong start and maybe you have a strong finish planned, but to hold up the belly of the book is the toughest part."[1] Editors want to know that you can sustain the characterization and narrative flow over the length of a manuscript before they fork over the money.

Of course, after your first couple of novels are hugely successful, you will have proven yourself. You can then sell a novel on the basis of a proposal, or maybe even a conversation with an editor over lunch. But to break in as a novelist, you almost always have to begin by writing an entire book on spec.

• **Keep multiple projects in the pipeline.** I rarely have fewer than three projects under contract at a time. I stagger the deadlines, usually three months apart. Sometimes I write a book straight through, start to finish, in a solid stretch, eight to twelve weeks. But usually I "leapfrog" between books. I may work four to six weeks on a sports book and send the first batch of chapters to my collaborator. While he's reading those chapters, I jump over to one of my own novels or nonfiction books for a few weeks. Toggling between projects every month or two keeps me fresh, keeps my interest from flagging, keeps me from going stale and getting bored. It also helps me to space out the publishers' advance checks to give me a stable cash flow.

While I'm working on projects already under contract, I'm also writing new proposals and developing new book ideas. It's important to schedule projects on a long-term calendar (I schedule book projects with deadlines as far as two years out). I keep my calendar handy, right next to my computer, and revise it as needed. When scheduling, it's important to allow space between books for rewrites and revisions, unexpected delays, reading and correcting proofs, promotional efforts, and vacation times.

• **Never be dull.** Grab the reader by the throat with the very first sentence—and don't let go. Don't give the reader any pause or excuse to put the book down. Make sure each chapter ends by propelling your readers helplessly along to the next chapter. Sustain this intensity throughout the book—show no mercy! And remember—editors are readers, too. Before you sell a million copies of your book, you have to sell *one* copy to *one* person—the editor. If you give an editor any excuse to put your manuscript down, you may never get a chance to reach the thousands of other people who would love to read your book.

One of the best ways to make sure your writing is fast-paced and exciting is by ruthless cutting in the rewrite stage. A book should always get shorter in the rewrite stage. If your second draft is longer than your first, you're doing something wrong.

I have recently written a series of science-fantasy novels for young readers (ages eight to twelve) called the Timebenders Series. When I submitted the concept for book one: *Battle Before Time*, I had plotted the book to fill 60,000 words. When the editors accepted it, they asked me to bring the books in at no more than 35,000 words.

To date, I have written four Timebenders books, and each one was from 45,000 to 60,000 words in first draft. So, after writing the first draft, I had to go back and cut from 22 to 42 percent of what I had just written— and I had to do it without sacrificing storyline. I couldn't just lop out whole scenes or chapters—I had to sculpt the text, removing a paragraph here, a sentence there, and even individual words. In all four books, I was able to fit the same amount of story into a more compressed space, and the result is that the story is tighter, more fast-paced, more exciting.

Were some of the cuts painful? Absolutely! If the edits you make don't make you wince and weep, you're not doing your job. A lot of your most cherished verbiage is really just froth and fluff that gets in the way of the story. Cut it! Simplify! Get to the point! Each time I turned in one of my 35,000-word Timebenders books, I was grateful for the discipline imposed by the limited format. Those books were improved immensely by the necessity to keep it short and simple (in fact, so was *this* book!). So I urge you to do the same: Keep it short, keep it simple, and never be dull!

• **Cultivate contacts.** Some say it's not *what* you know, it's *who* you know. I say it's both. First, you've got to be good at what you do; second, you've got to let people know you are good at what you do. So take control of your craft, and become a great writer. But also take control of your career by getting to know as many different kinds of people as you can: publishers, editors, writers, and influential people in all walks of life. You never know where your next sale or winning book idea may come from.

When you build a network of relationships, you create an environment where the lightning of "good luck" is more likely to strike you. Of the sixty-plus books I've written to date, only a few have been sold to an editor who didn't know me. In almost every case, I either knew the editor or knew someone who knew the editor. But first I had to be good at what I do. To be successful, it's not enough to know a lot of editors; it's much more important that the editors know me—to know that I deliver excellence, I deliver on-time, and I can be trusted with a hefty advance.

> "One of the best ways to make sure your writing is fast-paced and exciting is by ruthless cutting in the rewrite stage."

How do you build a network of relationships? For writers who live and work in solitary confinement, networking takes extra effort. We have to make the effort to get out of our lonely cells and out into the community of writers, editors, publishers, agents, and other contacts. The Internet can provide a certain limited level of contact through bulletin boards and websites. But a much more effective way is through writers' workshops and conferences.

When you attend a conference, meet as many people as you can. Don't be shy about approaching speakers—they enjoy talking to people who want to write. And remember that it can be just as helpful to make friends with other attendees as it is to become acquainted with the pros. There are many workshop attendees who can critique your work, inspire you, and introduce you to valuable contacts from *their* network of relationships.

An important rule in networking is the Golden Rule: Be as generous in helping others as you would have them be generous unto you. Exchange contacts, favors, resources, ideas, and information. You never know which of your wannabe-writer friends might suddenly hit the bigtime—and would remember your many acts of kindness by introducing you to a high-powered agent or editor.

• **Focus on excellence, but don't obsess over minutiae.** Many writers are overly obsessed with details, like the placement of commas or whether or not to put a copyright notice on the manuscript. Forget flyspecks. Focus on the big picture. Your manuscript should be neat, professional, literate, and presentable—but a little broken syntax or a misplaced comma won't kill a sale.

When you write a book, story, or article, focus on writing your first draft as quickly as possible. Sprint through it, allowing your own enthusiasm to carry you along. Novelist-essayist Anne Lamott (*Blue Shoe* and *Traveling Mercies*) put it this way in her book *Bird by Bird*: "You need to trust yourself, especially on a first draft, where amid the anxiety and self-doubt, there should be a real sense of your imagination and your memories walking and woolgathering, tramping the hills, romping all over the place. Trust them. Don't look at your feet to see if you are doing it right. Just dance."[2]

Once you have a first draft, let it sit for a few days or a couple of weeks, then go back to the beginning and rewrite. Do a computerized spell-check and grammar-check. At most, give it one final read-through, then let go of it. You're done. Stick it into an envelope and submit it.

• **Never accept rejection as final—keep submitting.** Before his first sale, novelist and playwright William Saroyan wrote dozens of short stories and sent them to every paying fiction market in the country. Eventually, every one of his stories was rejected by every one of those magazines—he had collected nothing but rejection slips. Undaunted, Saroyan simply turned around and sent the *same* stories to the *same* publications— and the second time around, they started selling. Why? Because there was a high turnover rate among the junior editors who sifted the slush piles at those magazines. The second time Saroyan sent out those stories, they went to a whole new round of editors. And you can do the same, because there is still a high turnover rate at publishing houses and magazines today.

Submit, submit, submit—and you will sell, sell, sell. As Lawrence Block put it in *Telling Lies for Fun and Profit*, "Once you've got a story to the point where you think it's worth submitting, you must submit it and submit it and submit it until someone somewhere breaks down and buys it."

• **Before launching your freelance career, write a business plan.**
It doesn't have to be lengthy or involved, but you must have a business plan from the get-go. A business plan is a roadmap to your goals. A written plan will give you a clear sense of how to get where you want to go in your writing career. Keep your plan flexible, and revise it on a regular basis—say, every six months. Your business plan should evolve as conditions change and your career grows.

> "When you write a book, story, or article, focus on writing your first draft as quickly as possible."

You might well object, "I don't write business plans! I write novels, stories, plays! Business is boring! I care about ideas, characters, and imagination—not marketing, cash flow, and pro forma income projections!" I understand. In fact, I fully empathize. But I have a two-part response to that:

First, as a full-time working writer, you are now a businessperson—like it or not. Writing is your vocation, not your avocation, so you've got to approach it seriously and professionally. And that means you must plan.

Second, planning isn't boring; it's fun and fascinating if you do it right. When you write a business plan, you envision your future on paper—and what could possibly be more exciting than anticipating and planning your brilliant future?

So what is a business plan and what does it do? Well, whenever an entrepreneur starts up a new company, he or she draws up a business plan to lay a firm foundation for the company. Normally, the purpose of a business plan is to prove to investors, such as banks and venture capitalists, that you know where you're going and what you're doing in this new business. Investors want to know what product the business will produce, how the company will market itself, how it will be capitalized, where the break-even point is, and how profitable it realistically projects to be a few years down the road.

You may think, "What does that have to do with me? I'm not going to ask venture capitalists to fund my writing career." True. Nevertheless, it is important that you answer *to your own satisfaction* all the same questions that a venture capitalist would ask:

(1) *What product will you produce as a freelance writer?* Novels, nonfiction books, short stories, magazine articles, screenplays, greeting card poems? Is there a market niche that you can target and take over as your exclusive domain? How big a market is there for the kind of writing you do? This portion of your business plan forces you to focus on your "product line" and think clearly and realistically about the kind of writing you will produce.

(2) *How will you market yourself to publishers?* Which publications and book publishers buy the kind of writing you produce? How will you make contact with editors in those companies? Are there people you know who are connected with the publishing industry and who can introduce you to editors and publishers? What steps will you take to build your list of published credits and make your name more marketable?

What professional and trade organizations should you join? What conventions and trade shows should you attend? Are there websites you can check on a regular basis that post opportunities for freelancers (example: www.writerswrite.com or www.authorlink.com)? Can you put up your own website on the Internet to promote your work (mine, by the way, is at www.denneybooks.com)? Can you take speaking engagements and do media appearances? In as many creative ways as you possibly can, you must answer the question, "How can I make publishers and editors aware of me, and how can I motivate them to buy my work?"

(3) *How will your writing business be capitalized?* Where will your funding come from? Do you have savings or an early retirement incentive that will carry you for a year or two until you get established? How much money do you have on hand? How much will you need, month by month, to stay in business? What are your anticipated expenses? What kind of cash flow can you expect? What net profit (or loss) can you expect in your first year of operation?

Ros Jay has a wise take on planning the financial side of a writing career. "Work out your figures in advance," she says, "how much you're likely to earn, what you need to live on and so on. Assume that you will only earn money three days a week—cost everything out on this basis. The other two days will be spent writing proposals, chasing work that doesn't come off, doing your accounts and all the other non-earning tasks you need to spend time on. Don't assume that everyone who says yes to the hypothetical question, 'If I became a writer, would you have any work for me?' will actually come up with any work when the question is for real."

Plan a sound, sober budget by determining the actual amount of money needed to open your writing business (start-up costs) and the amount needed to keep it open over the long haul (operating costs). Your start-up budget includes one-time-only costs such as office setup (furnishings and supplies), computer and software, legal and professional fees (particularly if you are incorporating), accounting (setting up your record keeping system), and so forth. Your operating budget describes the ongoing expenses you will incur and how you will cover them, including insurance, rent, loan payments, travel, supplies, utilities, legal and professional fees, dues and subscriptions, repairs and maintenance, taxes, depreciation, and miscellaneous costs.

> "Submit, submit, submit—and you will sell, sell, sell."

If you write shorter freelance pieces, such as stories, magazine articles, or advertising copy, long-term budgeting is largely a matter of guesswork, at least until you have established a steady work flow and cash flow. Writing books makes it a little easier to budget for a year or more at a time, because the money comes in large lump sums that are easy to plot out on a calendar. But it can still get tricky.

Let's say that every month you need $5,000 to meet your personal and business expenses. A publisher offers you a $15,000 advance to write a book—half on signing the contract, half on delivery of a complete manuscript. You know that it takes you three months to write a book, so you figure you have met your budget for those three months, right? Wrong. Let's walk through it.

You sign the contract, and the publisher writes you a check for $7,500, or half of the advance (the "front end" of the advance). Notice, first of all, that $7,500 only covers a month and a half worth of living expenses. Just forty-five days into the project, you are out of money, and you still have to keep writing. When do you get the second half of the advance (the "back end")? Check your contract. It probably states that the back end will be paid within thirty days after you turn in a manuscript that is "in quality, length, content, and form satisfactory to the publisher," or words to that effect. In other words, your back end check may not be cut until a month after the manuscript has been read and accepted by the editors. In fact, you may be called upon to make time-consuming revisions before the manuscript is accepted. Did you think you could write the book in three months, then pick up your check? Ain't gonna happen.

So as you budget, you need to make sure you have a constant stream of new contract signings—and a constant stream of books rolling off the assembly line, one after the other. You can't afford to line up book projects end to end—finish one project and then contract for another. You must schedule projects on top of each other, overlapping each other. I always have at least three books under contract at once. Fewer than that, and my cash flow is liable to dry up just when I need it most. Cash flow, scheduling, operating costs—these are some of the hard realities of the life of a working writer, and they must be carefully accounted for in your business plan.

(4) *What risks does your writing business face—and how will you insure against them?* What sources of emergency funds do you have if there is a big air bubble in your cash-flow pipeline? Can you tap into savings? Credit cards? A line of credit? If push comes to shove, do you have a Rolls Royce or a Rolex you can pawn? Do you have a spare kidney or other organ you could sell on eBay? It's crucial to know where your money is coming from—and if the money doesn't come, what emergency measures you can take to carry you through the crisis.

Also, the publishing industry is cyclical. Those red-hot crime novels you are churning out now could be market poison next year—but don't let that stop you from writing. If there is a slump in your preferred field, find another field, perhaps a related field. If your novels aren't selling, can you turn to nonfiction or collaborative writing? Can you reinvent yourself and your career as market conditions change? For every problem or risk you can think of, be prepared with a solution.

(5) *What are your goals as a writer?* You should have clear, well-defined goals for your writing career, segmented by time frame. They should be ambitious, but achievable and realistic (realistic goals encourage you to reach for success; unrealistic goals set you up for failure and discouragement). Here are some examples:

Time frame:	Goal:
Every month:	Produce one book proposal and three queries.
In six months:	Save enough to quit day job and write full time.
In one year:	Earn $25,000 per year from writing. Complete first draft of my novel.
In three years:	Earn $50,000 per year from writing. Make enough from fiction to quit ghostwriting and concentrate on novels and stories.
In five years:	Write best-seller, sell movie rights, income unlimited, move to Tahiti.

Your goals are not carved in stone. You can adjust them periodically as circumstances change. The purpose of goals is to inspire you and enable you to plan and prioritize, both short-term and long-range. It's a good idea to attach a five-year calendar to your business plan, and to plot your projects on that calendar. It helps to have a visual blueprint of the next few years of your writing career, with contractual deadlines marked in red, with start and stop points of various projects shown, and with holiday lead times noted (for example, you should write down "send queries for Christmas articles" in the box for March). Also, having your writing schedule calendarized will show you, in clear visual terms, where there may be gaps in your cash flow that need to be filled.

A final word on your business plan: Keep a paper copy of it handy for quick referral. Keep a file of it on your hard drive, so that you can easily revise it and print out a new one. Revise it every six months. Review it every week, to remind yourself of your goals. Follow it religiously. It's your road map to success.

• **Study the markets.** Shape your writing for the particular publishing house or magazine you wish to write for. Research the market online and in person at your local bookstore. Find out which books lead the field—and study them to understand why. Study the magazines to find out what kinds of articles and stories are the most saleable and why. When you make an intense study of the market, you not only learn how to target your work to fit a particular editorial slant, you also immerse yourself in the moods, modes, and influences of that market, which helps to make you a better writer—and a better-*selling* writer.

Familiarize yourself with publishers' wants, contact information, submission policies, and ranges of payment by consulting the latest editions of *The American Directory of Writer's Guidelines* and *Writer's Market* and by following the market updates in the magazine *Writer's Digest*. If you write in a specialty market, be aware of specialized information on your field in such books as *Novel and Short Story Writer's Market*, and *Children's Writer's and Illustrator's Market*. Most book publishers and magazine publishers post their writer's guidelines on their websites, or you can request writer's guidelines by mail (send an SASE).

• **Ask for the money.** According to the National Writers Union, only 15 percent of working writers earn over $30,000 a year.[3] But there's no reason why you should remain in the bottom 85 percent. Many writers starve needlessly because they lack the confidence to ask for what's coming to them. Elmore Leonard, best-selling author of such thrillers as *Get Shorty*, *Glitz*, and *Freaky Deaky*, says, "Fifty percent of writing is asking for the money. If you can't ask for the money, you have no business being in business."

The highest-paid freelancers tend to work in the business field, largely in advertising and public relations. The mid-level field is magazine and book publishing. The worst-paid field is freelance journalism—newspapers are notorious for exploiting and underpaying freelance "stringers." But generalizations are meaningless. The truth is that if you are skilled, hard working, savvy, and have confidence in yourself, you can make good money in even the lowest-paid sector of the writing industry.

Be aware of the many different ways writers are paid: contractual advance plus royalties, flat fee (work for hire), by the word, by the hour or day, and on retainer. The best form of payment by far is an advance plus royalties, because that means you own an asset with a virtually unlimited upside potential. As long as the book keeps selling, you keep making money. If you can write a book that never goes out of print, you'll have money coming in for the rest of your life.

Ray Bradbury's *The Martian Chronicles*, *Fahrenheit 451*, and *The Illustrated Man* have remained continuously in print for the past one-half century. Og Mandino's *The Greatest Salesman in the World* has never been out of print since it was originally published in 1968, and it has sold over 16 million copies. And *The One-Minute Manager* by Kenneth Blanchard and Spencer Johnson has remained in print since it first appeared in 1982, selling over 10 million copies.

When you are starting out, you generally don't have the leverage to demand many concessions from a publisher. That's okay. That's what the phrase "entry level" is all about. You are paying your dues and building your list of credits. But once your dues have been paid and your reputation has been established, it's time to be confident and assertive. Be bold. Dare to negotiate. Ask for the money.

> "Shape your writing for the particular publishing house or magazine you wish to write for."

How much money should you ask for? For current guidelines on what to charge for practically every kind of writing under the sun, consult the "How Much Should I Charge?" section in the latest edition of *Writer's Market*. It lists pay ranges for everything from advertising copywriting to speechwriting to screenwriting to book and magazine writing to business writing to Internet web page writing. Whatever kind of writing you do, it's covered in that section.

Whenever possible, charge a lump sum for the project. Don't charge by the hour. The reason is obvious: If you write quickly and produce efficiently, you should be rewarded for your speed. The writer who charges by the hour actually penalizes himself or herself for working efficiently, because in that situation speed only cuts down on billable hours—the faster you work, the more your income shrinks. You should always structure your rates in such a way that you have an incentive to work efficiently, so that you are motivated to earn more by working faster and smarter.

How to handle your success

> If [financial success] came early enough and you loved life as much as you loved your work, it would take much character to resist the temptations. Once writing has become your major vice and greatest pleasure, only death can stop it. Financial security then is a great help as it keeps you from worrying. Worry destroys the ability to write.
>
> **Ernest Hemingway**

In 1920, Aldous Huxley was a struggling, unknown writer. He eked out a living writing reviews for the *Athenaeum* and the *Westminster Gazette*. The pittance he earned allowed him to barely support his wife and child. They lived in a spartan coldwater flat in Hampstead, living on canned soup and boiled potatoes. Discouraged, Huxley wrote his father, "There is nothing but a commercial success that can free one from this deadly hustle."

Two years later, Huxley's first novel, *Crome Yellow*, was published and met with critical praise and modest commercial success: 2,500 copies sold the first year. Those may be dismal numbers by today's standards, but they were solidly respectable sales for the time, and Huxley was delighted. After several years of the "deadly hustle" of writing articles and reviews, the twenty-eight-year-old writer had achieved success. He moved his family from the Hampstead flat to a comfortable home in Kensington. He quit his day job at the magazine and became a full-time working writer, devoting his time and energy to his novels, including *Eyeless in Gaza* and *Brave New World*.

I know exactly what Huxley meant when he talked about the "deadly hustle." You probably do, too. But with persistence, planning, and hard work, you can achieve the success that will bring an end to the hustle. You can achieve the dream of becoming a writer on your own terms, writing the books you want to write, commanding huge advances, collecting obscene royalties. In time, you'll look back and know that the struggles and lean times were worth it.

Once you've achieved success, then what? Literary history is strewn with the broken lives of authors who became extraordinarily successful for a time, only to end their lives in destitution. Don't let this happen to you. Once you've earned your success, hold onto it, manage it, invest, and watch your success and security grow. Here's how:

• **Eliminate debt.** Novelist Robert J. Sawyer (*Hominids* and *Iterations*) carefully organized his life and his writing career to avoid falling into the debt trap. He says, "The best advice I have is this: Live a debt-free lifestyle. It's meeting debt payments—mortgages, cars, credit cards—that kills most freelancers. You can always squeak by a lean month if you don't have any huge bills to pay. My wife and I bought our first home with cash—we didn't want a mortgage, and so we saved brutally for eight years to buy a home, cutting back on everything."

Eliminating debt comes before investing. It makes no sense to invest money at 8 percent interest while you are paying 22 percent interest to the credit card companies. That high interest debt is eating you alive. So start with your highest-interest debt, then go down to the next highest-interest debt on the list, and the next and the next, until you have zero-balanced every account. Once you've eliminated debt, you are ready to start saving and investing.

• **Invest.** There are many ways of investing your hard-earned success: real estate, stocks, bonds, mutual funds, and so forth. The stock market boomed in the 1990s, then went bust in 2001, but it is still one of the safest places to invest your royalty checks. Even after the dot-com bust, the Motley Fool investors' website (www.fool.com) says that the Standard & Poor 500 (an index of 500 blue-chip stocks, considered the benchmark of the overall stock market) continues to average 11 percent growth per year. In fact, the annual stock market return since 1926 has steadily averaged 11 percent over the long haul. Let's look at what an 11 percent return can do for you over time:

Let's say you get an unexpected royalty check for $2,000 and you don't need it to pay the mortgage. It's yours to blow or invest, as you see fit. If you put that $2,000 in stocks or a mutual fund that yields an 11 percent annual return, it will grow to $53,416 in 30 years. And if you set aside just $1,000 a year every year (roughly the cost of a Starbucks latté every weekday morning), you'll have over a million dollars after forty-six years.

Dennis E. Hensley is the prolific author of over 3,000 articles for *Reader's Digest, The Writer, People, The Detroit Free Press*, and many other publications. Known to his friends as "Doc," Hensley has written six novels and twenty-seven nonfiction books (*Writing for Profit, The Jesus Effect*), in addition to ghostwriting eighteen nonfiction books for noted celebrities. He became successful as a full-time writer, and went on to manage his success well through prudent investing.

Doc Hensley told me, "In 1978, I was married with two kids and working full time as director of publications for Manchester College. It paid fairly well and had a good benefits package. However, that year I completed my doctor's degree in English and I sold my second book, so I shocked everyone and resigned my job and went full time into writing. It wasn't a foolhardy decision. First, I had received an advance for a third book and I was still getting royalties on the first two books. Second, I was an active stringer for two newspapers and three magazines, so I had plenty of small writing assignments to keep me busy. Third, I was able to supplement my writing income by teaching night school at a local college during the first year I was on my own.

"As the years passed, I worked hard and steadily. Whenever one of my books became a best-seller, I invested the money wisely. I paid off my home, then I bought three other homes as rental properties. I invested in stocks and bonds, too. By having other ways of earning money beyond just writing, I was never in a panic as to how I would pay my bills, educate my children, or take time off for vacations.

"I worked full time as a freelance writer from 1978 through 1997. I then was asked to accept a full-time position with Taylor University as an English professor, with the mission of developing a professional writing major. I accepted the challenge and have enjoyed teaching classes and mentoring students since then. I still stay very active as a writer. I have written one new book each year and have written dozens of articles since joining the Taylor faculty."

The key to Doc Hensley's long-term success is also the key to yours and mine: hard work, diversified fields of writing, diversified sources of income, and savvy investing.

• **Pay yourself first.** This is age-old investing principle for all self-employed people: Before you pay any bills, pay yourself. That is, put some money aside (a good goal is 10 percent of your income before taxes) in an investment vehicle—stocks, bonds, certificates of deposit, a mutual fund. As a self-employed writer, you never know how much income you'll receive in a given month or a given year. So every time you get a check, from whatever source, in whatever amount, sock away a certain percentage as part of a wealth-building strategy.

• **Consider incorporating.** Not long after I became a full-time freelancer, I went to Dallas to take part in a large multibook publishing project. There were several writers besides myself, plus our editor, meeting with a group of psychiatrists and psychologists to produce a line of books on psychology, marriage relationships, and recovery. For me, it was like a mini-workshop environment, where I got to meet and talk with other writers, all of whom had been writing full time several years longer than I had.

During a conversation over lunch with one of those writers, I mentioned the struggles I had experienced with irregular cash flow, and I asked him how he handled it. "I incorporated," he said. "Everything I earn is paid to the corporation, and the corporation pays me a regular salary."

At that time, this writer's answer did me no good. If I had incorporated, I would have still been in the same dismal financial shape. The corporation would have had a cash flow problem—and I would have had trouble collecting my paycheck from the corporation. To this day, I am not incorporated. I am simply self-employed. I have explored with my accountant the pros and cons of incorporating, and have decided it's not for me—but it does work for many other writers. It could be a good strategy for you.

Some of the advantages for writers who incorporate:

(1) *Corporate tax rates are lower than personal tax rates, so taxes on money left in the corporation are reduced.* But there's a drawback: Until you take it out of the corporation, it's not your money—and as soon as you *do* take it out, the taxman grabs his cut.

(2) *The "corporate veil" creates a layer of protection against lawsuits.* In theory, the writer's personal assets are kept separate from the assets of the corporation. The corporate veil, however, does not afford as much protection as many people think. If you, the incorporated writer, are ever sued for something you wrote that harmed someone else, the courts would have no trouble figuring out that you and the corporation are one and the same—and your assets will be as vulnerable as they ever were. And another thing: There is no corporate veil to protect you from bankruptcy.

(3) *Disability insurance, medical insurance, and healthcare costs are deductible as a business expense.* Incorporation can significantly reduce the cost of your insurance premiums—an expense that eats many freelancers alive. The corporation can also provide, tax free, up to $50,000 in life insurance coverage. These benefits can provide significant savings—but this advantage of incorporation disappears if your spouse's employer provides these same benefits.

The disadvantages of incorporating include:

(1) *The corporation has to pay taxes that you, as merely a self-employed writer, do not*: workers compensation, unemployment tax, and a slightly higher Social Security and Medicare tax (aka the Federal Insurance Contributions Act or FICA).

(2) *You get taxed twice on money you receive from the corporation as dividends.* It's taxed once under the corporation tax, then again when you declare your dividends on your personal 1040.

(3) *It is against the law to incorporate merely to lower your taxes.* If the IRS decides that your corporate identity is nothing but a tax dodge, it may decide to ignore the corporate shell and tax you as a self-employed individual.

(4) *Running a corporation can be complex and expensive.* You usually need an attorney and accountant to set it up, and it takes time and paperwork to keep it running.

With the aid of your attorney and CPA, you have to weigh the advantages and disadvantages of incorporating for your specific situation. If you decide to incorporate, you'll need to decide if you wish to form a Subchapter C Corporation (a business that is a completely separate entity from its owners, unlike a partnership; so-called because it is taxed under Subchapter C of the Internal Revenue Code) or a Subchapter S Corporation (a form of corporation which enables the company to enjoy the benefits of incorporation but be taxed as if it were a partnership).

There is no one-size-fits-all answer to the question, "Should I incorporate?" The answer depends on you. In general, incorporation is for those who earn a ton of money from their writing, who don't need to take it all out in salary, who are well-advised by able professionals, and who are meticulous record keepers and receipt savers.

INVEST IN *YOU*

> What is a writer's greatest asset? Faith in oneself.
> *Horror novelist **Anne Rice***

Here's a simple rule of thumb when it comes to investing: Accumulate assets, not liabilities. A *liability* is a financial obligation. An *asset* is an item on your balance sheet that offsets your liabilities; an asset could be cash, stock, inventory, property rights, or even goodwill. In the financial best-seller *Rich Dad, Poor Dad*, Robert T. Kiyosaki defines these terms even more simply: An asset is something that puts money in your pocket; a liability is something that takes money out of your pocket.

So as a writer, what is your best asset? Answer: You.

I'm not talking in some vague metaphoric sense. I literally mean that your own best financial asset is the work you produce as a writer. There is a term for the work you create: *intellectual property*. When you sit down and write an article, a nonfiction book, a story, a novel, or a poem, you actually *invent an asset*, using nothing but your imagination. You create a piece of property that puts money into your pocket—and the copyright law says that the moment you create it, you own it.

Of course, you have to make sure you protect your right of ownership in order to hold onto that asset. How do you do that? Well, when you sell your work to a publisher, you insist on the protection of your ownership rights. You protect your copyright. You protect your subsidiary rights, electronic rights, and reprint rights. If you write books, you make sure your book contract is structured so that you are paid royalties on all sales of your work—you don't hand this asset to a publisher for a flat fee. If you write magazine pieces, you make sure you sell only "first North American serial rights" (if you are handed a contract that takes electronic and reprint rights without giving you extra payment, cross out that clause).

Once you have protected your ownership of the intellectual property, you can then take steps to increase the value of that property. Isn't that amazing? Through your own efforts, you can actually drive up the value of your own property! Can you increase the value of a share of stock or a mutual fund or a municipal bond? Of course not. (Well, there are ways—but you can go to jail for it.) The truth is, there are *scores* of things, *hundreds* of things you can do to increase the value of intellectual property: You can focus on craft and excellence in your work, so that it will be highly prized and sought-after. You can promote, publicize, and advertise your work, so more people will hear of it and clamor to buy it. You can write more works and turn your name into a recognized brand name that people look for and seek out. You can create whole series of stories or books, taking advantage of the fact that groups of similar works create a synergy that multiplies sales.

If you want to invest in yourself and increase the value of your intellectual property, the guiding principle is very simple: The more people who want to buy your work, the more valuable your intellectual property becomes. Soon, you'll receive phone calls from people wanting to adapt it to film or television, translate it and sell it overseas, market it via electronic media, and make plastic Happy Meal toys out of it. If you create a work that has a classic, enduring quality to it, it will remain in print for years or even decades, attracting new generations of readers and devotees—and putting money into your pocket well into your old age.

> "So as a writer, what is your best asset? Answer: You. "

Can you name just one Wall Street stock that has performed as well, as long, and as consistently as *The Lord of the Rings*, *The Cat in the Hat*, *The Chronicles of Narnia*, *Catcher in the Rye*, *Carrie*, or *The Martian Chronicles*? Neither can I. If you create a perennial best-seller, you own an asset that is better than a blue-chip stock.

What are the odds of creating a work that has that kind of limitless upside potential? Well, let me ask you this: How much do you believe in *you*? Are you willing to take a gamble on your own hard work, imagination, and genius? If not, then why bother writing at all?

You might ask, "What if I invest in myself and fail? What if I flop as a writer? All the time, money, and effort I put into my writing will have been wasted. I'll lose my entire investment."

All of that is true. But every investment has an element of risk. The stock market can crash. Even a blue-chip company like an electric utility can go bankrupt. There are no guarantees in life. Everything is a gamble. Why not bet on something you can control? Why not bet on your writing? Why would you rather gamble on the stock market or porkbelly futures when you can bet on *you*?

Oh, sure, it's smart to diversify. It's wise to spread your portfolio around a bit—Wall Street, real estate, precious metals, works of art. But first and foremost, if you truly believe in yourself, invest in *you*.

So that's the business side of writing. It's a living. In fact, writing can provide a very *good* living, if you work hard, work smart, and plan wisely. And wise planning begins, as we are about to see, with a wise understanding of your contract.

What Have I Signed?

At no time are you, as a writer, more vulnerable than when you're confronted with your first book contract. At last you're being "recognized." For months, perhaps years, you may have been the only one with faith in your own work; you may, in fact, have been willing to pay a publisher to get published. Now, all of a sudden, someone else has faith in you and is willing to pay you. Where will you summon the nerve to ask questions, to bargain with your benefactor?

Literary agent **Georges Borchardt**

You can't get very far into a discussion of economic survival as a writer without rather quickly coming up against both issues of justice and the internal economics of the publishing industry itself.

Science fiction writer **Norman Spinrad**

THE FIRST BOOK CONTRACT I SIGNED contained an option clause, giving the publisher first right of refusal on my next book. It meant that I had to show my next proposal to that publisher, giving him the chance to accept or reject, before I could show it to any other publisher. I noticed the option clause and asked to have it deleted. The publisher said, "That's a standard clause. It's in all our contracts. Just sign it."

I didn't want to blow the sale, and it didn't seem like such a big deal, so I signed it.

A year or so later, I was approached by a second publishing house. Publisher Number Two was a small but aggressive house on the West Coast. The president of the company was personally involved in all acquisitions. He had seen the first book I did, and was favorably impressed.

"I'd like to see a proposal for a new book," he told me over the phone. "Write up some ideas and send them to me."

"I wish I could," I said, "but there's an option clause in my contract with Publisher Number One. I'm obligated to show them my next proposal before I send it anywhere else."

"Oh, you should never sign a contract with an option clause," he said. "That just ties your hands."

"Well, I asked to have the option clause removed," I said, "but they wouldn't do it. They said it's standard in all their contracts."

"I'm sure it's *printed* in all their contracts," he replied, "but if you had just crossed out that paragraph and initialed in the margin, I'm sure they would have let it slide."

"Ah," I said. "I'll keep that in mind for the future."

So I sent a proposal to Publisher Number One to fulfill the terms of the option clause. After about eight weeks, they rejected it. That was fine with me. Now I could take the proposal to Publisher Number Two. I did so, and the president of the company loved it and sent me a contract. I wrote the book, and it was well received.

My first two books got the attention of a third publisher, who contacted me and wanted me to write a book for them. Great! I came up with another proposal, sold it to Publisher Number Three, and wrote the book.

A few weeks before that third book came out, I got a call from the president of Publisher Number Two. He had been reading the trades, and had seen the notices for my forthcoming book. "Jim," he said, "we were very distressed to learn that you have a book coming out with another publisher."

"Distressed?" I said. "Why were you distressed?"

"Well, Jim," he said, "there's an option clause in the contract you signed with us. We have first right of refusal on your next book, and here you have a book coming out with another publisher—"

"What?!" I couldn't believe what I was hearing. "But you're the one who told me never to sign a contract with an option clause! Are you telling me you have an option clause in your own contracts?"

"That's correct," he said. "And you signed it."

I asked him to hold, and I dashed to my filing cabinet, pulled out the contract, and *boiiinnng!* There it was, just as he said. The blood in my veins turned to quivering lime Jell-O. I went back to the phone.

"Heh-heh," I said nervously, "there it is. Option clause. Whaddaya know?"

"Now, Jim," the president of Publisher Number Two continued, "as you know, we *could* enforce our rights in a court of law."

I gulped.

"But we don't want to do anything that drastic."

I was certainly glad to hear *that*.

"If you'll just show us your next book, Jim," he said, "we'll agree to let this matter slide." And that is how we resolved it.

But to this day, I wonder why the president of Publisher Number Two told me *never* to sign an option clause—then gave me a contract with an option clause in it.

Even more to the point, I wonder how the heck I *missed* it.

THE FINE-PRINT MINEFIELD

In a movie contract, I was asked to grant the right to my book to the producers, in perpetuity, throughout the universe. When I wrote in, "With the exception of Sagittarius and the Andromeda galaxy," it was accepted. Evidently the lawyers, who are writing to avoid litigation in a litigious world, did not anticipate a lawsuit from Sagittarius.

Fantasy writer **Madeleine L'Engle**

I am fully responsible to know what is in every contract I sign. This is true even if the contract is reviewed by an attorney or an agent. A contract is not light reading. It must be studied line by line and word by word. Understand: I am not an attorney and I am not giving legal advice in this chapter. What I am giving you is the benefit of my experience (including my regrets) after having signed some sixty-odd book contracts during my career. My intention is to alert you to the contract issues you should be aware of and which you, along with your attorney, should carefully explore before you sign.

Don't believe it when a publisher hands you a sheaf of papers and says, "That's our standard contract—just sign it." Take your time to read the contract carefully and run it past your attorney. Of course, most of what you find in a contract is "boilerplate"—standard language found in most such documents. Much of that boilerplate language is designed to protect you as well as the publisher.

But the fundamental negotiable issues of a contract—the so-called "deal points"—are all negotiable and deserve your careful attention. Deal points include the advance, royalty percentages, option clause, reversion clause, and subsidiary rights. Some of the contract language regarding those deal points will not be in your best interests—but those deal points can be balanced in your favor with a little polite dickering.

If you find language you don't understand, have your attorney explain it to you. If you encounter clauses that are unfair or unacceptable to you, negotiate and ask for changes. If this is a first-time contract, you probably won't have much leverage to get all the terms you want, but don't hesitate to ask. The worst that can happen is that the publisher will say no—and publishers will sometimes bend in your favor, even on a first-time contract, just to make you happy. They do, after all, want to publish your book.

Now, let's look at some of the most important clauses in your contract and see what they mean:

• **Grant of Rights.** We often talk about "selling" a book to a publisher, but if you look closely at the language of a normal royalty-based book contract, you'll see that you aren't actually *selling* anything. In reality, you are licensing and authorizing the publisher to print, distribute, and market your book for a defined period of time—typically until sales fall to a sufficiently low level that the book is deemed to have run it course and is declared "out of print."

The moment you created your book or other written work, you instantly owned all the rights to that work. Even if you didn't register a copyright with the Library of Congress, you still own the copyright. So the Grant of Rights clause in your contract licenses the publisher to exercise the various rights that are contained within that stack of papers you created.

The Grant of Rights clause also specifies in what part of the world the publisher may sell copies of your work—usually, "throughout the world," or even "throughout the universe." I actually signed one of those "throughout the universe" contracts once, and I'm looking forward to seeing a Klingon edition of that book someday.

Understand, everything I've said about the Grant of Rights clause applies only to a contract that pays you royalties. If the contract is a "work-for-hire" agreement, all of that goes out the window. A work-for-hire agreement pays you a flat fee for the work you create, and that's the end of it. If you have written a book on a work-for-hire basis, you actually *did* sell your book. The publisher owns everything, and you own nothing. It's gone, outta here, *phhhht*! Does that mean you should never write a book on a work-for-hire basis? You didn't hear that from me.

Fact is, I've written a number of books for a flat fee. Those books enhanced my resumé and led to other books that are now earning royalties.

> "Don't believe it when a publisher hands you a sheaf of papers and says, 'That's our standard contract—just sign it.'"

But it's also a fact that my two best-selling books to date were both written for a flat fee (I was a collaborator, not the sole author). Those books made a ton of money, but not for me. I got my flat fee and I was out of the picture. Am I bitter? No. I agreed to those terms going in, knowing full well what could happen. But the experience of writing two very successful books without getting to share in their success steels my resolve to always seek a share of the royalties.

• **Reversion of Rights.** This is crucially important: Make sure your contract contains a carefully worded reversion clause. This clause states that all the rights you have licensed to the publisher revert back to you when the book goes out of print. Those rights can often be relicensed to another publisher. In fact, there are many stories of authors whose books flopped with one publisher, went out of print, then soared under the aegis of a new publisher.

If your contract does not contain a reversion clause that is worded in your favor, you may *never* get the rights back to your book. You will have effectively *sold* the rights to your book for all eternity. The emergence of new technologies such as e-publishing (making a book available for download over the Internet) and print-on-demand (which enables books to be published one copy at a time for a reasonable price) has proven to be a double-edged sword for writers. If your book is declared out of print by a publisher and the rights revert to you, then even if you can't get another publisher to put it back in print, you can always sell it through e-publishing and print-on-demand outlets.

But those same new technologies can also be used by publishers to technically keep your book "in print"—conceivably by selling as few as one or two copies per year through e-publishing or print-on-demand. For example, a typical reversion clause might contain such language as, "The Work shall not be considered to be out of print if it is available for sale in any printed edition, including reprints...."

> "The moment you created your book or other written work, you instantly owned all the rights to that work. Even if you didn't register a copyright... ."

And those reprints can be construed as including the publisher's own e-books or print-on-demand editions. Owning a piece of intellectual property does you little good if the publisher locks up your book, refuses to reprint it, and refuses to revert the rights to you.

Tell your attorney and your publisher that you want that little loophole closed up. Clarifying that point can be in your publisher's best interest as well as your own. After all, it doesn't do you or your publisher any good to have ambiguity in your contract (contractual ambiguity is fertile ground for litigation). A working draft of the "Author's Bill of Rights," drafted by the Writers Group Summit (with delegates from Romance Writers of America, Science Fiction Writers of America, the Authors Guild, and other major writers' organizations) suggests this author-friendly definition of "out of print" in its model reversion clause:

> *Reversion of rights.* Authors shall be informed immediately when a book meets the Out of Print criteria as defined in the contract. If the author requests reversion of rights and the reversion criteria are met, said reversion will be granted in a timely manner, not longer than sixty days after the receipt of a written request. Print-on-Demand, electronic, or other "one at a time" print methods will not be acceptable as constituting a "reprint." In order to be considered a reprint, the publisher must prove a print run of a minimum of 1,000 paperback or 500 hardcover copies. Any book declared "Out of Stock" for more than three months shall be deemed Out of Print. Any book selling fewer than 200 copies in a calendar year shall be deemed Out of Print.[1]

Don't forget: Your book may have a lot of commercial life left in it, even after your publisher has lost interest. A book pronounced dead by Publisher A could be resurrected and given a whole new life by Publisher B—but only if you are able to reclaim the rights to your book from Publisher A! Don't surrender any potential second-chance earnings from your book. Nail down that reversion clause and protect your intellectual property rights.

• **Delivery of a Satisfactory Manuscript.** The publisher has probably accepted your book for publication on the basis of a proposal you submitted. The publisher liked your proposal, sent you a contract, paid you an advance—and now you must write the complete book. This clause typically requires you to deliver a manuscript that is satisfactory to the publisher "in style, content, length and form"—usually at the publisher's "sole discretion." It also must be delivered by a certain deadline. If it is not satisfactory, the publisher will usually require that revisions be made to bring it to a "satisfactory" condition. In extreme cases, the publisher can reject the manuscript, terminate the contract, and (if the contract stipulates) demand return of the advance from the author.

On rare occasions, that word "satisfactory" can be a writer's worst nightmare. Novelist Herbert Gold once signed a four-book contract with a major New York publishing house. He turned in the first two books, which were accepted and published. Apparently, the publisher was not happy with the sales of those two titles. When Gold turned in the third book, the publishing house rejected it as "unsatisfactory." Gold found another publisher, and the book was published. At that point, his first publisher sued to recover the entire advance for all four books, less royalties paid for actual sales. Gold filed a countersuit on the grounds that his manuscript must have been "satisfactory," as the contract demanded, because it had been published. The court ruled against Gold because the language of the contract gave the publishing house "sole discretion" to accept or reject the book. However, the court ruled that Gold only had to repay one-fourth of the advance for the four-book contract, less royalties Gold had earned on sales of the first two books.[2]

What constitutes a "satisfactory" manuscript? The Satisfactory Manuscript clause gives publishers complete authority in a realm of utter subjectivity. But don't worry. This clause rarely comes back to bite any competent, diligent writer. There have been a few times when I have turned in a draft that my editor did not consider "satisfactory." Usually, all that's needed to bring it up to "satisfactory" is a little tweaking. This clause has never troubled my sleep.

• **Advance.** The advance is money paid to the author by the publisher upon signing of the contract. The traditional and standard practice is for the publisher to pay half of the advance on signing the contract and half on delivery of a complete and acceptable manuscript. An advance is paid against future royalties. This means that the author will not receive any additional money unless and until sales of the book have earned royalties in excess of the amount of the paid advance.

In recent years, I have seen a few publishers inflicting an unfortunate practice on their authors: Instead of breaking an advance into two halves, they break it into thirds: one-third on signing, one-third on manuscript acceptance, and one-third on publication. That's right, *on publication*. Remember, the normal span of time from manuscript acceptance to publication date is about six to twelve months. To my knowledge, writers are the only class of workers who are routinely expected to wait six to twelve months to be paid for their work. (For the sake of full disclosure, I have to confess that I actually signed such a contract—*once*. Never again.)

• **Royalties.** Royalties are percentage-based shares paid to the writer from proceeds resulting from the sale of his or her work. The bigger the royalty percentages you negotiate, the more money you earn. Royalties are calculated in one of two ways: net (sometimes called "wholesale price") and gross (or "retail price"). It is important to know the difference between the two, and to understand which method is used in your contract.

A royalty on the gross is the simplest to compute and understand— it's a percentage of the retail price of your book. A royalty on the net is based on net receipts to the publisher—typically the cover price less discounts to distributors, wholesalers, and booksellers, which generally average around 50 percent. So if you receive a royalty on the net, you will be paid a percentage of the discounted price instead of a percentage of the full retail price.

The first time I ever saw a contract that paid a net royalty, I was astonished. I was used to a royalty of 10 percent of the gross; this contract offered a 16 percent royalty—and I thought I had died and gone to heaven. But when I re-read the royalty clause, I realized I was being offered 16 percent of the *net*, not the gross. When I asked about it, the publisher assured me that 16 percent of the net worked out to roughly the same as 10 percent of the gross.

But let's do the math, shall we? The publisher's net receipts on a given book, after being sold at discount to distributors, wholesalers, and booksellers, averages around 50 percent. What is 50 percent of a 16 percent royalty? Simple: It's 8 percent—a full two points *less* than the 10 percent of the gross I was accustomed to getting. On average, in order to get the equivalent of 10 percent of the gross, I should have been offered a 20 percent royalty on a net contract.

> "Royalties are percentage-based shares paid to the writer from pro-ceeds resulting from the sale of his or her work. The bigger the royalty percentages you negotiate, the more money you earn."

Look at it another way: Let's say you write a book that sells for $20 retail. Let's further say that, after discounting your book 50 percent to a distributor or retailer, the publisher receives $10 for that book. Obviously, if your contract gives you a 10 percent royalty on the retail price, you will receive a $2.00 royalty on that book. But if your contract gives you a 16 percent royalty on the net, you'll only receive $1.60; an 18 percent royalty on the net will yield $1.80; a 20 percent royalty on the net will yield $2.00. The point is that you must be aware of exactly what you are being offered. A supposedly "fat" 16 percent royalty may actually be a "lite royalty" comprised entirely of "nonfat skim money."

An author-friendly contract should contain "escalators"—levels of sales at which a higher royalty rate kicks in. Royalty rate structures and escalators tend to vary between hardcover, trade paperback, and mass-market paperback editions. An average royalty rate for hardcover books is 10 percent of the retail price on up to 10,000 copies sold; 12.5 percent on 10,001 to 25,000 copies sold; and 15 percent thereafter.

For trade paperbacks—softcover books with a trim size similar to hardcover books, sold primarily in bookstores—a typical royalty rate is around 7 to 10 percent of the retail price, often with escalators at the 10,000 and 25,000 levels or so.

For mass-market paperback originals—pocket-size softcover books sold in newsstands, drugstores, and supermarkets—the royalty rates are much less, frequently starting as low as 6 percent of retail. The first escalator usually kicks in at a much higher sales figure, often 100,000 or 150,000. But sales figures for mass-market paperbacks are usually much higher than for hardcover and trade paper editions. Because of bigger sales figures (that's why they call it "mass-market") and despite the lower royalty rate, authors often make far more money from mass-market paperback editions than from hardcovers or trade paperbacks. Mass-market paperback originals do not offer the prestige of a hardcover edition, but they often help you pay off the mortgage more quickly.

Understand, however, that there is a distinction between contracting to write a mass-market paperback original versus contracting to write a hardcover or trade paper original that is later reprinted as a mass-market paperback. There are few trade publishers who also publish mass-market paperbacks. So if your book is successful enough to warrant mass-market publication, your trade publisher will try to sell the mass-market rights to a mass-market publisher. You will find this covered under the Subsidiary Rights section of your contract, and normal practice is for the proceeds from a mass-market sale to be divided, 50 percent to the publisher, 50 percent to the author.

Be aware, too, that royalty rates are usually halved for sales to book clubs and overseas markets. One irony for Canadian authors publishing with U.S. houses is that sales in the author's own country are regarded as "foreign" sales. So a Canadian author's efforts to promote his or her own books at home only receive half as much reward.

A bit of historical perspective: Prior to the Great Depression, it was standard practice for authors to receive a 15 percent royalty on the cover price—sometimes even 20 percent. After the stock market crash of 1929 and the resulting economic hard times, publishers asked authors to share in the national sacrifice and accept rates of around 10 percent. To this day, despite intervening eras of enormous prosperity for the publishing industry, royalty rates remain at the Depression Era levels—which may explain why so many writers suffer from depression!

• **Statements and Payments.** Your contract spells out how often you will receive a royalty statement. The most author-friendly publishers issue statements quarterly. The minimum you should accept is two statements a year. Royalty statements should be issued within 60 days of the close of the reporting period. The advance you receive is paid against future royalties, so your first few statements may show that your book is in the hole. Once your book "earns out" (that is, once your royalties on sales exceed the advance you were originally paid), you will start getting royalty checks along with your statements.

It is common for a book to sell well for the first six months or year, then drop off the charts. If the book no longer warrants a major promotional push from the publisher, but continues to sell well enough to keep it in the catalog or on the publisher's order form, it is called a "backlist title." Having backlist books in print is a good thing—they bring in steady royalty checks (which can range from dinner-and-a-movie money to serious windfalls). The smartest strategy is to generate books of perennial interest and longevity in the marketplace. [For advice on how to write books that maintain their shelflife, see *Damn! Why Didn't I Write That?* by Marc McCutcheon (Quill Driver Books, 2001).]

• **Reserve Against Returns.** Most publishers withhold a "reserve against returns" from your royalties. That is, they anticipate that a certain percentage of books will be returned by booksellers as unsold. In effect, the publisher places your books in bookstores on consignment. In the end, you receive royalties on books that "sell through" (books that are actually purchased by customers) and your royalties are docked for unsold books that are returned (usually mangled and dog-eared) by booksellers. The reserve clause is usually worded rather vaguely: "Publisher may maintain a reasonable reserve against anticipated returns." If possible, the author should try to get this "reasonable reserve" changed to a hard number—preferably no more than 10 percent (though some publishers consider as much as 50 percent to be "reasonable").

• **Author's Warranty.** In this clause, the author promises that the work is original, is not obscene (in a legal sense), is not libelous, does not invade anyone's privacy, and does not expose the publisher to criminal penalties or civil litigation. Usually, the author agrees not only to cooperate with the publisher's legal defense, but also to *indemnify* the publisher against loss—that is, to protect the publisher against loss and compensate the publisher for costs arising from a legal defense. If the publisher's editors and attorneys determine that your book contains material that may create legal problems, you agree to fix those problems before the book is published.

As you write, it is best to think of all possible ways to avoid the slightest risk of litigation (you may want to reconsider that thinly veiled *roman à clef* you've been planning). It's not enough to say, "If I get sued, I know I can win." Getting sued is a very expensive proposition, and even if you win in court, the Author's Warranty clause probably requires you to pay a substantial portion of the legal costs. Even being in the right could ruin you.

> "It is common for a book to sell well for the first six months or year, then drop off the charts."

Novelist Gwen Davis Mitchell became painfully aware of the terms of her Author's Warranty clause when she was sued for libel over her novel *Touching*, published by Doubleday. The plaintiff contended that a character in the novel was a thinly disguised and libelous version of himself—and the court agreed. The plaintiff was awarded $75,000 in damages—and Doubleday in turn sued Mitchell to recover its losses. That case was settled out of court for an undisclosed amount.[3] The moral of the story: If you are thinking of writing *anything* that could land you in court, it just might cost you—big time.

• **Option Clause.** In May 1996, the book publisher Scribner exercised an option clause signed in 1935, obtaining the right to publish a book written in 1916 by an author who died in 1949. The option clause was in the contract for Margaret Mitchell's *Gone With the Wind*. That option gave Scribner the right to publish Mitchell's manuscript entitled *Lost Laysen*—a romance tale set in the South Pacific.

Mitchell had penned the tale in two handwritten notebooks when she was sixteen, and the manuscript came to light among the personal effects of the late author's friend, Henry Love Angel. When the legal eagles at Scribner heard that the Mitchell estate planned to auction the book for publication, they checked the contract Mitchell had signed with the original publisher, Macmillan. (Both Scribner and Macmillan were part of the Simon & Schuster group by this time.) They found that the company had a binding option on "future" books—even "future" books that were written in the past.

The moral of the story: Don't ignore that option clause—it can have a long reach.

An option clause isn't necessarily a bad thing. It gives your publisher the right of first refusal on your next book—and that means the welcome mat is already out for your next book. The option clause should stipulate that the publisher will report back to you within a reasonable period, usually ninety days—though some contracts stipulate ninety days after publication of your present book. (Publishers often want to wait and see what kind of reception your first book gets before signing on for a second.)

The option clause doesn't obligate you to publish your next book with the same publisher. You can refuse the publisher's offer. You can seek an offer from another publisher. But, in general, an option clause prevents you from publishing with another house unless that house offers better terms than your present publisher is willing to match.

The publisher's argument in favor of the option clause certainly has merit. A publishing house makes an investment—a somewhat risky investment, it's true—when it publishes a book by an unknown, first-time author. Publishers want to protect that investment and develop the author's byline into a trademark that sells many books over the long haul. Long-lasting, mutually beneficial author-publisher relationships tend to produce the best books and the biggest long-term sales.

Of course, when the author-publisher relationship is strong, neither side needs an option clause to enforce it. That's one reason option clauses should disappear from your contracts after the first or second book. If you've done one or two books that are even modestly successful, you should have no trouble getting an option clause deleted on request.

• **Basket Accounting.** I call this a "stealth clause," because you will have to hunt for it—you won't find a big bold heading in your contract announcing, "Basket Accounting Clause." In fact, you probably won't find the phrase "basket accounting" anywhere in your contract, so you will have to read your contract carefully and spot the practice of "basket accounting," regardless of how it is phrased. Recently, the term "cross-collateralizing" has come into vogue as a description of basket accounting. For example: "The royalty advance shall be cross-collateralized among all works between Author and Publisher, past, current, and future," or similar wording. Here's how basket accounting or cross-collateralizing works:

Let's say you publish two books with the same publisher. You get a $10,000 advance for each book. Book 1 only earns $9,000 in royalties—$1,000 short of earning back the advance. The good news is that Book 2 earned $11,000 in royalties—the full advance plus $1,000. But where is your check for $1,000? You don't get one. The publisher grabbed the royalties you earned on Book 2 and applied them against the shortfall on Book 1. The publisher put both of your books in one "basket" and treated them as a single earning unit.

Is that fair? Well, look at it this way: Suppose you only published Book 1 and never published another book. Would the publisher come and demand the unearned portion of the advance back? Of course not. The advance is yours to keep no matter how well or how poorly the book performs. That's just part of the risk a publisher takes for being in business. The publishing house paid you that advance because, in its best business judgment, it believed your book would earn that much and more. Anyone in business knows that you win some, you lose some. So is it fair for the publisher to rob your future books to make up the deficit on Book 1? Not in my opinion.

> "As you write, it is best to think of all possible ways to avoid the slightest risk of litigation (you may want to reconsider that thinly veiled *roman à clef* you've been planning)."

Let's look at it from another angle: Suppose you published Book 1 with Publisher A and Book 2 with Publisher B. Book 1 loses money, and Book 2 makes money. Does Publisher A have the right to knock on your door and demand that you hand over your royalty check from Publisher B? Of course not.

So do you see what basket accounting does to you, the author? It *penalizes* you for publishing multiple books with the same publisher! If you have one book that flops, that book will *steal earnings* from your successful books.

Now, a publisher might say, "Well, if you hadn't written a flop, then you wouldn't have anything to complain about." But that statement assumes the book flopped because the author wrote a bad book (and it makes one wonder why the publisher willingly published a bad book). Fact is, books often fail because of factors beyond an author's control. They sometimes fail because the publisher did a poor job of promotion. And sometimes books fail even when both author and publisher do everything right. Go figure.

The fact remains that there is a long-standing tradition and accepted practice in the publishing industry: When the author receives an advance, it is not a loan to be paid back. It is payment that the author may keep, (if he tuns in an acceptable manuscript) regardless of future earnings or lack thereof. Siphoning earnings from his other books is an author-unfriendly practice.

• **Subsidiary Rights.** This is an often-overlooked section of the book contract. "Sub rights" have to do with the licensing of your book (or portions thereof) to alternate outlets. Sub rights may be marketed by your publisher, your agent, or both. Typical sub right usages include magazine excerpts, serializations, syndications, abridgments, book clubs, foreign publishers, reprints by other publishers, workbooks, advertising, live stage plays, computer software or other electronic versions, video recordings, sound recordings, TV and motion picture adaptations, merchandising (calendars, posters, toys and plush figures, clothing, electronic or board games, school supplies or lunch boxes, and so forth), so-called "future technology versions," or (even more all-inclusive) "all rights not specifically enumerated, whether now in existence or hereinafter coming into existence."

Publishers are understandably unwilling to give up 100 percent of the "sub rights," since these rights are often highly lucrative. You never know when a book might attract the attention of Hollywood and generate an unexpected potful of money—and I'm not just talking about novels, either. Even nonfiction books occasionally get the Hollywood treatment, as when David Reuben's bestselling sex manual, *Everything You Always Wanted to Know About Sex* (*But Were Afraid to Ask)* was adapted as a Woody Allen sketch-comedy movie in 1972.

Your book may be so vivid and exciting that it practically screams "Movie deal!" In that case, offering the publisher a share in the movie rights just makes your book that much more attractive. By the same token, taking those rights off the table can make your project considerably less attractive.

Some would argue that if a movie studio comes along and makes a blockbuster film based on your book, the publisher doesn't deserve any of that money. Publishers are in the book business, and they should be happy just getting the boost in book sales that a movie deal brings. Maybe so. Of course, the folks at the publishing house would argue that your book would never have come to the attention of those Hollywood moguls if the publishing house hadn't published it. Their position is that they are entitled to a piece of the action because they took the original risk on your book and believed in it. Well, there's merit in that position, too.

> "When the author receives an advance, it is not a loan to be paid back. It is payment that the author may keep, regardless of future earnings or lack thereof."

When negotiating your contract, you'll have to take all the factors and competing philosophies into account and make up your own mind: Would agreeing to give up half of the film rights help you sell your book? Would demanding 100 percent of the sub rights be a deal breaker? Can you arrive at a compromise split—say, 60-40 or 75-25? It's all blue sky at this point, so it doesn't cost either side anything out-of-pocket to find a yes-yes solution. Ultimately, there is no one-size-fits-all answer to the question of sub rights. But here are a few key points to ponder:

• The smaller the percentage of sub rights you give the publisher, the less incentive the publisher has to go out and sell those rights.

• If you allow the publisher to take half of the proceeds from TV and film adaptation, you are in effect *trusting* the publisher to get you the best possible deal—and the publisher may not be competent or well-connected in that area.

• If you manage to keep 100 percent of the sub rights for yourself, then you'd better have an aggressive, well-connected agent who can sell them for you. The average author is in no position to shop those rights around Tinseltown, and must rely on the professionals. Make sure you've got a good professional in your corner.

• Don't get too starry-eyed about having your book made into a movie or TV show. It could happen, but the odds are somewhere between slim and none. Instead, focus on writing the very best book you can. And if some film producer happens to notice what a wonderful book you've written—well, who knows?

A "THROWAWAY CLAUSE" COULD CHANGE YOUR LIFE

> I was put on earth to make people laugh. Everything that has happened to me, including all that misery and suffering, was designed to bring this about. I am where I am today because God arranged it.
>
> *Novelist* **Irene Kampen**

Irene Kampen worked for eight years as a reporter and gossip columnist for the *Tribune* in Levittown, Pennsylvania. In 1954, she quit her job and moved with her husband and young daughter to the quaint town of Ridgefield, Connecticut. There they built their dream house. The dream turned sour when Irene's husband took off with the wife of the architect who designed the house. That was the end of their fifteen-year marriage.

Newly divorced, Irene Kampen took a day job in her father's New York City florist shop to support herself and her daughter. She commuted daily from Connecticut, and the meager pay didn't meet her monthly expenses. To help with the mortgage, she took in a boarder—another woman who was recently divorced and caring for a young son.

In an interview with Max Gunther (author of *The Luck Factor*), she said, "I was divorced, broke, trying to raise a child. I was utterly miserable. There was nowhere to turn. Life seemed to be over for me.... It was in this dark time, the late 1950s, that I started going to church. I hadn't been seriously interested in religion before, but now I was desperate for any comfort I could get. I didn't pray for things to get better. I was too pessimistic for that. My prayer was, 'I know I'm finished and I'm not asking for any fairy-tale surprises. Just, please, don't let things get any worse.'"

One day, she went to the local library to return a book. It was ostensibly a book of humor, written by a woman author. Handing the book to the librarian, she said, "I could write a funnier book than that."

The librarian had heard it all before. "It's easy to say you can write a book," replied the woman at the desk. "Once—just once!—I'd like to meet somebody who doesn't just *talk* about writing a book, but actually *does* it."

The librarian's words stung—but Irene thought, *Why shouldn't I write a book?* She had worked as a newspaper reporter and columnist. She knew syntax and punctuation. She could type with all ten fingers. So she went home and began writing a book about two divorced women raising their kids in one house. Despite the emotional exhaustion she felt as a struggling single mother, she could find humor in her most painful problems. The book she wrote was a wry, upbeat comedy.

It took Irene Kampen a year to write the book, working in the few free hours she had. "I didn't even know why I was writing it," she later recalled. "It was more or less a hobby, something to keep my mind off my troubles. I guess I must have dreamed about getting it published, but I didn't seriously believe it would ever happen."

Shortly after completing the book, she was invited to a party in Ridgefield. There, she met a screenwriter from Hollywood and shyly told him, "I've got something I'm working on. I think it's a book." The writer said he'd like to see it. She dashed home, grabbed her typescript, and took it back to him.

A few days after the party, the writer called her. "It's good," he said. "I'm showing it to a friend of mine, a story editor at Twentieth Century-Fox."

The story editor referred Irene Kampen to a New York literary agent. The agent sent her manuscript to a publisher, who offered Irene a $1,000 advance and a standard contract. She felt she had just won the lottery. "I would have been happy just to have somebody publish the book," she said, "but to have them actually give me money in advance—this was fantastic!"

Her agent knew that $1,000 was chickenfeed. It meant the publisher didn't expect the book to sell at all, but figured it was good enough to take a small chance on. The agent asked the publisher for more money; the publisher said, "That's my offer—take it or leave it." So, in a face-saving gesture, the agent responded, "All right—we'll take the thousand-dollar advance, but we want a concession. In the event the book is adapted for film or television, all earnings go to the author."

The publisher, knowing the long odds of selling a first novel to Hollywood, figured he was giving up precisely nothing. "Agreed," he replied. And the deal was done.

Irene Kampen had no idea that her life was about to intersect with the life of the famous red-haired comedienne, Lucille Ball. The actress's long-running TV sitcom, *I Love Lucy*, had ended production—and her long-running marriage to bandleader Desi Arnaz had ended in divorce. Lucy was looking for a new sitcom for herself and her friend, Vivian Vance, and she wanted a show without major roles for men.

Soon after Irene Kampen's book, *Life Without George*, was published, Lucille Ball's agent picked up a copy at an L.A. bookstore and gave it to Lucy. The actress said, "This is it!" Lucy bought the screen rights and Irene Kampen's story of two struggling single mothers became the basis of *The Lucy Show*. The series ran for eight years, and is still shown in reruns today. The show made Irene Kampen a very wealthy woman.

Thanks to *The Lucy Show*, *Life Without George* became a bestseller. Irene went on to write ten successful books, including *Europe Without George*, *Last Year at Sugarbush*, *Here Comes the Bride*, and *Due to Lack of Interest Tomorrow Has Been Canceled*. She published numerous short stories and articles in *McCalls*, *Redbook*, *Ladies Home Journal*, and *Reader's Digest*, and maintained an active schedule on the lecture circuit.[4]

There is a lesson for all of us in this story. Irene Kampen came very close to splitting that huge pot of TV money with her publisher, and ending up with only half a fortune. The advance clause turned out to be the *least* important deal point in her contract. The *big* money was tucked away in a little sub rights clause that the publisher dismissed without a second thought. The moral of the story: Don't take anything in your contract for granted. Read it carefully. Understand it. Ask questions. Negotiate. Get the very best deal you possibly can.

Don't think that contracts are just for lawyers and agents. To be a working writer, you *must* know what you're signing. The smallest "throwaway" clause could change your life—just as it changed the life of Irene Kampen.

THE SEVEN ESSENTIAL HABITS
OF A WORKING WRITER

Each morning I rose at seven, dashed cold water on my face, combed my hair, brushed my teeth, drank a large glass of unsweetened grapefruit juice and went directly to my typewriter, where I worked without interruption until twelve-thirty, by which time I was exhausted.

Writer Lukas Yoder in **James A. Michener's** The Novel

In writing, habit seems to be a much stronger force than either willpower or inspiration.

John Steinbeck

IN 1982, A MAN ASKED ME TO HELP HIM WRITE A BOOK. Because of some celebrity status he had achieved, he had three or four publishers pursuing him, but he wasn't a writer. He knew I had written a number of magazine pieces, so he showed me his notes and asked if I could turn them into a book.

"I've never written a book before," I said. "I don't know if I can."

"Well," he said, "this would be a way to find out."

I couldn't argue with that. So we met with an acquisitions editor from a large house that published over 150 titles a year. I was impressed by the fact that the editor flew out from the East Coast just to have lunch with us and discuss our book idea. We pitched it and he liked it—but I could tell he had reservations about me. "Jim," he said, looking me straight in the eye, "have you ever written a book before?"

"No," I replied firmly, "but I've written around a hundred magazine articles. The way I look at it, this book will be ten chapters long.

That's just ten magazine pieces in a row." Outside, I exuded confidence. Inside, I honestly didn't know if I could pull it off.

It took me about four months, working in my spare time, to finish the book. It turned out to be a lot easier than I expected. Once I was finished, I knew I could write a book. I also learned a valuable principle: Every time you take on something you've never done before—and you *do* it—your confidence and skill levels go up a notch.

Six years after that first book was published, I made the jump to full-time freelance writing. Soon after that, I got a call from an editor with whom I had done several books. "How would you like to write a book about football?" she asked. Well, I had never written a sports book before. I had read a lot of sports writing, and I knew it was a different breed of cat from the kind of writing I had done before. I didn't know if I could pull it off or not. Naturally, I said, "Sure!"

Turned out the book in question was the autobiography of Reggie White, the legendary defensive end of the Green Bay Packers. A few hundred sports writers around the country would have killed to get that assignment (and I was the guy they would've killed). But this assignment just fell into my lap. Working with Reggie turned out to be one of the most enjoyable assignments of my career. In fact, I think my nonsports-writing background enabled me to ask the questions and find the story angles that the average sportswriter might have missed.

Working with Reggie gave me some terrific stories and insights for my own book, *Answers to Satisfy the Soul* (Quill Driver Books, 2002). It also led to other sports projects, including *Undefeated* (working with father-son NFL stars Bob Griese and Brian Griese), *It Happens on Sunday* (an illustrated football gift book, written with Pat Williams, foreword by Reggie White), and *Got Game: Living Life Above the Rim* (an NBA gift book, also with Pat Williams, foreword by David Robinson).

Over the years, I've learned that it doesn't matter that I'm being asked to attempt something I've never done before. I have learned that whenever I attempt a book, I achieve it. Whenever I tackle a subject, the material is always there to support it. If an editor asks if I can do it, I always say, "Sure, no problem." That's not arrogance or braggadocio. I'm not just blowing smoke. I really *know* I can do it. Why? Because I always have.

Confidence produces opportunities. Opportunities produce experience. Experience produces more confidence. That is how your career spirals upward. You've got to have faith in yourself, a rock-steady assurance that you *can* do it, even when you can't imagine *how* you are going to do it.

An attitude of confidence is one of the seven essential habits you need to succeed as a working writer.

HABITS ARE BETTER THAN INSPIRATION

> There must be some little quality of fierceness until the habit pattern of a certain number of words is established. There is no possibility, in me at least, of saying. "I'll do it if I feel like it." Perhaps there are people who can work that way, but I cannot. I must get my words down every day whether they are any good or not.
>
> *John Steinbeck*

Over the dozen or so years that I've been writing full-time, I've discovered something about myself: My creative energies rise and fall. I have learned to become keenly aware of those energy levels. There are days when I feel creatively depleted. I don't feel that inner motivation, intensity, and drive to write. It's not that I feel *physically* tired. I just feel creatively spent, listless, and uninspired.

Yet there are other days when I wake up full of an inner fire, my mind bursting with ideas, my fingers eager to dance on the keyboard. I think that's the experience some people describe when they say they feel "inspired" to write. I enjoy writing on days when I feel inspired—but I have found that such days are rare. Most days, writing is work. I enjoy my work, so that's okay, but rarely do I feel "inspired" when I work. I get my work done by simply being there and slogging through it, hour by hour, day after day.

It's my habit. I write every day. On those rare occasions that I go a whole day without writing (Christmases and family vacations, for example), I have a vague, nagging sense that I *should* be writing. Something inside tells me that it's not right to not write.

That's the power of a habit.

If I only wrote when inspired, my output of published books would be a slim fraction of what it is today—and you wouldn't be reading this book right now. Fact is, there are many days I drag my unwilling carcass to the computer, slump in my chair, groan inarticulately, and begin grinding out my day's allotment of words. Occasionally, while I am sitting in that unwilling, uninspired state, I feel something come over me: the magic of inspiration. The words on the screen take on a life of their own. Ideas start flowing like wine. Soon, I find I can't type fast enough to keep up with the magic.

By the time I'm ready to stop, I've racked up two or three thousand words. If I hadn't started writing purely by habit, I would have *missed* the lightning bolt of inspiration when it finally struck. So I write daily and diligently, inspired or not. As someone once observed, "The art of writing is the art of applying the seat of the pants to the seat of the chair."

> "Confidence produces opportunities. Opportunities produce experience. Experience produces more confidence. That is how your career spirals upward."

Habits are constant. Inspiration is variable—it comes and goes. That's why habits are better than inspiration. It is habit, not inspiration, that builds writing careers. Inspiration makes you feel energized while you write, but inspiration isn't writing. Only writing is writing, and you can write whether you feel inspired or not.

For me, writing is frequently the first thing I do each day, even before breakfast. I'll work for an hour or two, then take a break for a bowl of Grape Nuts, then go right back to work. I find that when I start writing soon after I get up, I'm charged up and ready to work. I find that it helps to pull away from my writing for short periods during the day. After I get back to work from picking up kids at school or running errands or exercising, I again feel refreshed and ready to plunge in again. Late afternoon and evening, when the whole family is together, is family time.

Sometimes, after everybody is in bed, I'll write for a couple hours again at night—it's a cool, quiet part of the day where I can usually crank out a few more pages without the phone ringing. It's also helpful to end the day by focusing on the project at hand. It means I have the project on my mind as I go to bed, and that glimmer of time before dreaming is when I often get ideas and insights to use the next morning.

I asked novelist Robert J. Sawyer about his habits and discipline as a writer, and how he responded to fluctuations in his creative energy.

He told me, "Writing is my job, and I'm my own boss. The keys to success are treating it like a job, and being a tough boss. I try to do some writing every single day—seven days a week. On weekdays, I don't call it quits until I've done 2,000 words. If that takes just ninety minutes—which, if I'm really cooking, is all it does—then I get to knock off early. If it takes twelve hours, which it sometimes does, then I'm at the keyboard for twelve hours.

"Sure, my creative energies do go up and down. My secret for dealing with this is to not write my novels in sequence from beginning to end. Rather, I do easy transitional scenes or descriptions when I'm at low ebb, and save the blockbuster action or dramatic scenes for when I'm firing on all cylinders."

I often experience times when it's obvious that I'm just not going to be productive. I can flail away at the keyboard all I want, but it's not going to get me anywhere. It's rare but it happens. Most writers experience it, but it doesn't mean we stop moving forward.

There's a lot of "writing" that takes place when you are not actually increasing the word count of your manuscript. Internet research, library research, and interviewing are all part of the writing process. Thinking is writing. Reading is writing. Daydreaming can even be writing. I get some of my best insights and ideas while I'm in the shower or driving my car. Some writers insist that they "write" while sleeping—that their dreaming subconscious actually hatches plot ideas and solves characterization problems during the REM stage. I dunno, maybe so.

> "If I only wrote when inspired, my output of published books would be a slim fraction of what it is today . . . ."

The point is, when you are at low ebb, keep doing tasks that advance your writing project toward completion. Make sure you don't rationalize away your writing time. Writers are the best rationalizers in the world: "I just spent the whole day in my hammock, and wrote a complete short story in my head. Now, all I have to do is type it up. I'll do that right after my nap...."

I have learned to be acutely aware of whether I am truly writing or merely procrastinating. There is a part of me that can always tell when I'm writing and when I'm "writing." Thinking, researching, phoning, e-mailing, and so forth are all part of the job description of a writer. If that's what needs to be done at the moment, fine. But if I'm only doing those things to avoid *writing*, I always know it. I can't kid myself.

"One hasn't become a writer until one has distilled writing into a habit, and that habit has been forced into an obsession," says African poet-essayist Niyi Osundare (*Pages From the Book of the Sun*). "Writing has to be an obsession. It has to be something as organic, physiological, and psychological as speaking or sleeping or eating."

> "Thinking is writing. Reading is writing. Daydreaming can even be writing. I get some of my best insights and ideas while I'm in the shower or driving my car."

The habits of a writer produce the *confidence* of a writer and the *identity* of a writer. Don't call yourself a writer if you haven't acquired the habits and discipline of the craft. Don't call yourself a writer if you don't write every day, if you aren't totally focused on your work and your success, every day of your life.

The habits of a writer begin with the simple act of sitting down to write. Then you repeat that act the following day. Then the day after that. And the day after that. And you keep doing that for however many days the good Lord gives you. Samuel Smiles (1812–1904), the English social reformer, invented a formula for building good habits. (Incidentally, he founded the self-help industry with his 1882 book *Self-Help*). His formula goes like this:

> Sow a thought, and you reap an act;
> Sow an act, and you reap a habit;
> Sow a habit, and you reap your character;
> Sow character, and you reap a destiny.

So you must begin thinking like a writer. If you think like a writer, then you will act like a writer. If you act like a writer, you will build the habits of a writer. These will produce the character of a writer, which will enable you to enjoy the destiny of a writer. Here, then, are the seven essential habits of a working writer. Think about them, act on them, habitualize them, and you will succeed.

HABIT 1: WRITE DAILY

I write six to eight hours a day. I have to treat it like a job, and as I was educated by the nuns, I have both guilt and discipline. This is a good thing. When I first started I wrote in longhand. My kids couldn't be trusted not to kill each other. I needed to be right there, and a notebook was portable. Later, I switched to a word processor, and finally to a PC. ... Habitually, I start writing first thing in the morning and go until about four or five. Occasionally, I go back and work at night when there won't be any phone calls to interrupt. Since I live in a rural and remote location, I don't have a lot of distractions.

Romantic suspense writer **Nora Roberts**

One of the writer's worst enemies is procrastination. Self-employed people have no boss to answer to, no time clock to punch, so a tendency to procrastinate is deadly. Working writers must be self-starters. The more regular and automatic your writing schedule, the less you are tempted to procrastinate. Causes of procrastination include self-doubt ("I don't know if I can do this"), a project that is intimidating because of its size, scope, or complexity ("I don't know where to begin"), and obsessive perfectionism ("I can't start until everything is just right").

The cure for procrastination is the knowledge that you *must* sit down at a specified time every day and you *must* write. When you allow yourself no option, no escape, then the temptation to procrastinate loses its hold over you.

On rare occasions when I don't feel enthusiastic about writing, I sometimes start the day with writing e-mails or other writing-related computer chores. It gets me in the chair, gets my fingers on the keyboard, and makes it a lot easier to simply toggle over to my book file and start writing.

During the early years of my writing career, I kept a book handy for a quick "jump-start" at the beginning of each writing day. That book was *Dare to Be a Great Writer: 329 Keys to Powerful Fiction* by Leonard Bishop, published by Writer's Digest Books. It's still in print, and I highly recommend it. I recently had the opportunity to meet Leonard Bishop at a writer's conference, and I shook his hand and said, "You don't realize it, but you saved my life." I was exaggerating—but not much. The advice and encouragement in that book got me through some very rough stretches in my early career. The entries are short, usually a page or less, but after reading just one, I felt revved up and ready to write. It really is a writer's lifesaver.

You may be planning a transition to full-time writing, but you wonder if you have the discipline to write every day. If you're still working at your day job, you may find it hard to carve out a daily writing time. If that's your situation, I have an idea that you can use right now, guaranteed to transform your life. It's called "The Grab 15 Principle."

I learned about Grab 15 from Bert Decker and his wife, Dru Scott Decker. Bert is the founder of Decker Communications, Inc., and author of *You've Got to be Believed to be Heard* and *Speaking With Bold Assurance*. Dru is a consultant in business management principles, customer satisfaction, and time management, and the author of *Finding More Time in Your Life* (Harvest House, 2001). Dru originated Grab 15, and that principle revolutionized my life. It is powerful because it is so incredibly simple. Here's how it works:

If you've got a book you want to write, but can't find a big chunk of free time in which to write it, then make a commitment to "grab fifteen minutes" every day to work on it. You may not be able to clear two weeks to get your novel started, but everyone can carve fifteen minutes out of every day to make *some* progress. You simply make a commitment to yourself that your head won't hit the pillow for the night until you've spent at least fifteen minutes on your project. I know it works because I wrote an entire novel in small, daily blocks of time that I carved out around my regular schedule as a nonfiction writer.

Sounds too easy, right? But there are a number of good reasons why this principle is so powerful.

First, those fifteen-minute snippets of time quickly add up. After all, what could you do if someone put two extra weeks in your year? Because if you Grab 15 every day, you will magically add 91.25 hours to your year—time that might otherwise just fall through the cracks. That's the equivalent of more than two full forty-hour work weeks—and you can add it to your schedule with hardly an ounce of inconvenience.

Second, the Grab 15 Principle boosts your creativity, concentration, and retention. It keeps your head in the game. Every day, you'll spend at least fifteen minutes concentrating on your Great American Novel. This provides reinforcement and continuity from day to day. Without the Grab 15 Principle, you'd be starting over from scratch every few months, whenever you happen to get around to your project. You'd lose tons of time just saying to yourself, "Now, where was I?" With the Grab 15 Principle, you never lose momentum. Because you remain focused on your goal every day, ideas and insights come to you even when you are not working on your book—and that makes each of your fifteen-minute sessions much more productive and effective.

Third, once you get started on your Grab 15 session, you'll find it hard to stop at fifteen minutes. When you are on a roll, you just keep going—and that's bonus time that moves you even closer to your goals.

Fourth and most important, the Grab 15 Principle builds good writing habits. If you are not a full-time writer yet but you want to be, then this is a good way to acquire a daily discipline—and a good way to prove to yourself that you have what it takes to write every day. Grab 15 helps you build a daily habit that soon becomes hard to break.

HABIT 2: CULTIVATE THE ART OF SOLITUDE AMID DISTRACTIONS

> The key to all writing is solitude, and the writer is that being who is most alive when alone. Being alone is the best preparation for writing.
> *Novelist **Martin Amis***

During his confinement in Soviet prisons, Alexander Solzhenitsyn became so accustomed to silence and solitude that he could no longer write without it. After his release and return to Moscow, he found he could no longer tolerate the noise of the trams, buses, and cars outside his window. It distracted him to the point where he couldn't write. So he had his wife lock him in the basement with nothing but a loaf of bread, a pitcher of water, and a metal pot for a privy. Once he was restored to the same solitary conditions he had "enjoyed" in prison, he could write again.

Writing is a solitary business, and you can't become a working writer without cultivating the art of solitude. In *The Power of Myth*, Joseph Campbell advocates having a place or time of complete insulation from the world, so that "creative incubation" may take place:

> You must have a room, or a certain hour or so a day, where
> you don't know what was in the newspapers that morning,
> you don't know who your friends are, you don't know what

you owe anybody, you don't know what anybody owes to you. This is a place where you can simply experience and bring forth what you are and what you might be. This is the place of creative incubation. At first you may find that nothing happens there. But if you have a sacred place and use it, something eventually will happen.[1]

Annie Dillard put it this way in *The Writing Life*: "The trick of writing, which drives previously sane people around the bend, is to locate some weird interior spot our brains don't seem well programmed for: the spot that enables you to be wholly alive while wholly alone." And feminist writer Andrea Dworkin offers this explanation of the power of solitude:

> The writer lives and works in solitude, no matter how many people surround her. Her most intensely lived hours are spent with herself. The pleasures and pains of writing are talked around or about but not shared. Her friends do not know what she does or how she does it. Like everyone else, they see only the results. The problems of her work are unique. The solution to one sentence is not the solution to any other sentence. No one else knows where she is going until she herself has gotten there. When others are contemplating the results, she is on her next project, all alone again. ... The solitude demanded by the work is extreme in and of itself. Others rarely live so alone, so self-created.[2]

One of the paradoxical discoveries I've made as a working writer is that it is possible to cultivate the art of solitude even when I am surrounded by interruptions, conversations, and people. If you are able to achieve absolute physical solitude, then I salute you. But I have never been able to find it—and I don't even desire it. I have found that, for me at least, solitude is not a physical *sanctum sanctorum* where I can go to shut out all the distractions of this world. Instead, my chosen form of solitude is *a place in the mind*, a sanctuary within the soul.

When I started as a full-time writer, I had children ages six and one. I worked in a room that was open to the family, and my kids were welcome to come and visit me any time. In fact, I saw that as one of the real advantages of writing for a living. My office was right in the heart of my family life, and that was the way I wanted it. Don't get me wrong—my kids weren't climbing on my back while I typed. I always had plenty of uninterrupted time to work while the kids were one or two rooms away.

But if my daughter wanted to show me something she had made in her first grade class, or my son wanted to share his handful of Cheerios with me, I could stop, look my kids in the eye, listen to them, talk to them, and be a full-time dad, as well as a full-time writer. I learned to "hold that thought" during each priceless interruption, and to pick up right where I left off as soon as the Little Interruption toddled off to watch the Disney Channel.

Of course, not all interruptions are priceless. Some are costly—such as the infamous "person from Porlock." In the year 1797, the poet Samuel Taylor Coleridge was living in a country home not far from the village of Porlock on the Bristol Channel. After an illness, for which a doctor had prescribed the opiate drug laudanum, Coleridge became addicted to opium. One evening, after taking a dose of the drug, he fell asleep while reading a book about the palace of Kubla Khan, the thirteenth century Mongol emperor who founded the city of Beijing. In his opium dream, Coleridge experienced a vision of an epic poem, about 300 lines long. He awoke from his dream with the entire poem burning in his mind. He went to his desk and immediately began writing down what had come to him in the dream:

> In Xanadu did Kubla Khan
> A stately pleasure-dome decree:
> Where Alph, the sacred river, ran
> Through caverns measureless to man
> Down to a sunless sea... .

By Coleridge's account, he had only written fifty-four lines when there was a knock on the door. The poet went to the door and found on his doorstep "a person on business from Porlock." This "person from Porlock" stayed for about an hour. After the unannounced visitor finally left, Coleridge went back to his desk—and discovered he could remember nothing more of the dream. The fifty-four lines he had written down before the interruption were all that remained of the opium-induced poem. And that is why the poem "Kubla Khan" was never finished.

The moral to the story: Don't let anyone distract you from your writing—and beware the person from Porlock.

Some writers can disappear into their mahogany-paneled study, bar the door, speak to no one, and write. I have not found such idyllic perfection in real life. And frankly, I'm not sure it's as idyllic as it's cracked up to be. I think the ideal environment for writing books is a house with little kids in it. Seriously.

Isaac Asimov learned early in his writing career how to find an inner solitude amid a noisy swirl of distractions. As a teenager, he worked in his family's candy store in New York City, tending the counter and selling candy, cigars, and magazines. In fact, it was while working in that store that he discovered the science fiction magazines that eventually bought and published his early stories. He would take his typewriter to the store, set it up behind the counter, and pound out stories until interrupted (usually in mid-sentence) by a customer. He would ring up the sale, then go right back to his story.

The writing conditions in Asimov's home were hardly more conducive. His family lived in a so-called "railroad apartment"—a long line of rooms without a hallway. Each room was a passageway to the next, so there was continual foot traffic through young Isaac's room. The atmosphere was enlivened by the sound of his sister's phonograph, his mother's stentorian voice, and the constant roar of New York City traffic outside the open window (this was in the days before air-conditioning).

"In short," Asimov concludes, "my apprenticeship as a writer took place in a boiler-factory under conditions of constant enforced interruption. I doubt if I ever had fifteen straight minutes of peace. Naturally, the fact that I continued to write meant that I had learned to withstand incredible noise and interruption. ... I was undistractable."[3]

And that is what you and I must be as writers: alone amid the crowd, finding solitude alongside a ringing phone, a neighbor's barking dog, and a child's inquisitive "Whatcha doing, Daddy?" I believe Martin Amis and Annie Dillard are right: A writer *is* wholly alive when wholly alone. I believe Andrea Dworkin is right: As writers, we *do* live and work in solitude, no matter how many people surround us. And I also believe that Isaac Asimov is right: We *must* find our solitude within. Regardless of the noise and distractions that swirl around us, we must be *undistractable*.

HABIT 3: WRITE QUICKLY AND WITH INTENSITY

Write quickly. Revise extensively.
F. L. Lucas (Style and Critical Thoughts in Critical Days)

Most people think of writing as a static, sedentary pursuit. I think of it as a performance, like an athletic or musical performance. Good writing is powered by emotional intensity. You must be swept away by the torrent of your words. You must tingle with their electricity. If you are moved by what you write, your reader will be moved as well. It's an amazing feeling when you get "in the zone" while writing. You feel pumped, you feel an adrenaline rush. When I'm writing with intensity, and I feel that emotion and enthusiasm flowing through me, I pound the keyboard of my Gateway like a pianist at the keyboard of a Steinway.

To have that kind of intense writing experience requires not only emotion but momentum. You must write quickly, always moving forward, never looking back. As you write your first draft, let it flow through you—bubbling from the wellspring of your soul, coursing through your cerebral cortex, pouring down your arms and out your fingertips, flooding your computer's Pentium memory with brilliance.

Don't stop to obsess over details or rewrite the same sentence over and over. Don't stop to check your facts in an encyclopedia or hunt for words in a thesaurus. If you can't remember if "interrogate" has one R or two, just spell it any old way and keep writing. Do all your nit-picking, fact-checking, and spell-checking later, when you rewrite and revise. If you use a word processor like MS Word, which checks grammar and spelling as you write, simply disable that feature; those squiggly underscores are distracting nuisances that slow you down and impede your creativity.

Writing is a magical process—but also a fragile one. As you write, don't allow anything to break that transcendent experience of being carried along on a river of thought, image, and emotion. Your writing—whether it is fiction or nonfiction, article-length or book-length—*must* have emotional intensity. That intensity of emotion serves three purposes:

First, it gets *you* involved in your story or message. It inspires you to do your best work, and to stick with it to completion.

During the Great Depression of the 1930s, John Steinbeck did a series of newspaper articles on the desperate conditions faced by migrant farm workers in California. While researching those articles, he met the workers, lived among them, interviewed them, listened to their stories, and absorbed their pain into his soul. What he heard and saw made him angry—*intensely* angry. He used that intense emotion, that social and moral outrage, to carry him through the process of writing one of the greatest novels of all time: *The Grapes of Wrath*.

> "As you write your first draft, let it flow through you—bubbling from the wellspring of your soul, coursing through your cerebral cortex, pouring down your arms and out your fingertips, flooding your computer's Pentium memory with brilliance."

Pick up a copy of that book and weigh it in your hands. It is roughly 500 pages long, and is brilliantly structured and written. It's hard to believe that the first draft was completed in a mere *five months*, from June through October 1938. Not only did Steinbeck receive the Pulitzer Prize for that novel, but he was later awarded the Nobel Prize for literature—and a 1940 film version of *The Grapes of Wrath* (starring Henry Fonda) was nominated for seven Academy Awards, including Best Picture. It is nothing short of miraculous that such an achievement could have been pounded out in only five months—but when you power your writing with intense emotion, anything is possible.

"Most negative emotions aren't helpful," says novelist David Brin. "But one of the most negative—righteous indignation—has proved to be useful to many writers over the years. So much so that they cannot imagine how calmer, happier people can write at all! I feel sorry for these guys—but not very much. Indignation is *fun*, you see. Angry, indignant writers really do have a great time, bouncing off walls, denouncing fools and enemies and the Powers-That-Be. Much of the writing that results is turgid and bombastic—it's hard to achieve subtlety when your blood is hot all of the time. But sometimes the best and most worthwhile denunciations of human hypocrisy arise from this roiling maelstrom of emotion."

Second, emotional intensity makes a powerful impact on the *editor* who buys your work. When your article, story, or book has the power to affect an editor's emotions, you are well on your way to a sale. Editors respond to writing that crackles with energy and emotion. James Michener, in his novel about the publishing trade, *The Novel*, illustrates this truth with these words by one of the book's viewpoint characters, book editor Yvonne Marmelle:

> I remained after class to tell him: "I'm in training at Kinetic Press to become an editor. You've taught me what to look for in a manuscript."
> "In one word, what is that?"
> "Intensity."[4]

Yes! Intensity! Emotional intensity, emotional power, emotional punch. If you don't feel it while you're writing, your editors won't feel it while they're reading. Romance writer Melissa James (*Her Galahad* and *Who Do You Trust?*) puts it this way:

> How many rejection letters have we all had, stating that our writing lacks those two awful words, "emotional punch"? I know I've had more than a few in the past. . . .
> What is emotion, then? It's the lifeblood of a story. . . . That's what editors look for in a book—the color, the life, the fire, the guts and depth of emotion, the unmistakable richness. It's what makes a book live in the reader's mind after she's closed the book, or keeps her up until three A.M. reading until the story's complete.[5]

Third, emotional intensity involves the *reader* in your work. When people are deeply impacted by something you have written, they cannot keep it inside. They have to tell other people about this wonderful book they've just discovered, written by this amazing new author. You already knew that word of mouth is the best advertising. Now you know where word of mouth advertising comes from: It comes from the emotional power and intensity that you put into every sentence you write.

Vicki Hinze, author of best-selling romantic suspense novels such as *All Due Respect* (St. Martin's, 2000) and *Lady Liberty* (Bantam, 2001), put it this way: "My creative energies are tied to strong emotions. If a situation or event enrages me, odds are I'm going to write about it. But rage isn't the only trigger—any emotion will do. Emotions are vital to writing. I don't think a reader can get anything out of a book that a writer doesn't first put into it. We attract readers by creating and maintaining the fictional dream in our work, and we create that dream through emotion."

HABIT 4: SET AMBITIOUS BUT ACHIEVABLE GOALS

> I accomplish a thousand times more when I write down my goals and keep them in a place where I have to stare at them *all* the time. It works! Writing is lots of fun and creativity, but it also requires problem-solving and time management—which is where goal-setting comes in.
>
> **Jessica Page Morrell**, *author of* Writing Out the Storm

Joseph Heller's brutal satire *Catch-22* was published in 1961 and became an instant best-seller. It took Heller ten years to write his second novel, *Something Happened*. Ten years! It seems like a lot of nothing happened before *Something Happened*. On the other hand, it is said that Voltaire wrote his great satiric novel *Candide* (1759) in just three days.

Why does it take one author three days to write a great novel and another author ten years? I have found that the most productive writers are those who have a goal. Goal-setting is a crucial habit for the working writer. Goals should be written down and posted prominently, and they should be broken down into long-range, mid-range, and short-term objectives.

Our long-range goals define what we expect to achieve from a career as a full-time writer. Big, broad, ambitious goals serve as a vision that keep us energized and enthused about our work over the long haul. They draw us toward a hoped-for destiny of successes and accomplishments.

Mid-range goals define the specific projects that we have under contract, and they specify our deadlines for completing them. We must meet our mid-range goals, knocking them down one after another, in order to achieve our lofty and ambitious long-range goals.

Our short-range goals define the daily and weekly objectives we must achieve in order to reach our mid-range goals. These are such goals as "write x number of words or pages per day," "complete chapters x through z by this Friday," or "mail three query letters by Monday." Focus on producing pages, not putting in time. "I will write from 10 till 4" is not a goal—it's a schedule.

English novelist Anthony Trollope (1815–1882) produced more than sixty novels and nonfiction books, plus hundreds of stories and essays. He set a steady productivity goal of seven pages per day—no more, no less—and he produced his daily quota with machinelike discipline and efficiency. If he finished one book after having written, say, three pages for the day, he would take another sheet, write "Chapter One" at the top of it, and write the first four pages of his *next* book. That's discipline.

> ". . . the most productive writers are those who have a goal."

British novelist-essayist-critic-composer Anthony Burgess published over fifty books, including the futuristic novel *A Clockwork Orange* (1962). During the 1950s, Burgess served as an educator in the Malay Archipelago. In late 1959, a doctor in Borneo examined Burgess and told him he had an inoperable brain tumor. "How long do I have?" asked Burgess; the doctor replied, "A year."

Burgess had already written a few modestly successful books in his spare time. He decided to spend the last year of his life writing as many books as he could. The royalties, he hoped, would provide his wife with a tidy little annuity after his death. Living on a small disability pension, he returned to England and plunged into full-time writing. He set a daily quota of 2,000 words a day, seven days a week. During 1960, his so-called "terminal year," he wrote five novels and sold them all.

By the end of that year, Burgess was amazed that he was still alive and feeling healthy. He went to a doctor and discovered that the original diagnosis was in error—he wasn't dying after all. And, there was more good news: Burgess had developed some excellent writing habits during his "pseudo-terminal year." He went on to enjoy three more decades of life, and he continued writing with the same intensity and discipline he had developed as a man under a death sentence.

As Samuel Johnson once said, "Depend upon it, sir—when a man knows he is to be hanged in a fortnight, it concentrates his mind wonderfully." Whether or not we have received bad news from the doctor, we should write as if our lives depend on it—because, for the working writer, life really *does* depend on it. So make every day count. Set your daily quotas and meet them. Write as if this year were the last year of your life.

One of the most gifted and prolific writers I know is Angela Elwell Hunt, author of such inspirational novels as *The Pearl*, *The Canopy*, and the children's Easter classic, *The Tale of Three Trees*. She writes brilliantly—and she writes *fast*. She uses daily quotas, but she uses them differently than any other writer I've known. For Angie Hunt, a quota is not a goal—it's a *limit*.

"There's no secret to writing as fast as I do," she told me. "You just have to be an obsessive-compulsive. I'm like a dog who just can't put a bone down until it's chewed to the marrow. That's why I give myself daily quotas. When I hit my allotment of words for the day, I know I have to quit. Otherwise I'd be writing all night long."

You may not be obsessively, compulsively blessed like Angela Hunt. You may be a mere mortal like me—a writer who must ruthlessly drive those synapses to keep firing, those ideas to keep flowing, those fingers to keep typing. It's all a matter of discipline—and that's okay. If I can do it, you can do it. Set your goals for the day, pound out your quota of words, and be a *writer*.

Your daily productivity goals should be high but realistic, based on what you *know* you can accomplish in light of past successes and accomplishments. I know that, on average, it takes me about three months to write an 80,000-word book. But I also know that I have sometimes written an 80,000-word book in a mere six weeks. So, I like to set daily productivity goals that are close to my best performance in the past. Setting high goals based on my best performances inspires my best effort.

Don't base your goals on what you've heard other writers accomplish. Maybe some writers really do produce 10,000 words a day, but some writers are also notorious liars! Focus your goals on what *you* can realistically and optimally achieve. Then review, monitor, and revise your goals on a regular basis.

What if you fail to meet your goals for the day or the week? Sharon Ihle, author of such sizzling romance novels as *Untamed*, *Maggie's Wish*, and *Wild Rose*, says, "Never, ever beat yourself up if you don't meet a specific goal. If you expect five, but only write three pages on Monday, odds are by Tuesday or Wednesday, you'll have made it up. If you consistently find yourself falling short of your goal, ease up on yourself and revise downward until you feel comfortable, but stretched."[6]

Science fiction writer Piers Anthony has over a hundred published novels to his credit, and he still produces three novels a year. He is a high achiever as a writer because he sets goals and meets them. He divides his day between writing text and making notes—and he has a "3,000/500" goal for each task. That is, he sets a goal of producing 3,000 words of fiction plus 500 words of notes and ideas for both the current book and future books every day.

John Steinbeck set daily productivity goals (about 2,000 words per day) that kept him on track as he was writing *The Grapes of Wrath*. He usually started his writing day at around 10 A.M., beginning by making a short entry in his journal, such as this one from September 3, 1938: "Today is Saturday and half a day's work will finish the chapter." At the end of half a day, he made another entry in his journal: "Finished the chapter."

Novelist Vicki Hinze told me, "I have daily, monthly, annual, and five-year goals. For a long time, I've tracked the time I spend on given projects, so I have a good grip on what I need to accomplish a project. I allow myself a little wiggle room for the unexpected, and I pretty much stick to a production schedule. I don't write at specific hours or at specific times. I produce a minimum amount of work before I do anything else. That works well for me since I'm not fond of clocks."

So set your goals and remain focused on them. The more productive you are every moment, the more pages you write in a day. The more pages you write, the more books you write. Ultimately, your success as a writer is measured by the body of work you create.

HABIT 5: FOCUS!

You write a novel a word at a time. And this will go on for hundreds of pages.
Novelist and comic book scriptwriter **Neil Gaiman** (Sandman)

Vineeta Vijayaraghavan's first novel, *Motherland* (Soho Press, 2001), is the story of Maya, a teenager born in India, but raised most of her life in America. Returning to India, she feels like an alien in her own homeland, a society in turmoil after the assassination of political leader Rajiv Gandhi in 1991. But the story of *Motherland* is also the story of a young author who learned the importance of *focus* while writing her first novel.

Vineeta Vijayaraghavan took a pragmatic, determined approach to the writing of her novel. First, she worked hard, lived a spartan lifestyle, and saved up a year's worth of income. Then she took a year off from her day job to write her novel. In fact, the novel *became* her day job—she "punched in" at 9 A.M. and "punched out" at 5 P.M. every day like clockwork. She described what it was like when she began her year of writing *Motherland*:

> The first couple of weeks I was so exhilarated by the long, open stretches of time I had to sit down and really work on this manuscript that I had only been able to attend to in odd twilight hours while I had been employed. Then I felt lots of panic—I was terrified I would soon run out of energy and ideas for the writing, and I wondered what I would do with myself if that were to happen. I started thinking about working part-time, even though I had saved up enough money to live on for the year.... [But] I resisted the urge to fill in my days, and just stayed home and wrote every weekday. Some days, I just sat there in front of the computer and didn't produce very much, but I didn't do anything else until five in the evening.[7]

To keep herself focused, she broke the novel down into segments and created a series of deadlines for each portion. She treated these deadlines as "absolutely nonnegotiable." She signed up for two workshops and asked the other members to hold her accountable for turning in new chapters every other week. Those self-imposed deadlines, she said, "made a big difference in getting the manuscript done." By staying intensely focused on her novel, Vineeta Vijayaraghavan was able to use her year of full-time writing to maximum effect. The result was a first novel that instantly garnered strong sales and critical acclaim.

Focus is a crucial habit for success as a writer. If you have ever used a camera with a focusing lens, then you know that by rotating the lens barrel, you can move the plane of focus from the bee on the flower six inches from the lens, to the stone wall behind the flower, to the house beyond the wall, to the mountains in the distance behind the house. By turning the lens barrel, you change the focus of the camera.

As writers, we must have that same ability to focus on the various planes of our writing. We must be able to focus on the big picture, the total scope of the project. Then we must be able to focus on the various segments of the work and to see how they relate to each other and flow into each other, creating a unity out of diverse parts. Then we must be able to focus on the segments within segments, on chapter divisions, subhead divisions, individual paragraphs, sentences, phrases, and even words. We must constantly rotate the barrel of our mental lens, focusing now on an idea or theme, now on an emotion or effect, now on the way a given phrase resonates in the mind.

Writing is *focus*—daily, hourly, moment-by-moment concentration on the goals ahead and on the task at hand. A successful writing career is the result of a habit of focus.

HABIT 6: FINISH WHAT YOU START AND SUBMIT WHAT YOU FINISH

> I went for years not finishing anything. Because, of course, when you finish something you can be judged.... I had poems which were rewritten so many times I suspect it was just a way of avoiding sending them out.
> *Poet-novelist* **Erica Jong**

Robert A. Heinlein graduated from Annapolis, studied math and physics at the graduate school of the University of California, and once owned a silver mine before turning to writing in 1939. He practiced his craft by writing and selling scores of short stories. His first book, a juvenile science fiction novel, *Rocket Ship Galileo*, was published in 1947. When he died in 1988, he left behind an enormous body of work, published under his own name plus five pseudonyms. Those works include *The Puppet Masters, Starship Troopers, The Door Into Summer, Farnham's Freehold, Job: A Comedy of Justice*, and the cult classic, *Stranger in a Strange Land*. He once formulated a set of principles that he called "Five Rules for Success in Writing." They are:

1. You Must Write
2. You Must Finish What You Write
3. You Must Refrain From Rewriting Except to Editorial Order
4. You Must Place It On The Market
5. You Must Keep It On The Market Until Sold

Or, to put it even more succinctly: Finish what you start and submit what you finish.

Notice that Heinlein also says, you must "refrain from rewriting except to editorial order." Understand, he's not saying you should turn in your first draft. "Finish what you write" means that you write a first draft, then you go back and rewrite, and at most do one more read-through for a final buff-and-polish. But once that is done, you must refrain from endlessly fussing and obsessing over your work. After one or two rewrites, it's done. Shove it into an envelope and mail it, for crying out loud. Then, if an editor buys it and asks for changes, you can rewrite it one last time.

If your story is rejected and returned, you stick it into another envelope and send it off again immediately. Do that on a consistent basis, and you can't help but succeed.

Now, it is true that there are times when a book (or other piece of writing) *should* be abandoned. It should be abandoned if you realize that you began the book on a completely faulty premise. It should be shelved, at least temporarily, if you determine that the project is so large, complex, or demanding that you need to acquire more skills in order to complete it. Unfortunately, all too many people abandon books because it has simply gotten hard, or it's not as much fun as it was at the beginning, or they're not sure what to do next, or they just got a new idea that they're even *more* excited about.

My experience is that no book is ever as much fun to write in the middle as it is at the beginning or end. But without the middle, the beginning and end don't matter. The trick is to find ways to jump-start your imagination and enthusiasm for the middle of the book. This can often be a good point at which to rethink your original plan for the book. What kinds of surprises can you throw in at this point that will make the book not only more exciting to read, but more exciting to write? Often, coming up with an exciting new twist in the middle of the book can pump new life and energy into the writing process—and that will translate into a more exciting experience for your readers.

Children's author Elizabeth Hawkins (*Sea of Peril*) says, "The best piece of advice I was given by a highly successful writer is to finish anything you start. This forces you to tussle out the problems, and it is the best way to learn. Constantly giving up and starting something else often leads nowhere."

What if you are just stuck? I find that I sometimes get too close to the writing. I'm looking at my word processor, and the screen only reveals a tiny slice of the total manuscript at a time. I can scroll up and down, but I can't gain a sense of the overall structure just from scrolling. I find that I need to pull back and get a broader perspective. I need to see how *this* little piece of the book relates to the total scope of the book—and then everything usually becomes more clear.

The way I do this is to reduce the complete book to an outline, then print the outline onto paper, and literally take a pair of scissors and start cutting it up and rearranging the different pieces on the dining room table. Suddenly, the entire structure of the book becomes malleable and workable in my mind, and I see new ways to structure the themes or storyline.

My approach may not work for you. But you need to find some way to push past the inertia that almost inevitably settles in around the one-half to two-thirds point in a book. You must find a way to finish what you start. The discipline of forcing yourself to complete difficult projects and solve difficult writing problems is an important part of mastering your craft. Think of it as "on the job training."

HABIT 7: BELIEVE YOU CAN

Most of the writers I know have tremendous self-doubt, but beyond that there's enough arrogance that they're willing to take the chance and put pen to paper. I don't know what was going through my mind when I wrote my first script other than I was just so unhappy and I wondered if I could write one.

Korby Siamis, *television writer-producer* (Kate & Allie, My Sister Sam, Murphy Brown)

Every writer doubts his or her ability at some point. The successful writer learns to say no to those doubts and keep going. Tell yourself, "I can"—even if you think you can't. Act on the belief that you can do this, even if you don't believe it. Make a decision to sit down and write, whether you feel like it or not. Act first, and the feelings will follow.

Some people wait for the *feelings* of a writer to come before they exhibit the *behavior* of a writer. That is a prescription for defeat. Always remember: *Feelings follow behavior*, not the other way around. So act like a writer. Only when you *act* like a writer and *produce* like a writer will you truly *feel* like a writer.

Many writers struggle with yo-yo emotions, an alternating sense of, "I'm a genius! I'm so great I amaze even myself," alongside, "I can't write worth beans! I'm a no-talent bum!" Both extremes lead to a dead-end. Both are rooted in insecurity

As novelist David Brin told me, "Purist positions rarely interest me. I particularly dislike romantic exaggerations about human creativity. So watch out for the dangers of ego. For some, this often manifests itself as a frantic need to see ourselves as great. That's fine. But if you listen to the voice saying 'Be great ... *be great*!' too much, it'll just stand in the way. Others often have the opposite problem: egos that are too easily quashed by all the fire-snorting fellows stomping around. Either extreme can produce paralysis."

It's true. The feeling of "I'm great!" is nothing more than the self overcompensating for feelings of inferiority; by the same token, the feeling of "I'm nothing!" is the self surrendering to feelings of inferiority. The writer who has a mature and healthy self-appraisal says, "I know I have talent and skill, and I am going to apply my energies to do the best work I can. I don't have to prove I'm great. I just need to write down my thoughts and tell my stories. If I do my work well, it will be enough."

CREATURES OF HABIT

[Your] writing time must become so vital and intrinsic to your life that whatever attempts to distract you should be regarded as a vicious threat to your welfare. This may seem fanatic, inconsiderate, ruthless. It is not. If anyone tried to prevent a lawyer, doctor, plumber, pastor, or musician from going to work, [that person] would be dealt with mercilessly.

Leonard Bishop, Dare to Be a Great Writer

Gigi Levangie Grazer is a screenwriter and novelist. Her screenplay *Stepmom* was made into a successful and critically acclaimed movie starring Julia Roberts and Susan Sarandon. Her first novel, *Rescue Me: A Love Story*, was released by Simon & Schuster in 2000. Grazer is not only a writer; she is also a mom. She finds it fulfilling to combine the habits of a full-time writer with the habits of a full-time mother. "My writing ritual now," she says, "is to write five days a week, from 9 A.M. on, broken up by my baby's incessant need to be fed. Go figure. Seriously, I view writing very much as a regular job. That means five days a week, starting in the morning and ending four to five hours after that. Consistency is my savior."[8]

Novelist Kurt Vonnegut (*Slaughterhouse Five, Breakfast of Champions*) has the same advice for writers: Patience, perseverance, persistence, doing the work of a writer day after day until the work is done and ready to take to market. "Novelists have, on the average, about the same IQs as the cosmetic consultants at Bloomingdale's department store," he says. "Our power is patience. We have discovered that writing allows even a stupid person to seem halfway intelligent, if only that person will write the same thought over and over again, improving it just a little bit each time. It is a lot like inflating a blimp with a bicycle pump. Anybody can do it. All it takes is time."

Consistent, persistent, daily effort is the salvation of every working writer. All human beings are creatures of habit. Some habits lead to success; other habits lead to failure and disappointment. If you want to be a successful working writer, you must cultivate the habits of success. These, then, are the Seven Essential Habits of a Working Writer:

Habit 1:	Write Daily
Habit 2:	Cultivate the Art of Solitude Amid Distractions
Habit 3:	Write Quickly and With Intensity
Habit 4:	Set Ambitious But Achievable Goals
Habit 5:	Focus!
Habit 6:	Finish What You Start and Submit What You Finish
Habit 7:	Believe You Can

Without these habits, how could you do anything but fail? But with *all* of these habits firmly in place in your life, you can't help but succeed.

In the next chapter, we'll examine one of the most important assets any working writer can have: *speed*.

THE NEED FOR SPEED:
WRITING IN OVERDRIVE

> It had at this time become my custom—and it still is my custom, though of late I have become a little lenient to myself—to write with my watch before me, and to require from myself 250 words every quarter of an hour.
> **Anthony Trollope**, Autobiography *(1883)*

> I just have a fast pace; it's like having green eyes.
> *Prolific romance novelist* **Nora Roberts** (Montana Sky, Secret Star)

Multi-book contracts are great. You get half the money for all the books up front, then you get the back end of the money on each individual book as it is completed. My first such contract was a two-book deal for a publisher of gift books. Gift books have two very attractive features: 1) They are short, so you don't have to write so many words; and 2) They are full of pictures, so (again) you don't have to write so many words. Whenever someone offers you more money to write fewer words, take it.

Before we signed the contract, I asked the acquisitions editor how long the manuscript should be. His answer: 35,000 words. I pondered that. I knew that the average 300-page manuscript I wrote for the trade book market was around 80,000 words long. The acquisition editor had sent me a stack of gift books his house had published so I could see what they looked like. They were smaller and considerably slimmer than the hardcovers and trade paperbacks I usually wrote. The length he had given me, 35,000 words, was just under half the length of a normal trade book (43.75 percent, to be exact), yet the gift books he had sent me seemed to be closer to 15 or 20 percent as long as a trade book.

I asked the editor if he was sure that 35,000 words was the length he needed—it seemed like too many words for the format. He assured me that was the length. So I started writing.

Before I completed the first book, the acquisitions editor left the company. I turned in the manuscript for the first book to the managing editor. It was 34,800 words long. The managing editor acknowledged receipt of the manuscript with an e-mail, saying, "Got the book—it looks great! Only problem is that it's long and will need some cutting." She didn't say how much cutting.

It turned out the length they needed was 20,000 words absolute max—and if I could get it down to 18,000, all the better. By the time we were done, I had made three trips through the manuscript, hunting for material to cut. I cut three complete chapters, from ten chapters to seven, and then I went through the remaining material, cutting paragraph by paragraph, sentence by sentence, and word by word. Achieving brevity turned out to be a time-consuming process, proving the adage of Lord Chesterfield, who once wrote to a friend, "I'm sorry that I have written you a five-page letter; I didn't have time to write a one-page letter."

To make matters worse, I had over-researched the project at the beginning, spending two whole weeks gathering material for the book, 80 percent of which I never used. From researching to writing to cutting to rewriting, I spent about eight weeks on that book—eight weeks for 19,000 words. That nets out to less than 500 words per weekday—a miserable productivity level.

That experience was an education for me. When I started the second book, I had the job of writing gift books down to a science. I vastly reduced the amount of research I put into the book. I laid out a seven-chapter outline, I wrote my seven chapters to a total length of 18,000 words, and then I *stopped*. I was done. The total elapsed time to write the second book: three weeks. My productivity, including time spent researching and rewriting, averaged 1,200 words per day. To top it off, I felt the second book was stronger than the first, because it didn't have to be surgically altered and stitched back together. So the economy measures I undertook also enhanced the quality of the book.

The point is this: The faster you write, the more you produce. The more you produce, the more money you make. So every working writer has a *need for speed*. You must be productive in order to write for a living. One of your most important assets is the ability to write in overdrive.

QUALITY AND QUANTITY—AND QUICKNESS

Talent is a matter of quantity. Talent doesn't write one page, it writes three hundred.

French playwright/author **Jules Renard** *(1864–1910)*

Alexandre Dumas père (1802–1870) wrote more than 1,500 books in his lifetime, including *The Three Musketeers*, *The Man in the Iron Mask*, and *The Count of Monte Cristo*. British novelist-playwright Edgar Wallace (1875–1932) wrote more than 170 novels and plays and was called "The King of the Thriller." His classic mysteries include *The Green Archer* (filmed three times) and *The Mind of Mr. J.G. Reeder*. Charles Hamilton (1875–1961) wrote under more than twenty pseudonyms (he was better known as "Frank Richards"), and averaged over 1.4 million words per year over a fifty-year career. At his peak, he turned out one 70,000-word novel per week. Romance and suspense writer Kathleen Lindsay (1903–1973) wrote over 900 novels using six different pseudonyms. John Creasey (1908–1973) published at least 565 books under his own name and twenty-five pseudonyms.

Some writers say that to write quickly, you must sacrifice quality. I've found that the opposite is frequently true: The best books are often the ones written in a rush of energy and enthusiasm, full of passion and dynamism (you'd be amazed at how fast I'm typing right now!). The more slowly a book is written, the greater the opportunity for ponderousness and pomposity to set in. Some of the finest writers of all time were also among the fastest writers of all time.

Case in point: I don't think I would get many arguments if I proclaimed Charles Dickens the greatest novelist in the English language. Dickens published twenty-three novels and numerous short stories from 1836 until his death in 1870. That may not sound like such a prodigious output until you consider that some of his novels were as long as four or five popular novels in today's market. *David Copperfield*, *Bleak House*, and *Dombey and Son* are *each* more than 350,000 words long. Dickens' thirty-four-year career produced a total oeuvre of about six million words (an average of about 175,000 words per year). And, he did it all in longhand, without the benefit of a computer. So it is clear that writing quickly and writing well certainly can and do go together.

Sustained, rapid writing produces a far better book than a plodding pace. Setting high productivity goals and working with alacrity helps you maintain your focus and enthusiasm. The faster you write, the greater the cohesion and stylistic flow of your book. You can ruin a book by lingering over it—especially when you obsessively rewrite, re-rewrite, and re-re-re-write.

Don't seek first-draft perfection. Write quickly, always moving forward, never looking back. When you do your second draft, focus on making it leaner and tighter. Eliminate repetition, cut excessive narration, fix inconsistencies, and take out all that flowery prose you were so in love with the first time around. (Remember, inside every fat book is a thin book trying to get out.) After the second draft, give it one final read-through, just to buff and polish. If you can't leave the book alone after that read-through, then go see a shrink about that obsessive-compulsive disorder.

> "The best books are often the ones written in a rush of energy and enthusiasm, full of passion and dynamism."

If you look back over the history of literature, you find that brilliance is usually blindingly fast, like Steinbeck's *The Grapes of Wrath*, a 500-page magnum opus written in five short months. The greatest books are those that are written quickly, with intensity, with a fire in the belly.

But quality aside, the fact remains that writing fast is a flat-out necessity for the working writer. Productivity is the key to your survival. If you don't write, you don't get paid. If you don't get paid, you can't pay your electric bill. Your computer goes dark. Your spouse leaves you and takes the kids. Soon, there is no food in the house. Then you die. Not a pretty picture.

To keep that from happening to you, you must produce quality, you must produce quantity, and you must produce quickly. Work must be planned and scheduled in advance, executed efficiently and without wasted motion, and completed on deadline. You must allow extra time for unexpected problems and delays—but not too much extra time. You must take on enough work to meet expenses and turn a profit—but not so much that you miss deadlines and alienate editors.

Can it be done? Yes, it can—and you can learn how to do it. Here are some tricks of the writing trade that will make you a faster—and better—writer.

FAST WRITING LESSON NO. 1:
ACCEPT THE FACT THAT WRITING IS HARD WORK

The act of writing is very hard work. It's not greater or nobler than being a good plumber, ballerina, mechanic, et cetera, but writers are vested with great mystery and magic. ...The imagination comes from your head, but the act of pen to paper, fingers to typewriter, is just work.

Short story writer **Harlan Ellison**

Belgian novelist Georges Simenon had his first book published in 1921, when he was eighteen. It was a comedy entitled *Au Pont des Arches*, which a publisher agreed to publish if Simenon could sign up 300 subscribers to advance-order the book. The book was successful, and launched a career that produced over 400 novels—193 "canonical" novels (mostly crime fiction) under his own name, and the rest consisting of pulp potboilers written under more than twenty pen names.

Simenon was a man of incredible energy as well as skill. In 1928, while at the peak of his productivity as a pulp writer, he produced forty-four novels in a single year. His fame rests not only on his vast body of work (particularly the novels featuring his fictional detective Maigret), but on a publicity stunt he did in 1927. A contract he signed with publisher Eugène Merle called for Simenon to write a complete novel in one week in a glass cage in front of the Moulin Rouge cabaret in Paris. He received a 50,000-franc advance for the novel, which he wrote in full view of hundreds of gawkers. The novel was later serialized in Merle's newspaper, *Paris-Matinal*.

In recent years, American writer Harlan Ellison has performed his own variation on the Simenon stunt, having written one-day short stories in the windows of bookstores in London, Washington, Boston, New York City, New Orleans, and San Francisco. In fact, Ellison credits Simenon as inspiration for his own deeds of literary daring—but he denies that it is a stunt. "I thought this was a great way to get people to see what writers do," he explains. As each page is completed, it is handed to a store clerk who posts it in the window. By the end of the day, a new Harlan Ellison story has been written—in full view of the watching public.

At first, many people assumed he was working from notes. He couldn't possibly write a story from scratch in a single day with the whole world's nose pressed up against the window—could he? Well, he could and he did, as he explains: "I go into a window—tabula rasa, from scratch. I write a story from beginning to end and finish it by five when the store closes."

For the New York City event, Ellison began with an appearance on NBC's *Today Show*. There, Tom Brokaw supplied Ellison with the first three lines, which were kept in a sealed envelope and handed to Ellison after he took his place in the window of the bookstore on Fifth Avenue. The lines Brokaw supplied were, "A man is walking along a rocky coast of Maine. He sees something glittering in the sand. It is a broken pair of sunglasses." Since Ellison had never visited the rocky coast of Maine, he began by researching the Maine coastline in some travel guidebooks he found in the store. Then he sat down and wrote a story. The entire time he wrote, a huge crowd (estimated at over 1,000 people), choked the sidewalk in front of the store. The next morning, Ellison returned to the *Today Show* and read his story on the air.

Ellison's San Francisco event was held at The Booksmith on Haight Street in 1994, with camera crews from the three major TV networks present. As Brokaw had done before, actor Robin Williams gave Ellison a prompt—a card with a line on it about a "computer that bytes." Ellison writes with a typewriter, and he readily admits he knows *bupkis* about computers. So he grabbed a couple of computer magazines off a nearby shelf and *voila*! Instant computer research. Once again, crowds gathered in front of the bookstore window to watch Ellison pound out his story. By the end of the day, Ellison had finished the story, "Keyboard," which was published in his short story collection *Slippage* (Houghton Mifflin, 1998).[1]

Now consider this: What is it about a man typing behind a plate glass window that draws huge crowds? Answer: Nobody ever sees writers write! And what did people see when they saw Simenon or Ellison write? They saw a man sitting at a typewriter, working.

Because that's all writing is: Hard work.

Writers have no bosses but themselves. So writers must have within themselves the ability to begin a task, to focus, to persevere, to stay motivated, and to finish what they start. Working writers accept the fact that writing is hard work, and they *force* themselves to stay in that chair, facing that screen, until the work is done.

So the first step in becoming a faster writer is this: You must sit down and write. This may seem like a good place to insert the word, "Duh!" But I know for a fact that many writers have trouble accepting this simple truth. They can't accept the fact that writing is just hard work.

People see the torrent of books pouring from the pens of Stephen King, Mary Higgins Clark, Tom Clancy, Dick Francis, R. L. Stine, Sue Grafton, Anne McCaffrey, Dean Koontz, Anne Rice, Beverly Cleary, and Danielle Steel. They know that lumberjacks are working day and night, felling trees and producing fresh white paper, desperately trying to keep up with the inhuman speed of these godlike writers. And, they plead, "Tell us the secret of being so fast, so prolific! Tell us how we can write like King, Clark, Clancy, et al.!"

Ready for the secret? The secret is this: *There is no secret!* King, Clark, Clancy, et al., are as prolific as they are for one simple reason: They sit down and they write. That's it. That's all. And that's enough.

Speaking before the Commonwealth Club in San Francisco, May 1, 2001, novelist Louise Erdrich (*The Beet Queen* and *The Last Report on the Miracles at Little No Horse*), described the unusual way she acquired the discipline to sit down and write. "When I first started writing, I was a poet," she said, "and I wrote in concentrated bursts of energy. I was so nervous that I couldn't sit still. I took a scarf and tied it around myself and around my chair so that I would sit still and write a longer piece of narrative—and it worked. Now I can't get out of my chair; I keep writing."

Taking the same idea to an even more painful extreme, Southern writer Rick Bragg (*Ava's Man* and *All Over But the Shoutin'*) tells of a writer he knew who would start every writing session by chugging down a two-liter bottle of Diet Coke. Then he would belt himself into his chair. He would not allow himself to get up and go to the bathroom until he had written his daily allotment of words. "That," says Bragg, "is *discipline.*"

A scarf, a belt, a two-liter bottle of Diet Coke—these are just metaphors for the discipline every writer needs in order to write quantity and to write quickly. If you have to strap yourself into your chair with duct tape—*do it.* Whatever it takes to get you sitting in that chair and pounding on those keys—*do it.*

The beginning of writing *fast* is writing, *period.*

FAST WRITING LESSON NO. 2:
MAINTAIN AN ORGANIZED WORKSPACE

I write from ten at night to four in the morning, about 7,000 words at a time. It's like being in the basket of a blimp, working at that hour. It's wonderful. There's just one little room with me in it, and I'm sailing through the night wherever the story will go. Just me, alone.

Mystery writer **Donald E. Westlake**

A lot of people have a romanticized notion that you can sit in a café, leisurely scribbling your random thoughts and snatches of brilliance in a notebook while sipping a latté, and at some point—a year, two years, five years down the road—you will have a novel. It is the ego-inflating fancy of daily occupying Your Table, of saying to the waitress, "My usual, please," and knowing all the other patrons are pointing and whispering, "Ah, look! The Writer is writing!"

Natalie Goldberg, in her book *Writing Down the Bones*, popularizes the notion of writing in restaurants and filling notebooks with random musings and unfocused observations. She even offers an entire page on café-writing etiquette. She calls writing in restaurants "a trick I use" to eliminate distractions such as "the telephone, the refrigerator, the dishes to be washed, the shower to be taken, the letter carrier to greet."[2] But you don't need a coffeehouse to eliminate distractions. You just need self-discipline.

True, J. K. Rowling wrote her first Harry Potter tale in a coffee shop—but that's because she was a poor single mother on welfare, there was no heat in her flat, and she couldn't afford a computer to work on. She *had* to work in the coffee shop because her fingers froze stiff at home. When Harry Potter became a hit, Rowling did the only sensible thing a working writer could do: She bought a computer, and quit writing in coffeehouses.

Working writers know that the *romanticism* of writing has little to do with the *reality* of writing. This is a business, not a hobby. To write efficiently, effectively, and fast, you need the best tools possible—a good computer loaded with powerful writing software. And you need a well-ordered office space in which to write. The keys to maintaining an organized workspace for writing are:

• Eliminate clutter, especially the papers that pile up and hide the things you need to do your job. Open mail immediately, file what is important, and discard the rest. Toss outdated drafts, old notes, and other "junk" papers. Keeping a clean, orderly workspace will enable you to research and write much more quickly.

• Maintain organized files, with separate folders for each book or project you are working on, so that everything you need is indexed and available at your fingertips. It doesn't matter if you store your folders in milk crates or in a top-of-the-line filing cabinet, just as long as it's organized. Maintain separate folders for correspondence, clippings, publisher's guidelines, research and reference material, tax and bookkeeping records, rejection letters (you've got to save those!), and so forth.

> "King, Clark, Clancy, et al., are as prolific as they are for one simple reason: They sit down and they write."

• Keep different projects organized and stored in boxes. If you're like me, you've got three, four, or five going at the same time—from projects in development to projects under contract to projects currently producing Maalox moments. I find that file folders or manila envelopes are not nearly big enough to hold the paperwork, correspondence, books, magazines, and other resource material for a given project, so I usually store each project in its own cardboard banker box.

• Keep the tools of your craft organized and accessible—phone, tape transcribing equipment, reference books and software, paper, ink cartridges or toner, pencils and pens, and so forth.

• Maintain a regular cleanup-and-organize time on your schedule. I suggest a light tidy-up at the end of each working day and a thorough cleaning every Friday afternoon, after you've completed a full, rich, productive writing week.

• When the mail or other paperwork arrives at your desk, open it, deal with it, and be done with it. Don't let it haunt you and rob your writing time. Never touch a piece of paper twice.

• Whatever you don't need, toss.

FAST WRITING LESSON NO. 3:
ORGANIZE YOUR TIME

In the journey from chaos to order, it is often easier to organize space than time, because space is something you can actually see. Time, on the other hand, is completely invisible. ...Some days go whizzing by, others crawl painfully along. Even your tasks seem hard to measure—infinite and endless in both quantity and duration. ...In my own journey to getting organized, my biggest breakthrough came when I realized that organizing time is really no different than organizing space.

Julie Morgenstern, Time Management from the Inside Out

I had this great idea for a new approach to time management for writers: a time machine. If you realize you're about to miss a deadline, you just step into your time machine, set the dial to take you two weeks into the past, and *zap*! You get a two-week deadline extension—just like that. So I built my time machine, plugged it into the wall socket, and flipped the power switch, and—*ooops*! The entire western power grid of the United States went black.

I've decided to stick with good old-fashioned time management principles. Here are some ways I've learned to better organize my writing time:

• Be aware of your mental, emotional, and creative rhythms. Let's say you tend to start the day with a lot of energy, then fade in the afternoons. Fine. Just schedule your prime writing time for the morning, to coincide with your peak energy times. Schedule errands, research, phone calls, e-mailing, and other non-writing chores for the afternoon when you normally fade. When you are writing at your peak, you write quickly and enthusiastically, and the work you produce will require less revision and rewriting.

• Be attentive to the warning signs of time mismanagement: You feel stressed, irritable, tired, and unable to concentrate. You can't find things when you need them. Your workspace and your schedule are filled with clutter. You arrive late and/or unprepared for appointments and meetings. You have trouble saying no when people ask you to volunteer your time.

• Prioritize your time. Plan. Set Goals for each day. Make "Things To Do" lists. Break down large, forbidding projects into smaller, simpler steps. Take each item on your list in order of priority, do it until you have completed it, then move on to the next item on your list.

• Stop doing things you don't need to do. Assess every task or project in light of these questions: Why am I doing this? What will I achieve by doing this? What will it cost me do this? What is the worst thing that will happen if I choose *not* to do it?

• Learn to say no to demands that other people make on your time.

• Delegate any chores that someone else can do. Ask for help from your spouse and even your kids. Hire professionals to do what you don't do very well (or very quickly) yourself.

• Keep phone calls short and focused. When you call someone, state your reason for calling, stick to it, and once you've achieved your goal for that call, say good-bye. Standing while you talk on the phone helps to put more energy in your voice, while also motivating you to keep the call short. Never put your feet up while you are on the phone. Save phoning for times when your creative energies are sagging.

• Don't procrastinate. Impose tough, hard-headed deadlines on yourself. If your contract calls for a book to be completed by June 1, determine to have it done by May 1.

FAST WRITING LESSON NO. 4: USE EVERY POSSIBLE SHORTCUT

> You can't waste time and you can't save time; you can only choose what you do at any given moment.
> **James Gleick** (Chaos *and* Faster)

There are still writers around who refuse to use a computer. They are perfectly content with their clunky old Underwood No. 5 typewriter, secure in the knowledge that there's no delete key to hit accidentally, no hard drive to crash, no power cord to trip over. Yessir, whatever you type on a good old-fashioned typewriter *stays* typed.

There's no use trying to convince technophobes to change their ways. There's no point telling them that all you have to do to save your work is a simple CONTROL-S function, and that CD burners give you cheap, dependable backups of your entire hard drive. If those folks don't want to dip their toes into the twenty-first century, you can't force them.

But you don't have to be like them.

Today, there are many proven techniques and technological tools that will enable you to write faster and write better. Some are high-tech approaches; others are dirt-simple and dirt-cheap. Let's take a quick survey:

• **Brainstorm and cluster.** I learned this technique from Bert Decker of Decker Communications, Inc., and I used it to structure the book you are reading right now. You can find a more in-depth explanation of this technique in Bert's new book, *Speaking With Bold Assurance*. But I can lay out the basics for you by showing how I structured this book.

First, I took a pad of Post-It Notes and sat down at my dining room table (it's important to have a big, broad working surface). Next, I *brainstormed*. I just thought of everything I wanted to say about writing for a living—quotes, anecdotes, personal experiences, principles, ideas, advice. As each thought occurred to me, I scribbled a key phrase on a Post-It Note (such as "Asimov—Candy Store" or "Jim D.—Option Clause"). I quickly peeled it off the pad, and stuck it somewhere on the tabletop, completely at random, then jotted down the next idea. I did this as hurriedly as I could, without editing or criticizing any idea. I continued this until I started to "dry up" and no more ideas would come. The entire brainstorming process took twenty minutes or less. At that point, I had about fifty or sixty Post-It Notes scattered across the tabletop.

Next, I clustered. I could see that certain ideas, stories, and principles "attracted" each other. The story about Isaac Asimov typing behind the counter of his parents' candy store connected with the principle of remaining focused amid distractions. The story about the option clause I forgot I signed had a magnetic affinity with my thoughts on understanding contracts. So I physically moved Post-It Notes around the table, linking ideas, principles, and stories together into clusters. As I did this, I saw a number of themes emerging, and I would go back to my Post-It pad and write a brief description of that theme on a Post-It Note. With these "theme notes," I used red ink and drew a box around the word or phrase so that it stood out from the "idea notes." So I eventually had several Post-It Notes with boxed words like "Contracts" and "Take the Leap" and "Habits" and "Write Fast." Each of these clusters became a chapter.

Then I took the Post-It Notes of each cluster and arranged them on sheets of typing paper, one cluster to a sheet, and I created a logical flow of the ideas and stories for each chapter. When I was done, I had the skeletal structure of the book completely nailed down. Total elapsed time: just over an hour. You can use this same technique to rapidly construct the outline for a nonfiction book, a novel, a magazine article, or a short story.

This technique is not only fast, but it gives you a bird's eye view of your project. You can envision your entire book at a glance. This "aerial view" of your book acts as a map to keep you from getting lost in the thicket of your ideas.

• **Try high-tech brainstorming and clustering.** Inspiration Software, Inc. (www.inspiration.com) makes the powerful Inspiration program for Macs and PCs. The software does everything I just described above—but it does it on a computer screen instead of on Post-It Notes. The software is designed to give you the creative freedom to brainstorm and generate ideas in the form of free-floating boxes or bubbles. You can then move and link and cluster those boxes or bubbles into an orderly structure. At any stage of the process, you can save your session, then return and continue it later. I have used Inspiration 6.0, and it is a powerful and user-friendly tool. In fact, it is so easy to use that the company's marketing strategy for Inspiration 6.0 is focused on school classrooms, elementary grades through high school.

• **Automate your writing tasks with specialized software tools for writers.** One that I've used extensively and highly recommend is the latest edition of *Writer's Market Online*, available from Writer's Digest Books, consisting of a 1,100-page book, a searchable, interactive CD, and a one-year subscription to WritersMarket.com.

Other software for writers (which I've never used and can't vouch for, but which are worth investigating) include: IdeaFisher, Writer's Edge (idea thesaurus and brainstorming); ComedyWriter (a comedy technique tutor); Character Pro for Writers (for creating fictional characters); Plots

Unlimited (a plot generator, offering 200,000 plot combinations involving scenarios such as deception, vengeance, mistaken judgment, romantic misadventure, and so forth); GRiM Software's Musings (tip-of-the-day, inspirational quotes about writing, creative writing exercises); Final Draft, The Mystic Writer, Screenplay Outliner, Movie Magic, Dramatica, Script Genie, Sophocles, StoryView, and Writer's Blocks (screenwriting software); StoryCraft (story development software); and The Working Writer (writing business software). Software is certainly no substitute for a writer's innate creativity, and some of these programs may not be worth the disks they're burned on—but if one of these programs can give you an edge and increase your productivity, why not give it a shot?

> "Automate your writing tasks with specialized software tools for writers."

- **Use voice recognition software to speed transcribing chores.** Over the years, I have taped a lot of interviews, which means I have come home and spent days doing nothing but transcribing tapes. I tried using an outside service, but the costs were horrendous and the accuracy was spotty. I also found that it was helpful for me to transcribe the tapes myself, particularly when I was, say, ghostwriting an autobiography. It helped me to steep my mind in the voice and thoughts of the interviewee, to listen for unique speech patterns, cadences, and vocabulary. That's where the personality is. The more clearly I heard the interviewee's voice in my mind as I wrote, the more that person's authentic persona was woven into the book. So I felt it was important for me to transcribe the tapes myself.

When I began doing ghostwriting, I used a dictation tape player, with a foot pedal to start and stop the tape. I'm a fast typist, but I can't type quickly enough to keep up with a conversation on tape. I was continually having to stop the tape and back it up in order to get a good transcript.

Then I tried voice recognition software—specifically Dragon NaturallySpeaking 5.0. You "train" the software to recognize your voice (a relatively brief and enjoyable procedure), and then you start using it right away. You can speak naturally, quickly, and conversationally, and the software easily keeps up with you. It is not error-free by a long shot—

but a few errors don't matter all that much when you are transcribing raw notes. And the good thing about voice recognition software is that it enables me to reduce my transcribing time by *at least 75 percent*. In other words, a transcribing project that used to take me four full days could be done in one day using Dragon NaturallySpeaking.

Can you use voice recognition software to generate actual first-draft text? Personally, I wouldn't. In my experience, it doesn't lend itself to the stopping and starting and backing up and deleting that is a normal part of composing at a keyboard. It also is not sufficiently accurate for generating text. But for quick-and-dirty transcribing, you can't beat it.

For voice recognition, you need a computer with a fast processor and a lot of memory. The software must process an enormous amount of speech-pattern information, so the faster your computer, the more quickly and accurately the software responds. The software also needs to "hear" your voice with clarity and high definition, so you will need a computer with a high-quality sound card.

• **Speed up research with reference software and websites.** There's no need to spend time thumbing through a reference book when you can zap right to the word or information you need with a few keystrokes or mouse clicks. One of the best reference tools I own is Microsoft Bookshelf on CD-ROM, which contains nine reference works, including a dictionary, thesaurus, quotations, encyclopedia, almanac, and more. But I have not used Bookshelf nearly as much since I got my high-speed Internet connection. A CD-ROM takes time to insert into the computer, and time to load into memory. Since I'm always connected to the Internet, it's easier and faster for me to do reference checking online at websites like www.dictionary.com, www.thesaurus.com, www.encyclopedia.com, www.findarticles.com, or www.elibrary.com.

• **Save and recycle your research.** Take old articles and book chapters apart and rewrite them for different markets. Go back to old notes and research files, dig out unused quotes, anecdotes, and information. Also, add late-breaking information and timely, relevant events to reshape old work into something new and fresh. By rewriting and reslanting your material, you can turn chapters from your new book into fresh new magazine articles, or you can turn a series of magazine pieces into a book. You'll be amazed at how many ways you can sell and resell the same work to different markets. The key to writing for a living is maximizing your productivity—and you do that not by working harder, but by working faster and smarter.

Use every conceptual and technological shortcut you can find in order to squeeze the maximum productivity out of your writing time.

FAST WRITING LESSON NO. 5: NEVER DO MORE WORK THAN IS NECESSARY

> An average English word is four letters and a half. By hard, honest labor I've dug all the large words out of my vocabulary and shaved it down till the average is three and a half. ...I never write "metropolis" for seven cents, because I can get the same money for "city." I never write "policeman," because I can get the same price for "cop." ...I never write "valetudinarian" at all, for not even hunger and wretchedness can humble me to the point where I will do a word like that for seven cents; I wouldn't do it for fifteen.
>
> *Novelist and humorist* **Mark Twain**

"Are Amazing Instant Novels a cheap trick, a cute gimmick? Are they the literary equivalent of McDonald's hamburgers? Am I a two-bit hack in a yellow suit who can type fast? Should my motto be, 'I'm not a writer, but I play one online'?"

Dan Hurley, who is known as "the 60-Second Novelist," poses these rhetorical questions at his website, www.instantnovelist.com. And the answer to questions 1, 2, and 4, of course, is yes. But as to question 3— no, Dan Hurley is no "two-bit hack." First, I wouldn't call anyone a "hack." And second, Dan Hurley charges considerably more for his 60-Second Novels than "two bits."

Most people who buy Dan Hurley's "60-Second Novels" are people who want to give a unique novelty gift to a friend. Here's how it works: You go to Dan's website (replete with photos of Dan in his trademark yellow suit and yellow hat, along with his trademark 1923 Remington typewriter), and you fill out a form: recipient's name, description, your relationship to the recipient, how you met, how you feel about the recipient, and so forth. Dan takes this information and proceeds to write a story about the recipient—in fact, he pounds the story out on his antique typewriter. A "60-Second Novel" may range from 250 to 500 words long— just one page, typed on special "60-Second Novel" paper. Then Dan signs it, frames it, and sends it wherever you direct— "a one-of-a-kind work of art ready for hanging or prominent display in your home or office!" Price for this one-page masterwork: a mere $98.

The idea came to Hurley while he was an editor for the American Bar Association in Chicago. Taking a day off from work, he set up a chair and typewriter on the sidewalk on Michigan Avenue. Dressed in a three-piece suit, holding up a sign that read "60-Second Novels Written While You Wait," he talked to strangers on the street, asked them a number of personal questions, then wrote a "novel" of their lives in a single minute. Charging about two dollars per "novel," he wrote seven "novels" and made fourteen dollars for the day. A year later, he quit his job and became a full-time "speed writer." His experiences eventually led him to write a real book, *The 60-Second Novelist: What 22,613 People Taught Me About Life*, published by Health Communications, Inc.

The moral to the story: If you can get paid more to write less, why write more? Write less! Never do more work than is necessary to get the job done right—

But make sure you get the job done right!

I'm not suggesting you should do sloppy or slipshod work. Far from it. You've got to practice excellence in everything you write. But when you take on a project, don't over-research it, don't overwrite it, don't over-revise it. If a publisher pays you to write 300 pages, don't write 301. If you can find a niche that pays well for a small amount of work, then master that niche and make it your own. Learn to do enough and no more, then move on to your next project.

FAST WRITING LESSON NO. 6:
PUT PERFECTIONISM TO DEATH

I spent the morning putting in a period—and the afternoon taking it out.
Poet Dylan Thomas

A young woman came up to me after a workshop where I spoke on writing for a living. "My problem," she said, "is that I never finish anything. I'm so afraid someone will see a mistake in my story that I go over it and over it, trying to make everything perfect. I write a paragraph, and then I rewrite it and rewrite it before going on to the next paragraph. Sometimes, I can't even get started on a story. I know what I want the story to be about, and I know my characters and my plot. But until I can think of the perfect opening sentence, I can't write the rest of the story."

Obsessive perfectionism is deadly to good writing. It not only keeps you from *finishing* a book or story—it can even keep you from *starting*. If you are obsessed with writing the perfect book, you'll end up with no book at all. The solution: Give yourself permission to write a bad book.

I give myself that permission all the time. When you are okay with the idea of writing badly, you allow the words to flow. A lot of them will be lousy words, formed into wretched sentences. But some of them will be good. A few will be great. You simply keep the good words and delete the rest.

The beauty of writing on computers is that you are not writing on paper—you're just shoving electrons around. Your words are not chiseled in stone or even typed on paper. Until you actually print out your manuscript, your sentences exist only as invisible traces on the ferromagnetic coating of your hard drive. So what have you got to lose by writing a bad sentence?

> "Obsessive perfectionism is deadly to good writing."

In the old days, a writer used to sit at a typewriter, with crumpled paper overflowing from a wastebasket, with scores of paper balls littering the floor. Back then, if you wrote a bad sentence, you defiled a sheet of paper. Today, if you write a bad sentence, you just highlight it, tap one key, and make it disappear. So relax. Have fun. Write badly. Brainstorm. Experiment. Throw some really awful sentences on the screen, then read them and laugh. Then think about it. Some little notion of genius may lurk in one of those bad sentences. A horrible sentence may give you a clue to a classic line that will live forever. It happens all the time.

Ray Bradbury describes the creative process this way: "Throw up in your typewriter every morning. Clean up every noon." In other words, write quickly, freely, letting everything that is inside you pour forth unedited and uncriticized. Spill everything onto the page in the first draft, in the morning. Then, in the afternoon, clean up, polish, and perfect it.

You want to write the perfect book? Then put perfectionism to death. Snuff it. Terminate with extreme prejudice. Give yourself permission to write badly—and soon you'll be writing brilliantly.

Fast Writing Lesson No. 7: Practice

> As a younger man I wrote for eight years without ever earning a nickel. It was a long apprenticeship, but in that time I learned a lot about my trade.
> *Novelist* **James Michener**

A lot of books on writing advocate "writing practice"—keeping journals or filling notebooks with observations and stream of consciousness jottings. I certainly agree that writing is a craft, and a craft must be practiced in order to approach mastery (keeping in mind what Hemingway said: "We are all apprentices in a craft where no one ever becomes a master"). But I also know that what most books teach about "writing practice" is bunk—at least for those who are serious about writing for a living.

If you intend to make a hobby out of writing, if you have no desire to quit your day job and build an honest-to-gosh career as a writer, then by all means, take a walk, observe everything along the path that is pink, then go home and fill a notebook with observations about pinkness (an actual writing exercise from a very popular book on writing). But those exercises won't take you one step closer to writing for a living. In fact, such writing exercises could actually ruin you as a working writer by suggesting that writing is merely a matter of scribbling random and disorganized observations. Somehow, I can't picture an editor saying, "If only some writer would send me a book about pinkness! What a bestseller *that* would be!"

What kind of practice do I advocate? I encourage people to practice *writing to sell*. Write stories, articles, and chapters of books. Write them—then submit them. Why is this kind of practice better than doing writing exercises and filling notebooks? Because when you write with the intention of submitting what you write, it changes the way you write. It forces you to think about the people who will read your manuscript—the editor, and ultimately, the reader. It gets you out of the mindset of a dilettante and a dabbler, and forces you to *think* like a working writer.

When you practice writing for publication, you approach your writing in a disciplined and concentrated way. You focus on the skills you need to impress an editor and sell your work. You focus on speed and productivity. You know that your writing won't just end up in a notebook. It's going to end up on an editor's desk, and it's going to be viewed with a critical, jaundiced eye. It will have to be good, it will have to draw the reader in from the very first sentence, it will have to keep the pages turning all the way to the end—

Or it will be *rejected*.

If you practice diligently, submit regularly, and collect a mountain of rejection slips along the way, you will eventually reap the reward for all that practice: You'll make a *sale*.

Some people object, "But I'm not writing to be commercial. I'm not writing to please anyone else. I write to please myself, period." Fine. If writing is your hobby, I have no quarrel with that. Enjoy yourself—there's a lot of satisfaction in writing as a hobby.

But remember the title of this book? It's about *writing for a living*—and you can't make a living by only pleasing yourself. Writing for a living is about writing to please readers, not just ourselves. In fact, it's about pleasing as many readers as possible. Ursula K. LeGuin said, "The unread story is not a story; it is little black marks on wood pulp. The reader, reading it, makes it live: a live thing, a story." And Blaise Pascal said, "Everything that is written merely to please the author is worthless."

When you write to please readers, you are practicing writing that sells. Of course, you can still take a notebook (or better yet, a notebook computer) when you go to the mall or a restaurant. You can make notes, jot down ideas, write down snatches of dialogue you overhear that might make a great scene-starter for your novel. But journaling and writing in notebooks should not take the place of a daily, disciplined effort to write for publication.

Here's a suggestion for your writing practice that will help you focus on speed and productivity: Make a commitment to write one short story or nonfiction article per week—finished, complete, buffed and polished, and ready to submit. At the end of that week, send your story or article to the top market in the field. Write another one the next week. And another the next. Do this every week for a year. At the end of a year, you will have generated fifty-two stories or articles, and that's a lot of valuable practice. If you are very good and a little bit lucky, you will have also made some sales.

(You can apply this same concept to writing a novel or nonfiction book—just write a chapter a week, and in ten to twenty weeks or so, you'll have a complete book, ready to submit.)

By practicing this way, you will build some crucial habits: writing quickly and productively; writing under deadline; brainstorming new ideas on a regular schedule; honing not only your craft, but your manuscript marketing skills. As Susan Sontag observes, "By writing much, one learns to write well."

As you write for publication, have your work critiqued on a regular basis. Get involved in a writer's workshop. There are many kinds of workshops: informal writers' groups that meet weekly, bi-weekly, or monthly; more formal workshops organized by writers' organizations; and online writers' workshops, where writers can upload their own work and download others' work for critique and advice.

Novelist David Brin told me, "My advice is to workshop with writers worthy of respect—but also with 'civilians,' nonwriters and unpublished writers, because they are the kind of people who will buy your books. If something in your writing is confusing to a normal reader, you're not doing it right. Criticism is the only known antidote to error, so writer's workshops are one of the most intensive ways to learn this craft."

FAST WRITING LESSON NO. 8:
PUSH YOURSELF TO COMPLETION

When I am all done I shall relax, but not until then. My life isn't very long and I must get *one* good book written before it ends.
John Steinbeck, *from his journal*

Anton Chekhov claimed that he wrote a new short story every day. By the age of twenty-six, he had published over 400 stories. After 1887, his output decreased in volume, but increased in maturity and power—the result of more care that Chekhov put into rewriting and polishing his stories. Born in 1860, Chekhov was in ill health much of his life, and he died in 1904, just forty-four years old. He seemed driven by an awareness of the brevity of life. While the actual number of his works is unknown (many have been lost), it is estimated that he produced some 600 to 800 short stories, novellas, and plays during his short lifetime.

After his untimely death, Chekhov's mother recalled, "When he was still an undergraduate, Anton would sit at the table in the morning, having his tea, and suddenly fall to thinking. He would look straight into my eyes, but I knew he saw nothing. Then he would get his notebook out of his pocket and write quickly, quickly."

Chekhov maintained a strict writing regimen. He pushed himself to complete any story he started—he couldn't tear himself away. He once explained his intense drive to finish his stories this way: "If I leave a story for a long time, I cannot make myself finish it afterwards. I have to begin again."

It may seem simplistic, but it is true—profoundly true: The best way to write quickly is to *push* yourself to write quickly. You have to set a goal: "I will not sleep until I finish this chapter." Then you must keep faith with that goal, even if it keeps you up until three in the morning. Does that sound hard? Well, it is. Writing is hard work. I push myself like that all the time, and I publish four or five books a year.

"People on the outside think there's something magical about writing," said Harlan Ellison, "that you go up in the attic at midnight and cast the bones and come down in the morning with a story, but it isn't like that. You sit down at your typewriter and you work, and that's all there is to it. ...Writing is the hardest work in the world. I have been a bricklayer and a truck driver, and I tell you—as if you haven't been told a million times already—that writing is harder. Lonelier. And nobler and more enriching."

Your goal should not be, "Make it as good as I can," but, "Write it as fast as I can." If you focus on "fast," the "good" will follow. If you focus on "good," it will be slow—and it won't be good. You may not believe me, but it's true. As evidence, I submit the book in your hands. Okay, it's not great literature, it's not Steinbeck or Mark Twain, but I think it's a *good* book on how to write for a living. I think I've written it well. And, I *know* I've written it quickly. I *pushed* myself to write it quickly.

Why does writing faster make you write better? Because the faster you write, the more you use the *creative* side of your brain. The more slowly and deliberately you write, the more you use the *critical* side of your brain. The critic in you is important—but not until you get to the rewriting and editing stage. When you are creating, you must create quickly, without self-criticism or analysis. You must lock the inner critic away in the closet of your brain and keep him there until you are done creating. Then—and only then—let him out to carp and cavil over what you've created.

So set high productivity goals for your writing, then push yourself to hit those goals. In the process, you will build the habits that make you a better, faster writer.

FAST WRITING LESSON NO. 9: PUNCH THROUGH WRITER'S BLOCK

> You want to write a story, see, and you sit down in front of the mill, wait until that certain feeling comes to you, hold off a second longer just to be quite sure that you know exactly what you want to do, take a deep breath, and get up and make a pot of coffee. This sort of thing is likely to go for days, until you are out of coffee and can't get more until you can pay for same, which you can do by writing a story and selling it, or until you get tired of messing around and sit down and write a yarn purely by means of knowing how to do it and applying the knowledge.
>
> *Theodore Sturgeon*, "The Perfect Host," *Weird Tales, 1948*

I haven't been troubled by writer's block for years—but I remember what it feels like. You sit at the keyboard and nothing flows. Soon you find yourself watching TV or rummaging in the refrigerator or twiddling your lips with your forefinger. If it goes on long enough, you find that weeks or months have passed while your magnum opus languishes on a shelf or on the forgotten sectors of your hard drive. The Great American Novel that was going to be becomes something that never was.

This thing we call "writer's block" is a different experience for different writers. For some, it manifests itself as an inability to come up with new ideas—imagination at an impasse. For others, it's an inability to organize words and ideas into a coherent work. It may feel like a complete lack of motivation, an inability to get started, a sense of terminal procrastination, a malignant laziness that kills one's self-esteem and self-confidence, creating a vicious cycle of self-doubt and malaise. Sometimes writer's block is the sense of devastation one feels after having a work savaged by malicious criticism (a thick hide is a real asset for a working writer).

At base, I think writer's block is simply not knowing what to write next. It's the paralysis that results when the ideas, scenes, and words you need are just not there. Fortunately, the causes of writer's block are easy to understand—and treat.

Writer's block is pandemic among writers who have no daily writing habit and who produce only when they feel "inspired." It also afflicts those who are deadline-phobic and who tend to procrastinate until the very last moment. It also afflicts those manic-depressive types who seesaw from thinking everything they write is brilliant to thinking everything they write is drivel. It severely afflicts those who cannot take responsibility for their own success or failure, but blame their failure on outside circumstances or other people. And, it is particularly acute among obsessive-compulsive perfectionists.

> "It may seem simplistic, but it is true—profoundly true: The best way to write quickly is to *push* yourself to write quickly."

There was a time, years ago, when writer's block could sidetrack me from my goals—but no more. Sure, I've been stumped or frustrated for an hour or two, but never as much as a whole day. The reason for that, I believe, is twofold: 1) I can't afford the luxury of writer's block. Writing is my day job. If I don't produce, I don't get paid. I have to generate four or five books a year in order to pay the mortgage, feed my kids, and keep electrical current coursing through the innards of my computer; and 2) I've acquired a few effective "block-busting" techniques to get me through the rough spots, which I now share with you:

• *Withdraw briefly and relax.* Sometimes you get blocked when you press too hard. You get too close to the problem and can't see your way through the tangle of ideas, thoughts, and feelings. You're not really blocked—you just need a break. You need to withdraw for a bit. Take thirty minutes away from your computer and:

Lie down on the couch, put your feet up, close your eyes, clear your mind, daydream, meditate, or pray.

Put on your jogging suit and run.

Take a hot shower.

Listen to music.

When you withdraw, avoid talky, distracting input, such as TV or talk radio. You want to back off from your project—but not too far. You want to keep the muse perched on the shoulder of your awareness, within easy reach. While you relax, a preconscious part of you is turning the writing problem over in your mind—exploring options and ideas, looking for new angles of attack, seeking solutions to writing problems. Your conscious mind will be totally unaware of this process—but it's happening all the same.

Eventually, "inspiration" will strike you—seemingly out of the blue. In reality, that "inspiration" is nothing more or less than the solution that arose as your creative mind continued to function just below the level of your awareness.

• *Leave a gap and move on.* Often, when I come to a tough passage in a book, I say to myself, "This is too tough now, so I'll come back to it later." I insert a note at that point that says: "[TO COME: SECTION ON BLAH-BLAH-BLAH.]" I usually write it in all caps so it stands out, and I sometimes use the bookmark feature in my word processor to make it easy to find. Later, when I come back to the difficult passage, I have written beyond the problem passage and I see how things turn out. That gives me a perspective I didn't have earlier. Sometimes I find out that the passage that stumped me was actually unnecessary and should be deleted. If I had spent hours trying to write it, I would have wasted precious time on a section that was destined for the cutting room floor.

Novelist and nonfiction writer Robert Darden agrees. "If I get to a point where I don't know what's going to happen next," he says, "I type GREAT STUFF HAPPENS HERE and move ahead in the story. It always works out later." Leaving a gap and moving on can save a lot of time, toil, and Tylenol.

• *Write garbage and move on.* Writing garbage and moving on is a lot like leaving a gap and moving on. You say to yourself, "It's lousy, but what the hey! I'll fix it later." Don't demand first-draft perfection of yourself. Go ahead and write garbage—and don't let it undermine your self-confidence. You know you're a good writer, so trust yourself to fix it later. By final draft, you'll turn that garbage into gold.

"Books have bad patches," says Lawrence Block. "The important thing is to get through them, to get the words down however ill-chosen they may seem. ...I tell myself that I'm going to do my five or ten pages no matter what, and that I can always tear them up the following morning if I want. I'll have lost nothing—writing and tearing up five pages would leave me no further behind than if I took the day off, and I'll have avoided guilt and at least kept my fingers limber."[3]

• **Stop while you're on a roll.** Sounds crazy, but it works. I always make sure I'm in the middle of an easy section when I quit writing for the day. That way, I know that when I sit down at the computer the next day, I won't feel blocked by a tough section. Instead, I'll feel eager to jump right in and keep going from where I left off.

Use momentum to your advantage. If possible, try to get through difficult sections while you've got energy and momentum working for you. Save the easy stuff for getting started the next time you start writing.

• **Build your book, story, or article on an outline.** A lot of people don't like to outline their projects. One of those is Stephen King. "I don't take notes," he says. "I don't outline, I don't do anything like that. I just flail away at the thing." King can flail away at his writing and be brilliant; maybe you can, too. If so, then ignore my advice. But I know I can't write like that. I've learned that I have to know where I'm going or I'll never get there.

What Stephen King calls "flailing away at the thing" is also known as the "narrative push" approach, in which you start writing, not knowing where you are going or how your story is going to end. The idea is that as you "push" the narrative forward, you make surprising plot discoveries as you go. Some very successful writers swear by this approach. One proponent was science fiction writer Theodore Sturgeon, who said, "If the writer has no idea what happens next, the reader certainly won't." It is important to note, however, that Sturgeon was chronically afflicted by writer's block throughout his career.

(Aside: Many people think that Kurt Vonnegut's famous recurring character Kilgore Trout—a down-and-out science fiction writer with a small cult following—is Vonnegut's own alter ego. Wrong! Vonnegut modeled Kilgore Trout on the brilliant but chronically blocked and struggling Theodore Sturgeon.)

An outline is merely a plan on paper, not a set of commandments carved in stone. A good outline is sufficiently structured to give you guidance as you write, but flexible enough to allow for discovery, serendipity, and surprise along the way. In my experience writing both fiction and nonfiction, an outline is essential to enabling me to write well and to write quickly.

When I submitted a proposal for a time-travel novel for young readers, the publisher surprised me by offering me a four-book contract—a pleasant surprise, to say the least. Suddenly, I had not *one* book to write but an entire *series*—the Timebenders Series. It was a challenging assignment. I would have three months to produce the first two books and another four months to produce the second two—a total of four books in seven months. I had only one book plotted out in detail; the rest of the series existed only as vague sketches in my imagination.

So I began outlining the rest of the books in the Timebenders Series. As I outlined, I made a fascinating discovery: I was experiencing the adventure of the "narrative push" while writing my outline. My outlines were filled with plot twists that surprised even me! I did my "flailing away at the thing" while I was hammering out the outline, so I didn't have to flail helplessly during the writing phase.

There were times when I invented scenes and even entire chapters as I was writing. The outline didn't hamper my imagination, but it did enable me to write quickly, without getting stuck or blocked. As a result, I not only wrote the four Timebenders books during that seven-month period, but I also coauthored a nonfiction business book during that same time frame. I couldn't have written five books in seven months without an outline to guide me through each book.

An outline is not a straightjacket, it's just a piece of paper. You can follow it when it's working for you, you can depart from it when a better idea comes along. You can introduce new characters, add subplots, change the ending—and I did all of those things while writing the Timebenders Series.

I follow roughly the same route with my nonfiction books. I assemble an outline, grow that outline into a book proposal, sell the proposal to the publisher, then I grow the proposal into a book. Far from being limiting or rigid, it's a very organic and satisfying way to write (notice that organized and organic come from the same root word).

Many people know that Erle Stanley Gardner, the creator of Perry Mason, "wrote" his novels (over 150 books in all) by dictating the text into a recording machine. He would have two or three secretaries type up the manuscript from those recordings, then he would pencil-correct the typescript and send it to the publisher. What few people realize is the extensive and careful groundwork Gardner did before dictating each of his books.

He began by plotting out his story in longhand on legal pads—a process that might take days or weeks for a single book. He constructed his characters in exacting detail, eliminated inconsistencies and contradictions, tied up loose ends, nailed down every twist and turn of the plot, and choreographed the climactic courtroom drama. Gardner could not afford to just "flail away at the thing." He had to know where his story was going at every step along the way—but without telegraphing the solution to the reader.

Once he had his story laid out in detail, he reduced the plot to a stack of 3x5 index cards—one key plot event per card. Then he taped the cards to the wall of his office. Now he was ready to dictate. Taking microphone in hand, he moved along the wall, literally walking through his plot, dictating his story as he went. He could dictate 10,000 words in a single day—an enormous output for any writer. But before he dictated the first sentence, he had the entire book outlined in detail.

Novelist Vicki Hinze calls outlining "prewriting," and she uses her outline to stay productive even when she doesn't feel particularly inspired. "I do a lot of prewriting," she told me, "which means on those days when I'm not feeling spunky or particularly creative, I already have a map of where I need to go. That means I don't have to slog through the 'what in the world am I going to do next' challenges. That prewritten outline is a lifesaver. When the draft is done, I can't tell the difference in scenes where I felt inspired and those where I didn't."

First-time novelist Vineeta Vijayaraghavan could not afford writer's block either. She had taken a year off from work to write her novel, *Motherland*, and she had to go back to work at the end of that year whether the novel was finished or not. So she used an outline to keep herself on-track. "I had outlined about half the book when I decided to take the year off," she explains. "The outline gave me so much support, because it meant I didn't have to write in a linear fashion. If I got stuck writing one chapter, I could switch to an earlier or later chapter because I knew exactly what needed to be accomplished in the plot at that point. Later, of course, I would have to go back and weave in character names or subplot points that I didn't realize would crop up, but it's great to have the opportunity for discovery without writing into a void."[4]

So, as you write, use an outline as your roadmap. But don't be afraid to take a detour or go off-road now and then.

• *Make sure you're having fun while you write.* After all, how can you get blocked if you're having fun? And if you *aren't* having fun, why write?

As you write, ask yourself, "Am I having fun?" If the answer is no, ask, "Why isn't this fun? What could I do to make it fun?" It could be that you aren't having fun because you aren't doing the kind of writing that truly interests and excites you—that's a matter of choosing the right projects. Or, it may be that you have lost sight of how to write material that is fun to write and to read—that's a matter of craft. Or, it may be that there arc problems and obstacles in your life that are hindering the fun of writing—financial pressures, personal problems, worries, and so forth. Solve those problems—and your writer's block may evaporate as well.

"I fear writer's block," novelist Paul Theroux said, speaking before the Commonwealth Club in San Francisco. "If I weren't writing, God knows what I'd do." You don't need to fear writer's block. You now have to tools to defeat it, and to press on to your goals.

TO WRITE WELL, WRITE QUICKLY

Being fast has been useful to me because I can make swift adjustments to the changing market.
Romance writer Jayne Ann Krentz (Sweet Fortune *and* A Coral Kiss)

Sean Stewart is the author of a number of critically acclaimed fantasy novels, including *Passion Play*, *Resurrection Man*, and *Galveston*. He says that his novel *Clouds End* (Ace Books, 1996) "is by far the most important of my books to me. On no other book have I even come close to working so hard, learning so much, failing, at times, so dramatically, or touching, at others, so deeply."

He set out to write a great, sweeping epic. "I decided I would write quickly," he recalls, "and follow the story, instead of making the story up to fit my little pet ideas." He sprinted through the first draft during one intense summer; an extraordinarily productive ten-day stretch produced 400 pages. When his wife became pregnant that fall, he took a full-time job—but he refused to let his day job interfere with his writing. "I worked thirty-five hours a week on the novel," he recalls. "I set the alarm many mornings for four A.M., wrote until seven, and then off to work."

His completed first draft was 1,400 manuscript pages long. After a ing and cutting, he brought in a final draft at 540 pages. The result a novel that was critically and commercially successful. Typical of the reviews Sean Stewart garnered for *Clouds End* was this notice in the science fiction trade magazine *Locus*: "Stewart doesn't make it easy for the reviewer to suggest the special wonders of *Clouds End* without blurting raves. Well, so be it: with this book, he has written an astonishing, wise, beautiful work, full of the terror and wonder and love and power of life and legend intertwined."[5]

The moral to this story: If you would write well, then write quickly, write in overdrive, push yourself to completion. Do I practice what I preach? Well, the first draft of the chapter you've been reading was written over three days: Day 1, 4,420 words. Day 2, 5,120 words. The morning of Day 3, 2,570 words. No question, that's fast.

Was it good? I'll let you be the judge.

But enough of that. Let's move quickly—*quickly*!—to the next chapter, an all-important exploration of the most important relationships in the professional life of a working writer: editors, agents, collaborators, and publishers.

7

Professional Relationships

EDITOR, n. . . .

Master of mysteries and lord of law, high-pinnacled upon the throne of thought, his face suffused with the dim splendors of the Transfiguration, his legs intertwisted and his tongue a-cheek, the editor spills his will along the paper and cuts it off in lengths to suit.

Ambrose Bierce, The Devil's Dictionary

Editors are extremely fallible people, all of them. Don't put too much trust in them.

Maxwell Perkins, *legendary Scribner's editor*

It was one of the most unpleasant experiences of my writing career. And I learned a lot from it.

My coauthor and I had just turned in the final draft of a book, and I felt good about the job we had done. The book contained a lot of information of a technical nature, so we had vetted the book with a couple of experts who had carefully checked all of our facts, footnotes, and sources. The text was as scrupulously accurate as we could possibly make it.

Our editor freely admitted to having no expertise in the subject matter, but I wasn't worried about that. I knew we had gotten our facts straight. Though I had never worked on a book with this editor before, I didn't foresee any difficulties ahead.

The editor read our manuscript, then called me and said, "Great job! The book reads well, tells great stories, and rivets your interest all the way through. One slight problem: The book is running long, so we need to cut some copy. If it's all right with you, I'll just make the edits, then e-mail you the revised file in Microsoft Word format."

"That'll be fine," I said.

A week later, the file arrived by e-mail. I opened it and began reading.

I think it's a good practice, when you read an edited manuscript, to simply go straight through it without comparing it against your original text. I figure that if you don't notice an edit, it's a good edit. All that matters is that the edited text reads cleanly and the author's language and thoughts are intact.

But as I began reading the edited version of the manuscript, I ran up against jarring passages—words I didn't remember using and poorly constructed sentences I didn't remember writing. I can only compare it to the experience of dining on a succulent, savory grilled filet of red salmon—and suddenly choking on a pin bone. I flagged those places to check later.

Then I hit a doozy of a factual error and I did a double take. Had I written that sentence? I couldn't have! I called up my original file, checked the passage in question, and found that it had been heavily altered. In the course of rewriting my original text, the editor had introduced a major factual gaffe. If a glaring error like that got into print, our readers wouldn't have thought, "Gee, some editor sure got that wrong!" They would have thought my coauthor and I were idiots.

Reading further, I found more places where sentences had been added or rewritten, the right word changed to the wrong word, transitions inserted that made no sense—and more factual errors. My heart sank into my shoes with a thud.

I spent the next two days undoing the damage.

TURF WAR

> I think editing is a dying craft, and it really is a craft.
> **Beena Kamlani**, *senior editor, Viking Penguin*

As I examined this editor's changes, I let the majority of them stand. In other cases, I saw that the edit attempted to fix a real problem, but the editor's way of fixing it didn't work for me, so I reworked it in my own words. In an alarming number of cases, the changes were simply disastrous. Some were accompanied by the editor's comments, such as "Transition sentence added here," or "Sentence frags—rewritten as one sentence."

Well, I didn't agree that a transition was needed where the editor indicated. What's more, the editor's sentence was clunky and misleading. I deleted it and inserted a note explaining my rationale.

As for those sentence frags—well, yes, your high school English teacher will tell you to always write in complete sentences, never in sentence fragments. But to write well, you must sometimes break the schoolmarm's rules. Sentence fragments magnify the power of your writing by creating a dramatic pause between thoughts. A pause that creates visual space. A pause that gives tempo and energy to your words. Sparingly and prudently used, sentence fragments turn prose into poetry. I reinserted my sentence frags, along with a note of explanation.

> "I figure that if you don't notice an edit, it's a good edit."

I went over the changes with my coauthor, and he agreed with my revisions. Then I e-mailed the revised file back to the editor.

Next, the manuscript was copyedited, and the copyedited manuscript was e-mailed to us. In addition to the copyedits for punctuation and house style, there were some additional text revisions. For example, the editor's clunky transition sentence, which I had cut, was back in the book—no explanation. I went over the copyedited manuscript and made as few changes as I could bear (I let some edits slide that I really didn't like). I deleted the clunky transition sentence, and again inserted a comment with an explanation of why the sentence wasn't needed. Then I turned it in.

A couple weeks later, the typeset page proofs arrived via FedEx. I read through them—and did another double take. There it was again: the clunky transition sentence that wouldn't die! Still worse, a number of *new* factual errors had crept in. Now I was getting worried. The page proofs are your last shot at the book, and if you don't get it fixed in the proofs, the book will be *published* that way. After all the pains we had taken to get our facts straight, I refused to let the book get into print with all of those errors.

Understand, I'm not accusing the editor of deliberate sabotage. The editor honestly believed that these changes would make our text clearer, cleaner, more grammatically correct, and more accessible to the reader. But in spite of those good intentions, our text kept coming out mangled.

Worse, the editor had *three times* inserted a sentence that I repeatedly insisted was not needed, not wanted, and would hurt the readability of the book. I had never had an editor do that before. *Never.* In my experience, the editor makes a suggestion and the authors either adopt that suggestion, reject that suggestion, or come up with a compromise. I had rejected the change, and had explained and supported my reasons for doing so. At that point, protocol says that you let the author have the text his way. Even if the author is wrong, one little passage will not ruin a book's sales.

For some reason, this editor had decided to get into a turf war over that transitional sentence, stubbornly insisting that the authors' wishes be overridden. I wondered: Whose book was it, anyway? Whose name is on the cover?

I corrected the page proofs and wrote a detailed memo that I sent back with the corrected proofs. An excerpt from my memo:

> P. 66 — There is a MAJOR ERROR here that resulted from not making the correction I requested in the previous go-round. It is EXTREMELY IMPORTANT that this be corrected with great care! We have a recurring problem where serious errors of fact and intent creep in when my wording is changed. I don't claim that my words are inscribed in stone; in fact, there have been a number of edits that have improved the text. But it is a little alarming that some of these problems have appeared in the text after I thought I had taken the final look at the manuscript and I thought all changes had been flagged to my attention.

As to the clunky sentence that wouldn't die, I was determined to pound a stake through its heart and kill it for all eternity. I wrote:

> I have tried repeatedly to delete the transitional sentence added by the editors. It keeps coming back and muddying up the thrust of the next section. We have already spent four pages telling the reader what this sentence says. I know this sen-

tence is intended as a transition, but it is worse than redundant—it actually destroys the transition to the next thought. It misleads the reader into thinking that this paragraph continues the preceding discussion, when in fact we have finished that subject. Now, in this new paragraph, we are addressing a new subject, and this supposed transitional sentence only throws the reader off track.

If we must have some sort of transition between the preceding thought and the next paragraph, then let's insert a subhead.

After I returned the page proofs to the publisher, I got back a lengthy, angry e-mail from the editor—and it was copied to several other people in the publishing house. I was stunned. While I knew my own memo had been emphatically worded, I hadn't intended to come across as angry or combative. Yet the editor perceived my memo that way—and responded in kind. Here is an excerpt from the editor's e-mail:

> Though I know it is difficult for any writer to fully let go of his "baby," you can rest assured that this book is in the careful hands of our team. Please read carefully these responses to your requests because I do have some concerns about the process of this project when it has been placed into your hands.
>
> While we appreciate and respect your writing style, we also ask that you respect our editorial decisions. Your comments are alarmingly inconsiderate of the editors' role. As we work hard to create a winning book for everyone, I would appreciate it if you would couch your suggestions in more considerate terms.

Hard to let go of my "baby"? I was doing everything in my power to get rid of it and get on to the next project! I had more deadlines to meet, and the extra time I spent correcting those proofs threatened my own schedule, costing me time and money.

"Concerns about the process of this project when it has been placed into your hands"? That said a lot about the attitude of this editor. That book was never "placed" into my hands by the editors; it was the *work* of my hands! I had conceived it, I had written the proposal, I had written the text, and everything I did was focused on protecting the truthfulness and integrity of that text.

Had I been "inconsiderate of the editors' role"? I hadn't thought so at the time. I certainly hadn't wanted to offend my editor. I just wanted to get a clean, accurate book, with all of its stylistic energy intact.

The editor went on to address the issue of the transitional sentence:

> Your frustration and anger are evident when you say you "have repeatedly tried to delete the sentence." Please also note that you have not offered help with the problem of the lack of transition until now.

True, I hadn't offered any help with that transitional sentence. I had *deleted* it. I had clearly, consistently stated my opinion that no transitional sentence was needed. And that, I submit, is a fair response to an editorial suggestion. Except in truly critical issues, such as libel or obscenity, editors should not dictate; they should suggest. Ultimately, the author—not the editor—is held responsible for every word contained in the book that bears his or her name. The author should certainly be open to editorial advice, but the author should have the final say over any individual word or sentence in the book.

And what about the claim that my "frustration and anger" were "evident" in my memo? I'll return to that in a moment.

In the end, the product that emerged from that tortured process was a fine book, of which I'm very proud. Some months later, I did a second book with the same editor, and the process went very smoothly—in part because I wrote the manuscript with a better understanding of the editor's preferences, and in part because the editor went over the manuscript with a lighter touch.

But I will always regret the aggravation and grief we inflicted on each other in that process.

THE EDITOR: ALLY OR ADVERSARY?

Brian Lamb: What role does the editor play, and does an editor really make a big difference?

Thomas Friedman: It depends on the writer what role the editor plays. Obviously, I came at the book with a lot of writing experience. I wasn't in any way a novice. But at the same time, my editor, I think, played a very important role in helping me with organization. Sometimes you don't really see the best way to organize the book as you're writing it. And it's very helpful to have someone say the second half of chapter five would really make a perfect first half of chapter three and the bottom half of chapter three should really be the second half of chapter seven, et cetera. Only an outsider can make those recommendations for you.

Thomas Friedman *(*From Beirut to Jerusalem*), interviewed on C-SPAN's Booknotes, September 10, 1989*

I respect and appreciate the role of editors. In at least nine cases out of ten, my editors have greatly improved the books I have written. I believe an editor's first concern has to be the excellence of the work, not the fragility of the writer's ego. I always appreciate getting a critique from a perceptive, knowledgeable editor, because I know that those criticisms will make my book stronger.

Of the sixty-odd books I've done, I can count three occasions where I experienced sharp conflict in the author-editor relationship. Three conflicts out of sixty isn't a bad ratio—it means I've had good, cordial author-editor relations in 95 percent of the books I've written. Considering how subjective the craft of writing is, considering how many arguments *could* arise during the process of bringing a book to market, considering the egos and tough personalities one often finds in the publishing world, a 95 percent success rate is not so bad.

But it doesn't satisfy me.

I've always gone out of my way to maintain cordial relationships with editors. I have prided myself on being professional and easy to work with. There are three editors who might argue the point, and I don't blame them—but that is honestly my goal on every book I write. I think the majority of editors I've worked with would say I *am* easy to work with.

Maintaining good professional relationships with publishers, editors, collaborators, and agents is a key aspect of writing for a living. Networking is a big factor in any writer's success, and you cannot build productive networking relationships on the basis of abrasiveness and conflict. Whenever you make contact with an editor, you are not just selling a book, story, or article—you are selling *yourself*. If you build a good relationship with an influential editor, one sale can become a string of sales, and even a career of sales.

So how do you build good working relationships with your editor? Here are some suggestions:

• View every contact with your editor as part of a long-term relationship, not an isolated sale of a single work.

• Go out of your way to make editors pleased with you and your work: Produce excellence. Deliver on time (or ahead of time). When asked to spend extra time on revisions, rewrites, or other related chores, do so without complaining. Show that you are willing to go above and beyond to make the editor's job easier and the project better.

• Never be rude to the people who buy your work. Never lose your temper. Always be patient and courteous.

• Maintain a personal connection. Send thank-you notes and positive e-mails.

• Be kind to the assistants of editors and publishers. Not only do they sometimes have more editorial influence than you realize, but it's just a good idea to be nice to people. (And assistants become full-fledged editors, too.)

If you practice all of these principles on a consistent basis, you will build healthy relationships and accumulate goodwill. I knew all of those principles before my unfortunate exchange with the editor—but something clearly went wrong. Who's fault was it?

Well, I think it was mine. True, the editor should not have gotten into a turf war with an author over transitions and so forth. But on rereading the memo I sent back with the page proofs, I realize I could have worded it more diplomatically.

Putting phrases like "MAJOR ERROR" and "EXTREMELY IMPORTANT" in all caps made my memo look angry instead of merely emphatic. When you use all caps in an e-mail, people take it as "shouting." Maybe, on a subliminal level, I *was* shouting—though I didn't consciously intend to. It was certainly frustrating that my efforts to eliminate factual errors and get the text I wanted were being thwarted. And, when people feel that they are not being heard, they tend to shout (or write in ALL CAPS) in order to make themselves heard.

There's also the fact that I'm used to blunt talk in my profession. In fact, I prefer blunt talk. It doesn't help me if an editor resorts to vague euphemisms, obliquities, and beating around the bush when telling me what's wrong with my manuscript. I always appreciate it when an editor gives it to me straight. I've had editors tell me such things as, "This three-page section doesn't relate to the rest of the book and needs to go," or even, "This chapter is boring—delete it and write a new one." I don't blow up, I don't get defensive, I just deal with it and fix the problem.

> "I always appreciate getting a critique from a perceptive, knowledgeable editor, because I know that those criticisms will make my book stronger."

In this situation, I expected to be able to deal with my editor straight from the shoulder. Editors have been that blunt and more with me, and I took no offense. I tend to assume that's what we do in this business: We speak plainly and we focus not on egos, turf, and territoriality, but on what's best for the book. Sometimes, however, that's not a safe assumption.

Editors come in all shapes, sizes, temperaments, and levels of courtesy (or arrogance) and acumen (or incompetence). Some editors have a sensitive ear for the music of language; others are tone-deaf, and freely substitute their leaden syntax for your golden phrases. Some editors have a collegial respect for authors; others are like the editor who once told me, "Let an author have his own way and he'll ruin the book." Some editors have a real respect and appreciation for the craft of writing and the skills of its practitioners; others seem to think that the role of a writer is to generate the raw material that editors use to make books. Some editors see themselves as libertarian facilitators of a freewheeling dialogue between author and reader; others see themselves as the Grammar Police, pulling over and arresting sentence fragments and other verbal violators.

While working on *The Lord of the Rings*, J. R. R. Tolkien had to deal with one of these Grammar Cops who sought to instruct him in proper English usage. The editor told Tolkien to change his "dwarves" to "dwarfs" and "elvish" to "elfin" on the grounds that these were the correct spellings in the Oxford English Dictionary. Never mind the fact that Tolkien was, at that time, Merton Professor of English Language and Literature at Oxford—and that he had served for two years as an editor of the Oxford English Dictionary! Fortunately, Tolkien stood his ground.

Even Winston Churchill had to deal with the Syntax Gestapo. When one straitlaced editor rewrote a Churchillian sentence to avoid ending with a preposition, Churchill responded with this fittingly punctilious response: "This is the kind of arrant pedantry up with which I shall not put."

Some editors' attempts to "fix" an author's copy produce unexpected results. In the mid-1970s, fantasy writer Anne McCaffrey turned in a short story collection called *Get of the Unicorn*. "Get," in this sense, is an Old English term referring to the offspring of an animal; it comes from the word "beget" which means to father or sire an offspring. But some editor spotted the "mistake" on the title page and promptly "corrected" it to *Get Off the Unicorn*. Ms. McCaffrey found the editor's "correction" amusing, so she left it intact, and the book was published as *Get Off the Unicorn*.

Robert Darden related this Abominable Editor story to me: "I once had a recent college graduate assigned to a book I did for a regional press. He rewrote the entire book and took out ninety percent of the direct quotes and turned them into passive, past tense, boring paraphrase. I pitched a fit, but was only able to salvage about half of the quotes before the drop-dead deadline. The book was a mess. The editor was fired shortly thereafter, but *I'm* the one whose name is on the book!"

Elbert Hubbard (1856–1915), author and founder of the Roycroft Press, once defined an editor as a person "whose business it is to separate the wheat from the chaff, and to see that the chaff is printed." There are times in the life of every working writer when it is tempting to believe those words—but the truth is: *Every book needs an editor.*

Writing and editing are two separate processes. One is creative and right-brain; the other is critical, analytical, and left-brain. Both processes are necessary to the creation of a professional-quality book. And both processes are deserving of respect.

I believe strongly in the all-important role of the editor as the gatekeeper and guardian of the special status of a published author. One of the major revolutions taking place in the communications world today is the rise of e-publishing and print-on-demand, which now makes it easier and cheaper than ever before to become a "vanity" author. Anyone with a couple hundred bucks to spare can get a book "published" and start selling it over the Internet. Some are predicting that the "middlemen" between author and reader (publishers, editors, distributors, wholesalers, books dealers) will eventually disappear, and readers will be able to buy directly from the author. If that is true, it is not a good thing. Just read any vanity press book and you will see just how much we need editors.

> Writing and editing are two separate processes. One is creative and right-brain; the other is critical, analytical, and left-brain.

I appreciate having a process in place that says, "These authors have run the publishing gantlet, they have impressed editors with their work, they have been approved and validated as people who have mastered a craft. They have done something that is difficult to do. This is their imprimatur: They are *published authors.*" I think it would be tragic if that distinction ever disappeared.

Editors are the unacknowledged shapers and arbiters of the literary corpus of their age. That role should not be dismissed lightly, nor should we ignore an editor's insights and judgment. A good editor can be a potent ally in the success of any book—and any writer.

Case in point: In April 1935, Harold Strong Latham, chief editor at the Macmillan Company in New York, went to Atlanta in search for regional talent. He visited with various people in Atlanta literary circles, asking for referrals to promising writers in the area. One name given him was that of a former newspaper reporter, Margaret Mitchell. Latham paid a visit to Mitchell at her home on Peachtree Street. When she answered the door, he introduced himself and said he had heard she was writing a book. She refused to discuss her book with him and closed the door in his face.

Later, Mitchell was talking to a friend—a young woman who was also writing a novel—and she told this friend what she had done. The friend was aghast. "A New York publisher asked to see your novel and you refused?" she said. "Margaret Mitchell, you don't have the seriousness to be a novelist!"

Stung and angered by those words, Mitchell went home, packed her sprawling, nearly complete manuscript in a large suitcase, and took it to Harold Latham's hotel. Latham received the suitcase without enthusiasm, unhappy at being brushed off before. He took the manuscript, suitcase and all, back to New York.

When Latham finally got around to opening the suitcase and inspecting the manuscript, he thought it was the worst-looking mess he had ever seen. Instead of a complete first chapter, it had several versions of a partial first chapter. There were gaping holes in the storyline where portions of the manuscript were missing. The heroine's name was obnoxiously cutesy: Pansy O'Hara. The title page bore the insipid title *Tomorrow Is Another Day* (other titles Mitchell suggested: *Not in Our Stars*, *Bugles Sang True*, and *Tote the Weary Load*).

Latham nearly shipped the manuscript back to Mitchell unread—but on a whim he started turning pages. Soon he became engrossed in the steamy romance between Pansy O'Hara and the roguish Rhett Butler, set against the epic backdrop of the American Civil War.

Meanwhile, Margaret Mitchell regretted having shown him the book. She sent Latham a telegram, asking for the book's return. He wired back that he thought the book had potential. Over the next few months, Harold Latham worked with Margaret Mitchell to reshape and transform her vast, inchoate tale. Pansy's name was changed to Scarlett, and *Tomorrow Is Another Day* became a runaway best-seller as *Gone With the Wind*. The result was an instant classic that sold over a million copies in its first six months. If not for the keen editorial judgment of Harold Strong Latham, however, *Gone With the Wind* would not exist.

THE MANY ROLES OF AN EDITOR

I cannot think of anybody who doesn't need an editor, even though some people claim they don't.

Novelist **Toni Morrison** (Paradise, Song of Solomon)

First, let's look at the various roles of magazine editors. Check the masthead of any large magazine, and you'll see a bewildering array of editorial titles. Unfortunately, there is very little title standardization in magazine publishing. It can become a tricky task to decode these titles so that you know which editor you need to reach with your query.

Many people with the word "editor" in their title don't actually edit anything—they don't buy manuscripts, they don't deal with writers, they don't edit copy. A "production editor," for example, usually works with layout and design, not manuscripts. If you send your query to the wrong editor, it may eventually get forwarded to the right editor—but then again, it may not. So it is vitally important that you do the research and address your query to the right person, or you're wasting your time.

In some publications, the "managing editor" is The Boss in the corner office; in other publications, the "managing editor" might be the editor who reads submissions, or even a person who manages the production end of the magazine (overseeing copyediting, proofreading, typesetting, art direction, and printing).

In small publications, a few people wear many hats. When I was fresh out of college, I worked for a very small magazine. My boss, the "editor-in-chief," read all submissions, assigned all articles, and personally edited all manuscripts. I was the assistant editor, and I did a lot of the in-house writing and rewriting. We divided up the art direction chores— my boss did half of the layout work; I did the rest. My boss's wife worked in the office part-time. The three of us *were* the magazine staff. It was a very short masthead.

The "editor-in-chief" of a large publication like *Time* or *Reader's Digest* never sees individual submissions, does not assign articles, and never blue-pencils manuscripts. He or she is an executive in charge of administration and editorial policy. This person may also be called "editor and publisher" or "editorial director."

The person *you* want to connect with is further down the masthead, and may simply be called "editor." The best way to find the person who receives submissions at a magazine is by checking the listing in the latest *Writer's Market*. Also recommended: Phone the magazine's switchboard to confirm that the editor listed in *Writer's Market* is still in that position; if not, get the name of the individual who has replaced him or her. Approaching an editor by name makes a much better impression than "Dear Sir or Madam."

Large publications also have editors for various departments. If you have an article idea that fits under one of the magazine's departments (such as Health, Travel, Family, Money, and so forth), then seek out the editor of that department. People who head these departments are commonly given the title "senior editor" or "feature editor." They are responsible for everything in their subject area, and often deal directly with writers.

These job descriptions tend to be the same for Internet magazines as well as print publications.

All initial communication with editors should be by mail or, if the publication's website invites it, by e-mail. Phone calls to editors are okay once an editor-writer relationship is established; keep calls brief, professional, and cordial. Ask, "Is this a good time to call?"

For detailed information on writing for magazines and working with magazine editors, see *Magazine Editors Talk to Writers* by Judy Mandell (John Wiley & Sons, 1996), *Writer's Guide To Magazine Editors and Publishers* by Judy Mandell (Prima Publishing, 1997), *Writing for Magazines: A Beginner's Guide* by Cheryl Sloan Wray (NTC Publishing, 1996), and *Writer's Digest Handbook of Magazine Article Writing* by Jean M. Fredette (Writer's Digest Books, 1990).

Next, let's look at the roles of editors in book publishing. When your book is accepted for publication, you can generally expect it to be handled by four different kinds of editors. Each editor has an important role or function:

• **Acquisition editor.** The acquisition editor reads book proposals and novel synopses (usually prescreened from the slush pile by an editorial assistant). The final decision to accept a book is usually made by an editorial committee or publishing board, but the acquisition editor will normally go into a pub board meeting and contend for the books she wants in her line. (The pub board also gives the editor a buffer when she doesn't want to offend an author by turning down his book: "I went into that meeting and pitched your book as hard as I could, but the pub board turned it down.") The acquisition editor is involved largely with 1) discovering and developing new talent and 2) maintaining good relations with already-acquired authors so that they do not bolt to other publishing houses. The acquisition editor seeks to develop books that will bring a profit to the publishing house, and does this by helping books (and their authors) to realize their full potential.

• **Content editor.** The content editor (also called the developmental editor, substantive editor, manuscript editor, or line editor) works with the author on the broad issues of the manuscript: structure, theme, organization, clarity, and expression. The content editor is the person at the publishing house with whom you will have the most continuous contact. In my experience, the acquisition editor often serves as the content editor as well—not only signing the author but helping the author to shape and develop the content of the book for publication. The best content editors are those who see themselves as the ally of the author, who are able to catch the author's vision for the book, and who are committed to helping the author convey that vision as clearly, powerfully, and effectively as possible.

Content editors walk a fine line with the author, sometimes pushing the writer to rewrite and refine his text in order to take it to the next level. Beena Kamlani, senior editor for Viking Penguin, tells the story of working with a brilliant writer who already had a number of books in print. This writer had turned in a very good novel that was flawed in one respect: The protagonist had become involved in a relationship for which there was no believable motivation—it seemed completely out of character. Kamlani asked him to work on that section. The author produced ten different versions, none of which solved the problem.

"I kept saying, 'You're not there yet, you're not there yet,'" Kamlani recalls, "though by this time I could sense he'd get there eventually." Six weeks later, the author faxed in revisions of three paragraphs. Kamlani read them—and knew that the author had nailed it. When *The New York Times* reviewed the book, the reviewer quoted those very passages as examples of the author's craft and brilliance. But those passages wouldn't have happened without the craft and brilliance of a great editor.

A content editor must also know when to let go. "As an editor," says Kamlani, "the most important thing is to keep your relationship with the author harmonious, constructive. The editor is the ideal reader of the book, which means that you don't come armed with personal biases, with prejudices, looking for reasons to shoot the book down. You're not judging it; you're protecting it. You come to it to learn what the author's trying to do. . . . It helps to remember that this isn't my book, it's the author's book, and I'm an editor, not a cowriter. It's got to be a relationship that ultimately sustains the author's endeavor."[1] The great Scribner's editor, Maxwell Perkins, once put it even more succinctly: "The book belongs to the author."

It is the content editor's responsibility to identify the audience for the book; to understand the author's vision and concerns; to consult with the author and answer questions; to analyze and strengthen the structure and organization of the book; to help the author make technical or complex passages reader-friendly; to clarify ambiguities, identify unclear writing or flawed logic, and suggest corrections; to help format the book with regard to such issues as chapter divisions, graphics, and bullet lists; to identify potential legal problems involving libel, copyright infringement, trademarks, permissions, and so forth; and to challenge the author to achieve his or her best effort.

A content editor is sometimes called upon to write original material to complement the author's text—as when, for example, a transition is needed. But when doing so, the editor has a responsibility to emulate the style and tone of the author, to always flag such changes to the author's attention, to permit the author to substitute his or her own wording, to listen sensitively to any objections the author might raise, and ultimately to respect the author's vision for the text. Ideally, a content editor who inserts his or her own writing into the manuscript should have a good ear for language, diction, idiom, dialogue, and style.

• **Copyeditor.** After hammering out the form and structure of the manuscript, the content editor typically passes the manuscript on to a copyeditor, who refines the text in terms of grammar, punctuation, spelling, active versus passive voice, and such technical matters as citations and cross-references. The copyeditor watches out for factual inconsistencies, repetition of words, and similar fine points. He or she has little flexibility or responsibility for changes regarding structure and form. Copyediting is often performed out-of-house by freelance copyeditors.

• **Managing editor.** The managing editor (sometimes called a production editor) manages the postediting production process. This involves preparing the manuscript for typesetting, interacting with the author on proofs, and sometimes even shepherding the book through printing, binding, and warehousing, so that release dates are met. The entire editing and production process—from the moment you turn in your manuscript until the first printed copy lands on your doorstep—usually takes about nine months to a year.

I have seen books nearly destroyed by a bad editor—and I have seen books saved by a great editor. I once had both experiences on one book. An acquisition editor had given my manuscript to an overly aggressive copyeditor who proceeded to completely rewrite the book in his own style. There was literally not one paragraph left untouched and unmutilated. In some places, he actually turned the meaning of my text upside-down, so that it said the *opposite* of what I had originally written. To top it off, this copyeditor had a bad case of what novelist James Blish used to call *said bookism*—the practice of peppering dialogue passages with every possible alternative to the perfectly good word "said." Wherever I had written "he said" or "she asked," this copyeditor substituted "murmured," "retorted," "proclaimed," "hissed," "whispered," "muttered," "inquired," "quizzed," "queried," "shouted," "spouted," "grated," "exclaimed," and even "ejaculated." My acquisition editor (to her everlasting credit) was as horrified as I was. She sent the manuscript—my *original* manuscript—to another copyeditor who (I'm happy to report) did a very careful, sensitive job of copyediting.

So let's not be too hard on editors. The bad ones are few and far between. The good ones are numerous and, in my experience, well versed in the specialized craft of editing. I vote for a little compassion, appreciation, and understanding for editors, most of whom do not receive the recognition they deserve for the contributions they make to an author's book—and to an author's career.

When the poet T. S. Eliot was an editor for a London book publisher, he was approached by a struggling young author. This author was still stinging from having his manuscript rejected by another publishing house. "Mr. Eliot," said the young author, "isn't it true that most editors are failed writers?"

"Perhaps," Eliot replied. "But then, so are most writers."

Editors and writers are in this business together and we need each other. As editors and writers, we must see each other as allies, not antagonists. Our mutual success depends upon it.

THE AGENT: DO YOU REALLY NEED ONE?

> I have spent too much time helping too many writers get out of bad agency relationships; it is better to have no agent than a bad one.
> *Science fiction writer* **Orson Scott Card**

In the 1970s, the prolific English novelist Ian Watson wrote a quirky deconstructionist novel called *The Woman Factory*. Years later, he told an interviewer, "*The Woman Factory* is one of the reasons why I don't have a literary agent." Watson had targeted the publisher he saw as a "dead cert" buyer for his offbeat work: Olympia Press in Soho, London. He turned the manuscript over to an agent who was located in the same building as Olympia Press, just one floor down. Then he went off and proceeded to write other books.

After a year, it occurred to Watson to inquire about the status of *The Woman Factor*. So he paid a visit to his agent's office and asked if there had been any nibbles. The agent claimed to have submitted it to numerous houses, all without success. Which houses? The agent named a series of wildly unlikely candidates for Watson's quirky tome. "Did you happen to pop upstairs with it," asked Watson, "and show it to the good people at Olympia Press, as I suggested a year ago?" The agent admitted he had not.

Watson snatched his manuscript away from the agent, took it himself to the editors at Olympia, and they loved it. "Just give us a few days to draw up a contract," they said. "You'll be hearing from us straightaway."

A few days later, Watson was reading the newspaper and happened to spot an article: Olympia Press had just gone bankrupt.

A few years later, he managed to sell the book to a French publisher—so there was a French language edition, but none in English. A few more years passed, and Playboy Paperbacks agreed to bring out an English language edition if the book could be rewritten and updated. Watson completed the rewrite as requested, and delivered the manuscript to Playboy Paperbacks, only to be told that the company was being sold and no new books were being acquired.[2] In 2001, Watson's novel was sold to a Japanese publisher for translation. To date, *The Woman Factory* exists only in French and Japanese editions.

Ian Watson's tale of publishing woes involves a combination of bad luck, bad timing, publishing industry travails—and a clearly less-than-competent agent. In the publishing industry, there are great agents, good agents, and horrible agents. Patricia Nell Warren, author of *The Wild Man* and *The Front Runner*, put it this way:

> Twenty-five years ago, when I published my first national best-seller, I believed that literary agents were gifts from God. While still a *Reader's Digest* book editor, I worked with a well-known author who had soured on agents...he had nothing good to say about them, and negotiated all his own contracts. I was mystified by his attitude, till I had my first Waterloo with an agent. Then I understood. There are agents...and agents.[3]

Horror writer Dean Koontz recalls that, early in his career, he had a *good* agent who was unfortunately the *wrong* agent. Koontz describes the man as intelligent, honest, and charming, a shrewd and aggressive negotiator who represented a number of high-powered talents. Koontz considered him a friend, and enjoyed working with him. One day, over lunch in an expensive restaurant, Koontz mentioned one of his novels to the agent and wondered why this eminently filmable book had never gotten an offer for film rights. "Oh, we had an offer," said the agent. "They offered a hundred-thousand. We turned it down."

It was several moments before Koontz was able to speak. "We turned it down?"

The agent explained that the offer came from a producer who wanted to direct the film himself—and the agent considered him a poor director. "It would be a lousy film. We'll sell the rights to someone who'll make a good film of that book—better for your career that way."

Koontz was young and he trusted the agent. He waited patiently—but no other film offers ever materialized for the book. One day, Koontz approached the agent with a book idea that was more ambitious than any he had ever done. The agent refused to represent it. He told Koontz to stay with the shorter, simpler novels he had been writing heretofore.

"*That*," says Koontz, "was what made me go elsewhere. An agent can offer guidance and market suggestions, but he must not be the absolute determiner of what stories his client will tell. He must encourage his client to grow, to try new ideas that challenge the client's talents. If an agent does not trust a client's artistic instincts, if he will not sell what the *client* wants to write, he is the wrong representative for that particular author."

Though it pained him to do so, Dean Koontz fired his old agent and hired a new one. His new agent sold the idea for the biggest advance Koontz had ever received. Once published, the book went through seven printings and sold over a million copies. "That novel was the turning point in my career," he concludes, "and it taught me a vital lesson...even a *good* agent is not always the right agent."[4]

The best agents are easy to spot: They are the ones who aren't taking on new clients. The worst are also easy to spot: They are advertising for new clients. If you do a lot of research and send out a lot of query letters, you *may* be able to land a good agent who can help your career. But first you need to ask yourself: "Do I really need an agent? Do I even want one?"

Fact is, you don't need an agent to get published. You don't need an agent to have a successful career as a writer. Most of my career, I have not been represented by an agent.

My experience, and the experience of many writers I've talked to, is that it is about as difficult and time-consuming to find an agent as it is to find a publisher. So if you are not an established author, the question you have to ask yourself is: Why waste time pursuing an agent? True, the largest book publishers won't read submissions that don't come from agents—but there are still many good, solid houses that will. So my advice would be to approach publishers who are approachable. Then, once you are offered a contract, it becomes an easy matter to interest an agent who will negotiate the contract for you.

How should you contact an agent when you have an offer from a publisher? Pick up the phone and call, or send an e-mail. I know, the agent's website says, "Write to us—don't call." But you've got an offer from a publisher and no time to waste. For an agent, that's found money. He or she doesn't have to go out and market your book, because you've already done that. All you want is to have your contract negotiated by someone who knows the ins and outs of the business. You are not pleading for the agent to do you a favor, you are doing the agent a favor. If an agent doesn't want to take your call, then: 1) it's his or her loss; 2) you have lost nothing by making the call; and 3) you have just screened out an agent you don't want to do business with anyway. If you'd rather send an e-mail than make a phone call, and if the agent offers an e-mail address in his or her listing, then by all means, use it.

What will the agent do for you? If this is your first book, an agent probably will not be able to get much more advance money for you. But there is a lot more to a book contract than the advance. An agent might be able to negotiate better royalty escalators, or a bigger percentage of the sub rights, or other deal points that you might not even be aware of.

Agents typically insist on a 15 percent commission for representing a book (and 20 percent for overseas sales)—but if you already have an offer from a publisher, you have already done half the agent's work. It is certainly fair to insist on a 10 percent commission. Incidentally, you will learn a lot about the agent by negotiating his or her commission. Does the agent view you with professional respect, or does he or she just want to exploit you? Is the agent interested in a long-term relationship or short-term gain? If you don't like what you see and hear, politcly close the discussion and continue your search for the right agent.

The best way to find a good agent is through a referral from a satisfied published writer. Another way is to look at books of authors in your chosen field. Authors will often thank their agents on the acknowledgments page. Writer's resources, such as *Writer's Market*, also list agents and their contact information.

Approach an agent as you would a publisher: Write an interesting, professional query letter. Describe your book in no more than two typed, single-spaced pages. List your credits and qualifications. Include clips (photocopies of your published work) and an SASE.

Then be patient—persistent, but patient. Responses from agents average six to eight weeks. Querying several agents at the same time is okay—in fact, you'd be foolish not to. If you don't hear anything after a reasonable time, send a follow-up letter. If an agent wants to scc your work, send exactly what he or she asks for—no more, no less.

> "The best way to find a good agent is through a referral from a satisfied published writer."

If you have the luxury of choosing between competing agents, choose the one who shows the most genuine enthusiasm for your work, and who seems to have the best track record in your field. The agent will market your book to publishers, negotiate the contract, act as a buffer or liaison with the publishing company, and give you advice and assistance if problems arise in the author-publisher relationship. Your advance and royalties are generally paid to the agent, who passes them along to you, less his or her commission and fees.

Do not expect an agent to be your writing coach (you should already know your craft), your banker (don't ask for a loan), your shrink (let writing be your therapy), your attorney or accountant (you should have an attorney and an accountant as well as an agent). Your agent is your advocate and your ally. If you both are very fortunate, you and your agent could even become genuine friends.

What should you look for in an agent—and what should you beware of? Here are some suggestions:

• Seek out an agent who is currently a member of the Association of

Authors Representatives (P.O. Box 237201, Ansonia Station, New York, NY 10003). AAR members adhere to a Canon of Ethics. To obtain a copy of the canon or a list of AAR members, visit the AAR website at www.publishersweekly.com/aar/.

• Agents today are highly specialized. Some only deal in fiction, some nonfiction. There are agents who specialize in children's books, science fiction and fantasy, romance, mystery, and other genres. Do your homework and find the agent who handles what you write.

• Avoid agents who charge fees of any kind, especially reading fees or editing fees. Such agents make their money off of fees you pay, not from commissions they earn. Also, avoid agents who want to steer you toward a "book doctor" or other paid editing service.

• Ask for a list of authors and books the agent has represented. The better agents have such a list printed up and on file, and they are eager to show it to you. If an agent is secretive about his or her supposed "successes," steer clear.

• Avoid agents who actively advertise or solicit clients. An agent who beats the bushes for work is not an agent you want.

• Avoid agents who try to push you toward the latest fad or hot genre; you want an agent who understands, appreciates, and encourages your work, and wants you to be *you*.

• Avoid agents who seem uncritically enthusiastic about your work ("Everything you write is absolutely brilliant!"), or who make grand, unrealistic promises ("This book will be snapped up right away," or, "With my guidance, you'll soon be a millionaire!"). Responsible agents usually try to dampen your expectations, not inflate your hopes.

• Don't sign any long-term contracts with an agent. Agree only to be represented on a book-by-book basis. Agent-author relationships go sour all the time, and you don't want to be locked into a bad relationship. The agent-author relationship should be based on mutual trust and mutual benefit, not on the threat of contract enforcement and litigation.

• If you have a problem with your agent, talk it over and seek a cordial solution. If you can't resolve the problem, it's perfectly reasonable to end the relationship, as long as you do so according to the terms of your written agreement.

• If you cannot get an agent or decide not to use one, have a good contract lawyer review all your contracts. An attorney should either advise you in negotiating your deal, or should negotiate for you. In fact, it's not a bad idea to have an attorney double-check your contract, even if it has been negotiated by an agent.

Finally, a word from the Master of Horror on finding an agent. "Remember Stephen King's First Rule of Writers and Agents," says the author of *Carrie* and *The Shining*, "learned by bitter personal experience: You don't need one until you're making enough for someone to steal...and if you're making that much, you'll be able to take your pick of good agents."[5]

COLLABORATORS: ARE TWO HEADS BETTER THAN ONE?

Trade nonfiction is the biggest market for ghostwritten books. Virtually every celebrity autobiography and memoir is ghosted, as are the overwhelming majority of books on any subject by a celebrity. However, for every celebrity bio, there are a hundred other ghostwriting assignments which often go unnoticed. For the working writer, the prime fields for ghostly plows include history, biography, autobiography, memoirs, how-to books, politics, religion, popular psychology, relationships, conspiracy theories, New Age, true-life stories, and true crime.

Ghostwriter **Richard M. Cote**

I got my start in this business by writing other people's books. I sometimes called myself a "ghostwriter," although technically a ghostwriter is someone who writes another person's book and receives no credit. To be more precise, I have been a "collaborative writer" and my role has always been credited on the cover or the title page. I usually worked with people who have a story to tell or an idea to expound, but who were not writers. In the process, I became acquainted with some truly outstanding and fascinating people, from business leaders to Super Bowl winners to an actress and a supermodel.

It sometimes happens that writers are brought in to write a book where there really is no book to write. A famous actor or sports figure is offered six figures for his or her "autobiography," but can't really be bothered with being interviewed for the book. The writer goes out and researches the book on his own, and then writes a manuscript that the so-called "author" never even reads. That's probably what happened when

NBA star Charles Barkley once claimed he was "misquoted" in his own autobiography.

Fortunately, I have never had to write such a book. The authors I've worked with have all been cordial to work with, articulate and thoughtful in their interviews, and extremely cooperative. As a result, every collaborative book I've written has been honest, and the words are the author's own words that I have shaped into a book, not words I've had to invent.

For example, I went to the home of football star Reggie White and recorded twenty hours of interview tape. When I was done, I had his story in his own words, and that's what you find in his autobiography, *Reggie White: In the Trenches*. Moreover, Reggie was closely involved in the structuring and editing of the book. He took ownership of the project and wanted to make sure it was honest and accurate, reflecting not only the details of his football career but his passion for racial reconciliation. Reggie would never say he was misquoted in his own book, because all the words in that book are *his* words.

If collaborative writing interests you, here are some suggestions for success in a collaborative career:

• **Capture the author's "voice."** Keep your own voice, style, and opinions out of the way. After you conduct your taped interviews, listen to the tapes until you can hear that person's voice playing in your mind—the cadences, the phrases, the idioms, the unique vocabulary.

A few years ago, an author I worked with sent me a copy of a book we had written together. Opening the book, I found he had inscribed it with these words: "To Jim—Thanks for making me read like I sound." That was the ultimate compliment.

• **Find or generate projects you can feel passionate about, books you can write with intensity, energy, and flair.** I've learned, gained, and grown from every book I've ever worked on. I've never had to take a project just to make a buck. I've never had to work with an author I didn't respect. Writing is hard enough when you love what you do; if you have to spend weeks or months on a project you detest, it's murder. If you have to write a book that bores you, the reader will be bored as well. So be selective about the projects you accept.

• **Make sure you have a written agreement with your collaborator.** In many cases, I have approached a celebrity or business leader and have suggested that we do a book proposal together and market it to a publisher. I've learned the hard way that it's smart to have a written agreement spelling out such matters as the division of advance and royalties, division of sub rights, who has final approval of content, and who owns what in case the partnership breaks down. You don't need a lengthy contract with a lot of fine print. All of these matters can be settled in a one-page letter of agreement signed by both parties.

On one occasion, I approached an entertainer and offered to help her write her autobiography. She was excited about the idea and we made a verbal agreement: At no charge to her, I would interview her, write a proposal, and market the proposal to publishers. If the book sold, we would split all the proceeds right down the middle. Over the next few weeks, I put an enormous amount of time and travel expense into that proposal. Finally, I had a draft ready to show her. I gave it to her for final approval and correction before sending it out to the publishers. She was speaking at a conference that weekend, so she took the proposal to read on the plane.

At the conference, she gave a talk in which she told of some of her life experiences. After her talk, a man approached her and said, "You've got a fascinating story. I'm a literary agent, and I think you should write a book."

"Well, that's a coincidence," she said, "because I'm working with a writer on a book right now. In fact, I have the proposal right here." She handed the proposal to the agent, he skimmed it, and offered to represent her on the spot.

"What sort of arrangement do you have with this writer?" the agent asked.

"If it sells," she said, "we split everything fifty-fifty."

"Oh, no!" he said. "He's not entitled to that much! It's lucky we met. You need an agent to look out for your interests." The agent proceeded to suggest to this lady that I was taking advantage of her.

The next thing I knew, I got a phone call from the agent. "I'm now representing Miss So-and-So. I understand you don't have a written agreement with her, so I'm sending you an agreement I have prepared. We are offering you thirty percent of the advance and royalties, and you must agree to relinquish all subsidiary rights. And, of course, fifteen percent of your earnings will be deducted for my commission."

I couldn't believe it. I had initiated the book, and I had invested time and money developing the project on spec. I had been completely fair to this lady, had taken no up-front money from her, and had offered her exactly the division of proceeds that was spelled out in *Writer's Market*. The agent had inserted himself into our arrangement, claiming to "protect Miss So-and-So's interests" as if I were some sort of con artist trying to fleece her. It was outrageous and insulting—but the agent had won her trust, so I had few options short of withdrawing from the book.

I argued and negotiated with the agent, got some small improvement in the terms, and finally signed the paper. Over the next few months, the agent tried to sell the book, but without success. Finally, he dropped the project.

At that point, the entertainer and I got together and wrote up a new agreement based on our original terms. I quickly sold the book to a good publisher via my own connections.

So the story had a happy ending. The book got published, and I learned a valuable lesson: When you collaborate with another person on a book, don't trust verbal agreements. Put everything in writing.

• **Remember whose book it is.** Sure, you care about the quality of the product—but always remember that it's the author's name on the jacket, not yours. Don't let your ego interfere with the working relationship. I always give the people I work with the benefit of my experience, and sometimes I politely argue with them, but I always frame it in terms like, "We both want this book to be the best it can be. Whatever you want in the end, that's what I'm going to do. But I wouldn't be serving you well if I didn't at least suggest to you another way of doing it."

• **Assess your career goals on a regular basis.** Do you want to be a collaborative writer for the rest of your career? Nothing wrong with that. In my own case, I knew that collaborative writing wasn't my ultimate goal. It was a good way to get into the writing business, gain some experience, and meet a lot of people. Still, I had my own books to write, my own stories to tell. After a few years of full-time writing, I realized that I was filling my schedule, year after year, with collaborative contracts—and I didn't have any time left over to write my own books. I had failed to think strategically about my career, I had lost sight of my goals.

Understand, I don't regret a single book I have written. In the process of writing books with so many accomplished people, I gained insights, experiences, and knowledge that I never could have discovered on my own. My years as a collaborative writer honed my skills and prepared me to write my own books.

Professionally, however, collaborative writing had become a treadmill—and I was finding it hard to get off. If I were going to achieve my own goals and write my own books, I would have to make sacrifices. I would have to focus on developing material under my own sole byline. That meant saying "no" to some lucrative collaboration projects in order to launch my own books.

So I sacrificed. My income took a sharp dip at first. But I wrote a number of proposals, and most of them sold. Within eighteen months of making a decision to concentrate on my own books, I had one solo book completed, five more under contract, and more on the way.

Collaborative writing has been good to me. I still do collaborative books today, though not as many as before. If you want to write for a living, there are certainly worse ways to break in than this. Many successful solo authors have learned and practiced their craft by collaborating. Just make sure you never lose sight of your goals and never step aboard a treadmill that you can't get off.

PUBLISHERS: "THE GOLDEN AGE" IS DEAD

> Oh Lord, forgive the misprints!
> *Last words of Pennsylvania book publisher **Andrew Bradford** (1686–1742)*

The poet Lord Byron once gave a rare, ornate Bible to his publisher, John Murray. On the flyleaf, Byron wrote a flattering inscription. Murray proudly displayed this gift on a table in his office so that his visitors could admire it. One day, a visiting author was examining the Bible. Turning the pages, he came upon a passage that had been altered in ink by the hand of Lord Byron. It was John 18:40, which contained the sentence, "Now Barabbas was a robber." Byron had crossed out "robber" and inserted the word "publisher." After that alteration was pointed out to John Murray, he removed the poet's gift from his office and it was never seen again.

Lewis A. Coser, Charles Kadushin, and Walter W. Powell, writing in *Books: The Culture and Commerce of Publishing*, offer a somewhat more ennobled view of publishers than that of Lord Byron:

Books are carriers and disseminators of ideas. More than any other means of communication, they are the most permanent, reasoned, and extensive repository of the thoughts of civilized man. Although the publishing industry may hold a more mundane view of itself, the book trade is, in fact, both the guardian and the constant creator of our written culture.[6]

Robbers? Or guardians of the culture? What is the role of publishers in our society and in the life of the working writer?

The publishing industry has a grand tradition. The decades of the 1920s, '30s, and '40s have been called "The Golden Age of Publishing." That was the era of Alfred A. Knopf, Bennett Cerf of Random House, and Maxwell Perkins of Scribner's (actually an editor, but with power and autonomy rivaling that of a publisher). These great publishers discovered and developed an extraordinary list of literary talents. Perkins alone was responsible for nurturing the careers of Thomas Wolfe, F. Scott Fitzgerald, Ezra Pound, and Ernest Hemingway.

During that era, two young editors of the Columbia University student newspaper founded a publishing firm in a two-room office on 57th Street in New York; their names were Simon and Schuster. Another pair of editors bolted from the august firm of Henry Holt and founded their own publishing house; their names were Harcourt and Brace. It was the era of Theodore Dreiser's *An American Tragedy*, Fitzgerald's *The Great Gatsby*, Hemingway's *The Sun Also Rises* and *A Farewell to Arms*, Gertrude Stein's *Lucy Church Amiably*, Sinclair Lewis' *Babbit*, Thomas Wolfe's *Look Homeward, Angel*, Faulkner's *The Sound and the Fury*, Willa Cather's *Death Comes for the Archbishop*, and Dashiell Hammett's *Red Harvest*.

How does today's crop of authors compare with that list? Dean Koontz, Anne Rice, Danielle Steel, John Saul, James Patterson, Dara Joy, Catherine Coulter, Patricia Cornwell, Stephen King, Philip Roth, Lalita Tademy, Elizabeth McCracken, John Irving, Michael Chabon, Alice Hoffman, John Grisham, Mary Higgins Clark, Dick Francis, Sue Grafton, Anne McCaffrey, William Goldman, Susanna Kaysen, Susan Isaacs, Clive Cussler, Sara Paretsky, Jerry Jenkins, Robin Cook, Nicholas Evans, Margaret Atwood, Tom Clancy, Joy Fielding, Nora Roberts...?

Personal opinion: That list brims with both brilliance and banality—just as the best-seller list that once touted the works of Hemingway and Faulkner also touted popular twaddle now long forgotten. But one thing the "Golden Age" publishers did not publish is the flood of movie tie-ins, celebrity bios, "get-thin-quick" fad diets, cutesy calendars, gimmick books, and formula best-sellers that are the bread and butter of commercial publishing today. American publishers now produce some 135,000 titles a year—which means that a lot of trees give up their lives for a lot of meaningless drivel.

The prevalence of mass-market drivel is, perhaps, necessitated by the economics of mass-market publishing today. Given the high costs of overhead, typesetting, printing, packaging, selling, marketing, shipping, warehousing, and returns, the cost of producing a single book title is estimated at around $40,000 and up. Publishers know there is a lot of money to be made down around the lowest common denominator, so that is where many of them have set their sights.

Meanwhile, we witness the concentration of decision making into fewer and fewer corporate hands with the mergers of HarperCollins and Morrow/Avon, Putnam and Penguin, Random House and Bantam Doubleday Dell. As publishing houses merge and consolidate, or get swallowed up by entertainment conglomerates, the only autonomous publishers today are the independent publishers—such as the one that published this book. The independents are the houses that go against the herd and take the bold gambles that Maxwell Perkins used to take, sixty or seventy years ago.

I have also found smaller houses to be generally more aggressive and creative when it comes to marketing and promotion. They may not have as much advertising money to spend, but the smaller budget is usually spent more strategically and effectively than the megapublisher's megabudget. So if you are looking for more personal attention from acquisition through production, if you want a publisher who will respect the uniqueness of your voice and your vision, you should at least consider publishing with an independent house.

One recent change in publishing is the way certain decisions that were once editorial in nature are now made by the sales and marketing departments. I once collaborated with a corporate CEO on a business-oriented book for a major New York publisher. Throughout the writing process, my collaborator and I had a title in mind that was short, memorable, and powerful. I built the book around that title, working the phrase into the text in various chapters. I *loved* that title.

We completed the book and shipped it off to New York. Weeks passed as the book worked its way through substantive editing, then copyediting. While on business in New York, my coauthor stopped by the publishing house and met with the editor and some people from sales. During the meeting, the sales people started brainstorming about titles. After the meeting, my coauthor called me. "Jim," he said, sounding pleased, "the book has a new title!"

My heart stopped. "Oh?"

"Tell me what you think of this." Then he told me the title.

My heart broke. "Let me think about it," I said. I instantly hated it—but maybe I could get used to it. It has been ten years, and I'm still not used to it. I am convinced the book could have been much more popular with the original title.

My title woes were a drop in the bucket next to what happened to Bob Blauner with his book *Our Mothers' Spirits: Great Writers on the Death of Mothers and the Grief of Men*. The book featured essays by a host of writers, including John Updike and John Cheever, all writing on the subject of grief and the mother-son relationship. A few weeks after Blauner turned in the manuscript, his publisher called him with the news that Diana, the Princess of Wales, had died in an auto accident in Paris. The original cover, featuring a Renaissance painting of Madonna and Child, would be replaced by a photo of Princess Diana, her two sons, and her flower-decked coffin—even though there was not one word in the book about Princess Diana.

"I knew immediately," Blauner recalls. "I told them that this was all wrong, that the cover was going to become the attention of the book and not the content."

But the publisher was adamant. It was a book about sons who had lost their mothers, right? Well, Prince William and Prince Harry had just lost their mother, so a Princess Di cover couldn't be more fitting, end of story. Blauner's heartsick objections fell on deaf corporate ears.

Next, the publisher asked Blauner to write a new preface for the book that would tie the content to the tragic story of Princess Diana and her sons. Blauner was reluctant to do so. He told the publisher it would appear exploitative. Book buyers would be misled, thinking they were buying a book about Diana. The publisher insisted. Blauner relented and wrote the preface.

The book appeared and was greeted by a brief but scathing review in *Time*, which dubbed the book "Di-ploitation." The review ignored the bulk of the book, focusing on the fact that the author had written a "lame" introduction in order to rationalize an exploitative cover. What should have been an author's most joyful experience—the release of a new book—became a painful experience for Bob Blauner. Such horror stories are not uncommon when boardroom thinking is substituted for sound editorial judgment.[7]

What about Lord Byron's accusation, "Now Barabbas was a publisher"? Any truth to it? Do publishers ever *steal*? It is very rare for publishers to steal ideas or money from writers. It has never happened to me—though it has happened to writers I know.

"I sent a proposal for a book to a publisher I'd done several books for already," recalls Ros Jay. "She was very enthusiastic, then suddenly went cold on the idea after a month or so. A year later, she brought out an almost identical book with a different author—unlike me, a 'name' in this particular field. She'd even used my title as the subtitle. I challenged her, of course, and she claimed the other author had come up with the same proposal as I but a few months earlier. This couldn't be true for a number of reasons I won't bore you with (not least, why didn't she say so when I first came up with the idea?). But I was in no position to sue—unless you're desperate that's a mug's game really. After all, you can copyright text but you can't copyright a format. I just have never given her any ideas since, and I'm careful who I do give them to."

> "I have also found smaller houses to be generally more aggressive and creative when it comes to marketing and promotion."

Ros Jay's husband, also a writer, had a bad experience of his own. "My husband once delivered a manuscript," she recalls, "which they tore to shreds. Their rejection letter opened, 'This manuscript is thin, ill-informed, and badly written.' They refused to pay his delivery share of the advance. They insisted he rewrite and then submit it again. His agent said she had a suspicion they had a cash flow problem, and this was their way of delaying payment. So he sat on the manuscript for six weeks, rewrote the opening sentence of each chapter (and nothing else), then resubmitted it. They accepted it without quibble."

Never assume that a religious publisher is automatically more ethical than a secular publisher. Some of the finest human beings I've ever known are in religious publishing—but also one or two of the lowest. For example, there was a Christian publisher who went behind my back and told my collaborator, "Let us get you a different writer for this book—he's asking for too much money." My collaborator, to his credit, pointed out that I had developed the project from scratch—without me, there wouldn't even be a book. Then he proceeded to lecture the Christian publisher on the subject of Christian ethics. He wisely waited until *after* the book was completed before he told me how the publisher had tried to sabotage our working relationship.

Robert Darden recalls one experience he had in religious publishing: "A well-known Christian publishing house contracted a book from me, liked the book, and put it in the catalogue—then they changed their minds about publishing it before they'd paid me the rest of my advance. They tried to come back and say that everything they'd said about liking the book wasn't, um, in fact true. Fortunately, I'd kept copies of the correspondence. So eventually they paid the rest of the advance."

Some of the worst things a publisher can do to an author are purely unintentional. For example, a publisher might release your book, then accidentally make it disappear. That was Carol Brightman's nightmare with the release of her book *Sweet Chaos: The Grateful Dead's American Adventure*. Shortly after the book's release, she called a bookstore to see if *Sweet Chaos* was in stock. "Sorry, we don't have it," said the clerk. "In fact, I don't think the book exists. The title doesn't appear in *Books In Print*."

"I know the book exists," said Brightman, "because I wrote it."

So the clerk went to her computer and searched all the titles under Carol Brightman's name, and then said, "Here are the books we have listed under your name, Ms. Brightman: *Larry Rivers—Drawings and Digressions, Writing Dangerously—Mary McCarthy and Her World, Fat Trip—*"

"*What*?! Did you say—"

"*Fat Trip.*"

Carol Brightman was stunned. *Fat Trip* was an early working title for the book, based on a phrase Jerry Garcia of the Grateful Dead used to describe anything strange and surprising. Like finding your book listed under the wrong title. It got worse.

"According to the description," the clerk continued, "*Fat Trip* is a weight loss book."

Disbelieving, Brightman went to her computer and looked up her book at the Barnes & Noble website. One-seventh of all books sold in the United States pass through the Barnes & Noble chain. Barnes & Noble listed her book as *Fat Trip*; so did Ingram, the largest book wholesaler in the country. And—horror of horrors—so did the Library of Congress.

In the weeks that followed, the publisher tried to rectify the error, but once the wrong information got into the various computer systems around the country, it became almost impossible to eradicate. Where did the error originate? Nobody knew. "Somewhere in the sales department," was the only answer Brightman's editor could offer.[8]

The horror stories I've cited are cautionary tales intended to alert you to the kinds of things that *could* happen to your book—and to let you know that you cannot simply write a book and leave its fate in the hands of a corporation. The fate of your book is in your own hands.

In the next chapter, we will look at the ways you can actively shape the destiny of your book—and your writing career.

Generate Your Own Success

You can either become like one of those guys in jail who blames his attorneys, or you can do your best to promote the book yourself.
*Mystery writer **Jan Burke*** (Goodnight, Irene *and* Bones)

Anyone who has received as many rejection slips as I have is not going to complain about signing autographs.
Madeleine L'Engle

I WAS PUTTING THE FINISHING TOUCHES ON A MANUSCRIPT that was a week past deadline. I had been averaging four hours of sleep per night, and I knew the night ahead would be no different. At that, I would be lucky to get the book done in time for the next day's FedEx pickup.

At about 11·30 in the morning, my phone rang. When I heard the voice on the line, I was taken by surprise. I instantly knew who the caller was, though we had never spoken. He was the top-rated talk show host on the local 50,000-watt radio station. "Is this Jim Denney, the writer?" he asked. "I just had a guest cancel out, and I have about forty minutes at the top of my show to fill. I'm sorry about the short notice, but we go on in ninety minutes. Could you come on the air and talk about your latest book?"

Before telling you what my answer was, I have to explain something about myself: One of my greatest strengths is my ability to *focus*. I can immerse myself completely in my writing, oblivious to distractions, interruptions, and outside interference, and that's good. But at the same time, my great strength, my ability to focus, can also be my greatest weakness. At times, I become so focused on a goal that it takes me a while to shift gears, to respond to new situations and new input.

Believe it or not, I told the talk show host I couldn't do the interview. I said I was past deadline and I didn't have the time to spare.

"Well, maybe some other time," he said. "Thanks anyway."

I hung up—and instantly thought, *What have I done? The biggest radio host in town just offered me forty minutes of free airtime—and I told him no! What was I thinking?* I stared uncomprehendingly at my computer screen. A minute passed, maybe two.

The phone rang. It was the talk show host again. He wanted to know if I had the phone number of a certain celebrity I had worked with. I gave him the number, then said, "Is it too late to change my mind about the show?"

"Not at all!" he said. "It would be great to have you. But what about your deadline?"

I said, "One more day won't make any difference. Let's do the show."

So I did the interview by phone, it went well, and I think it did some good for the book. For weeks afterwards, I continued to get comments from people who heard the interview. What's more, the publisher of the book I was writing at the time was also the publisher of the book I promoted on the radio. When I told my editor about the interview, she was so pleased that she didn't even mind that I missed the deadline on the new book.

The moral of the story: Never pass up an opportunity to promote.

It's in your hands

> Most publishers have a front-list mentality. They put all their sales efforts into the first six months the book is out. That doesn't give you enough time for word of mouth to help. Make your readers your marketing team. Stay focused on the project for at least two to three years.
>
> *Canadian author-publisher-stockbroker* **Dave Chilton** (The Wealthy Barber)

The success of your book—and your career—depends entirely on you. If your books find an audience and a loyal following of readers, odds are it will not be the result of luck or your publisher's promotional dollars. It will be the result of your own hard work and perseverance.

But, you may ask, doesn't the publisher have departments devoted to advertising, promotion, marketing, and sales? Of course they do. And all of those glorious promotional resources are going to be lavished on the publisher's front-list authors—the ones, ironically, who *least* need to be promoted.

You can't afford to entrust your career to anyone but *you*. No one cares about you and your success as much as you do. Especially if you are a new author, odds are that your book will receive cover art that is anywhere from lackluster to bug-ugly, your book will occupy the bottommost slots of the publisher's list, you will get zero promotion effort, and the sales-people will not even bother mentioning your book when they call on bookstores.

> "Never pass up an opportunity to promote."

Your book may represent a year or two of your life, but to a bookseller it is just a line of six-point type near the bottom of an order form. Even if your book miraculously manages to find its way to a bookstore shelf (one copy, spine-out, virtually invisible on the shelf), there's no guarantee that readers will find it. *You* have to create demand for your book if you want it to sell.

Is that unfair? I don't know. I don't even care. I just know it's the way things are. Is that bad news? No. It's *great* news, because it means that the fate of your book is in *your* own hands. It means your career doesn't depend on the whims of others. *You* can do something to magnify the success of your writing labors.

Here, then, are some ways you can take command of your book's future—and your own:

• **Make sure your book generates *excitement*.** There is something about your book that was so exciting and powerful that it sustained you through weeks and months of solitary labor. Now you have distilled all of that excitement and enthusiasm into a book, and you must find a way to stir up that same emotion among thousands, even millions, of potential readers. How will your book wow your readers, change their lives, make them rich, or give them the thrill of a lifetime?

One of the best ways to generate excitement is to *make news* with your book. If you are a children's author and the topic of violence in children's entertainment hits the headlines, fax a news release to the media, explaining your qualifications and your point of view, with contact numbers for an interview. If you have written a book about a country that suddenly becomes a major hotspot, make yourself available for interviews as an expert. Also, build marketable, newsworthy "hooks" into your book. Whether you have written a novel or a nonfiction book, make sure it includes some angle or feature that is newsworthy in and of itself—a novel that takes place in a truly "novel" locale, or a nonfiction book that contains an astonishing piece of news that no one has ever heard before.

Canadian novelist Robert J. Sawyer is a master of self-promotion. He writes his own press releases, then broadcasts them to a list of forty or so media outlets by fax. "Press releases," he says, "must be timely: I've seen many writers win awards, then, a month later, decide to snail-mail out a press release. Of course, they end up getting no coverage at all." He also counsels patience, persistence, and repetition when sending out press releases.

"The first time you send out a press release," says Sawyer, "you won't get much response—maybe a couple of column-inches in the local weekly paper, and that's only if you're lucky. But it's just like sending out short stories. You can't give up after the first rejection. A little while ago, *Imprint* (a weekly book program produced by TVOntario and also carried nationally on CBC Newsworld) phoned me and said, 'We've got a thick file folder about you, and we've been meaning to do a piece on you for a long time. Now's the time.' Unless you win a major award, or a movie is made of your novel, not much will happen around the publication of a single book—but if you draw attention to your work on a regular basis, you will become a media presence, and that translates directly into book sales."[1] So first write headline-grabbing books, then promote them boldly. Do whatever it takes to make headlines and sell books.

• **Become a public speaker.** Many of today's biggest-selling authors got their books off the ground by becoming public speakers: John Gray, Wayne Dyer, John C. Maxwell, Stephen R. Covey, Zig Ziglar, Deepak Chopra, and on and on. Speaking is the most powerful way to promote books, and for a number of reasons: You can usually get an audience for free—and sometimes organizations will even pay you to come and promote your books. You can set up a back-of-the-room book table and make immediate money from selling and signing your books.

When people hear you speak and are impressed by what you have to say, they tell other people—and word-of-mouth is advertising that money just can't buy.

Publicizing books isn't the only reason for getting out and speaking to groups. At speaking events, you meet people and expand your network of acquaintances—and out of that circle of new acquaintances could come an important career contact, an idea for a new book or story, or a new friend (and we can always use more friends). From interacting with people before, during, and after your speaking event, you pick up anecdotes and experiences, plus names and e-mail addresses you can add to your mailing list (you do publish an e-newsletter, don't you?). You can also "test drive" ideas for future books by getting immediate feedback when you speak. And, you can add the event to your resumé.

> "Speaking is the most powerful way to promote books . . . ."

When you speak, make sure you are energetic, fascinating, animated, and fun to listen to. If you need insight and advice on how to be a more effective public speaker, read *Speaking With Bold Assurance: How to Become a Persuasive Communicator* by Bert Decker with Hershael W. York, or *You've Got to Be Believed to Be Heard* by Bert Decker with Jim Denney. Make sure that you do more than just talk. Create an *experience* that your audience will never forget—one which will move them to buy books for themselves plus extra copies for friends.

Make the local media aware of your speaking event. Come up with a good news angle for your speaking appearance, something that ties into current events or major issues that people are talking about. Your public appearance should be more than just a lecture. It should be *news* that people need to hear.

Invite friends and fans to your speaking appearances. Not only will they swell the numbers of your event—which is good for your stature as an author—but their enthusiasm will be infectious and they can offer good questions during Q&A sessions.

• **Become a talker.** Always be ready and prepared to talk about your book. Make sure you always have copies in the trunk of your car, or better yet, in your purse or briefcase. If you can't have the book with you wherever you go, carry some printed bookmarks in your pocket with the cover of the book, some big-name endorsements, the ISBN, and your website address. Strike up conversations with people in the movie theater ticket line or the checkout line at the supermarket. You never know when the person next to you might buy a book (or ten)—or maybe even introduce you to Oprah's producer!

• **Work the web.** It's not hard to create your own website and submit it to search engines. Also, visit various Internet forums—communities of involved, thoughtful people who just might be interested in your books. Get involved in the discussions, and add the name of your book and the address of your website to the "signature" at the end of each message you post. You can find Internet forums by using a search engine or by checking the forum directories at http://groups.google.com/, http://www.liszt.com/, and http://www.forumone.com/. Enlist friends and relatives in your cause—invite them to write glowing reviews for bookstore websites such as Amazon.com and BN.com.

• **Become a radio personality.** Radio talk shows yield an enormous amount of publicity—and it's free. You get anywhere from a half hour to two hours to really explore your ideas and give book buyers in the audience a good, tasty sampling of your wares. Best of all, you don't even have to go to the studio to be interviewed—you can appear on talk shows all around the country from the comfort of your home via your telephone. Here are some ways you can get the most promotional bang out of a talk show appearance:

Be well prepared. Have key talking points, quotations, anecdotes, and other information at your fingertips on 3x5 cards or in some similar handy format. It also helps to have key information written down, such as the city and station call letters, the host's name (don't call her by the wrong name!), the producer's name, and even a bit about the audience demographics, if you can.

Also, be prepared to talk about subjects that your book doesn't cover. Your interview should not sound like a long infomercial for your book— if you come off sounding like a salesman instead of an expert, you'll never get called back. You are there to do a show on a topic, and your job is to be interesting and entertaining. Be expansive and expressive. I find that I sound better on the radio if I am in a high-energy mode—standing rather than sitting, and freely gesturing and even pacing as I talk.

Whatever you do, don't come across as defensive or argumentative. If an interviewer asks you a tough question, or even a stupid question, find a pleasant, intelligent way to answer it. If the host hasn't read your book, don't take offense. Do everything you can to make the host look good. Better yet, mail or fax a set of prepared interview questions to the host a day or two before the show. This will enable the interviewer to ask intelligent questions, and you'll be prepared with some terrific answers.

If you do your interview in-studio, then be sure to leave some of your flyers or bookmarks at the reception desk of the radio station. Sometimes listeners will catch the tag-end of a show, then call and ask the receptionist, "Who was that writer on your show today? What bookstore was he appearing at?" And, the receptionist probably won't have an answer—unless you leave the information at her fingertips.

Make it easy for people to order your books. With your host's permission, give out a toll-free number, either yours or your publisher's, or give the address of your website. Make sure your website is packed with quality information that people can use—not just a sales pitch and a shopping cart. For example, I don't say, "You can order my book at www.denneybooks.com." I say, "If you want more information on such-and-such subject, I have some free articles you can download from my website." Big difference.

• **Cultivate a good relationship with your publisher.** Make sure your publisher has all the information needed to support your promotion efforts. Fill out the author information questionnaire. Include such information as: unique angles or ideas for publicity; opinion leaders and media personalities in your geographic area and subject area; smaller "niche" media, both broadcast and print, that might be missed by your publisher, but which would reach a desirable audience; and local bookstores and their contact people. Keep your publisher's publicity people aware of your travel itinerary and speaking engagements so they can magnify the publicity impact by scheduling additional appearances and interviews.

• **Maximize the effectiveness of book signings.** Before a signing event, make sure that the local media are informed. The publisher and bookstore should both send out news releases—and it wouldn't hurt to send out one of your own. A couple of weeks out, call the local radio and

TV stations and the newspapers to request interviews and coverage. Send a promotional copy of your book.

Your publisher should provide poster-size enlargements of your book cover for display at your book table. If not, you can get enlargements made at a photocopy shop and mount them on foam core board. Also, have business cards, bookmarks, and a sign-up sheet for your e-mail newsletter ready for the book table.

> "Keep your publisher's publicity people aware of your travel itinerary and speaking engagements so they can magnify the publicity impact by scheduling additional appearances and interviews."

Make sure the bookstore receives a nicely printed copy of all the big-name endorsements for your book and copies of the book cover. The store should use these on posters to advertise your appearance during the week or two before the event.

Very important: Arrive early, stay late. And, whatever you do, do it with energy and enthusiasm. The average book signing involves an author sitting alone at a table, being ignored by the browsers in the bookstore. You don't have to accept that passive role. Stand, walk, roam, smile, greet people, introduce yourself. You are meeting your public, your readers, your fans—so enjoy each personal connection you make. James Michener, in *The Novel*, expressed his own feelings about book signings through his fictional protagonist, author Lukas Yoder:

> I signed till my right hand was numb, and since I liked to look directly at the person requesting my autograph and exchange a few words, the process went slowly. This irritated Emma, who whispered: "Sign the things. Don't hold little cocktail parties with everyone who comes by." I could never explain to her or to the bookstore people who gave the same advice that at such moments I was not in Williamsburg or St. Louis autographing books by the hundreds, I was back in the Hess store in Allentown on that terrible day when not a single customer showed up. The difference between then and now was that more than a million people had read each of my last

three books and many of them had found them meaningful and their author a responsible man. They were people to whom I was indebted, and if they had come out on a warm evening for an autograph, I had to give it in a way that was not perfunctory.[2]

Make sure you have lots of copies available at the table—some bookstores, believe it or not, will only order five or six copies for a signing! If people come by and appear interested, introduce yourself, and put a book in their hands. Invite them to take a seat by the window and look the book over. Give out bookmarks. Many people view authors as inaccessible and aloof. Show them you are friendly and easy to talk to.

Invite people to sign up for your e-mail newsletter (it helps to have a "dummy entry" or two at the top of the list—for some reason, people don't like to be the first to sign). Enlist their help in getting the word out: "I'd appreciate it if you'd tell your friends about my book."

Get to know the people at the bookstore—the manager, the community relations coordinator, and the sales people. Build rapport. Make sure, at the beginning of the event, that everyone understands what your book is about, so they can recommend it to people who come into the store. Volunteer to sign stock before you leave. If you don't sell a lot of books, don't let it throw you. Fact is, non-celebrity authors are hitting a home run if they sell four or five books. Signings rarely produce huge sales, but they do produce goodwill that engenders positive word-of-mouth.

Follow-up is crucial. After the event, thank everyone personally, and mail a thank-you note to the bookstore manager. A gift that you either bring with you or send after the event is a nice touch. Stop by the store in weeks to come, say hello to the manager and staff, and while you're at it, see if your book is well displayed with the cover showing.

Another twist on the classic book signing: Arrange invitation-only book signings and talks at clubs or in the homes of friends or relatives.

• **Become a guerilla marketer.** Big publishers employ old-style marketing techniques, usually involving some combination of print ads, radio and TV buys, and sending the author on a multicity book tour. The tab for old-style book marketing efforts can quickly rise to six figures. As a working writer, I can't afford to buy that kind of campaign, and I'm betting you can't either. So you and I have to become guerillas, fighting our wars in the jungles of the marketplace, promoting creatively but on the cheap, scrounging for publicity advantages that the big publishing corporations would either disdain or never even think of.

Three indispensable books for guerilla marketers are *Guerilla Marketing for Writers* by Jay Conrad Levinson, Rick Frishman, and Michael Larsen (Writer's Digest Books, 2001), *The Writer's Guide to Self-Promotion and Publicity* by Elane Feldman (Writer's Digest Books, 1990), and *1001 Ways to Market Your Books* by John Kremer (Fifth Edition, Open Horizons, 1998).

One of the hallmarks of a guerilla book marketer is being available to your public. Guerilla writers make their e-mail addresses available to the public, because they want to maintain contact with readers and fans. Guerillas use the Internet to make themselves and their ideas accessible around the world, twenty-four/seven. And, they use e-mail to inform readers of new events and books, and to thank them for their support.

This is a new era of information and publishing, and we must respond by becoming a new breed of writers. We are not content to surrender our fate to publishers and publicity people. We have taken control of our own destiny—and that is the key to our success as working writers.

CREATE A BUZZ

> There's a poster showing a caterpillar on a branch and a butterfly hovering in the air above it saying, "You can fly but that cocoon has to go." You should be perpetually breathless from the opportunities for writing, promoting, and profiting from your books. ...If you believe you can become a successful author—however you define the word *successful*—you can.
>
> *Jay Conrad Levinson, Rick Frishman, and Michael Larsen,*
> Guerilla Marketing for Writers

In 1998, mystery writer Martin J. Smith and fellow writer Philip Reed hatched a plan to turn book promotion into a family business. Leaving their wives at home to maintain a steady paycheck, Smith and Reed scooped up the kids and set off from Los Angeles in a pair of minivans on a 6,500-mile cross-country odyssey. Smith had his nine-year-old daughter Lanie and six-year-old son Parker as assistants, while Reed brought his sons, Andrew, twelve, and Tony, eight. Both minivans were well-stocked with snacks, CDs, and games for the trip.

Smith was promoting his psychological thriller *Shadow Image* (Jove, 1998), while Reed was touting his book *Low Rider* (Pocket Books, 1998). Along the way, they signed countless books for fans, conducted readings, handed out free copies to influential booksellers, and gave interviews to media people who were fascinated by the novelty of the "Dads' Tour." Sometimes, to liven up the proceedings, Smith would haul out his harmonica and wail the blues to attract a crowd. It never failed.

During the road trip, the question was asked again and again: "Are we there yet?" But it wasn't just the kids who wanted to know. Smith later reflected in an article for the *Los Angeles Times* that the question haunted him. He continually asked himself, "Am I there yet? Am I reaching my goals as a writer?" And, the answer he kept hearing was, "No, not yet. You have to work a little harder." And that's why Martin J. Smith and Philip Reed were on the road, hawking their books.

Before his first novel was published, Smith asked best-selling novelist Dean Koontz what it would take for a writer to break into the best-seller level like Stephen King, John Grisham and Koontz himself. The author of *Whispers* and *The Vision* replied, "Figure you've got five books to make it." Koontz went on to explain that the industry has become much more celebrity-driven in years past, and it is becoming less common for writers to earn a decent living writing midlist books. You must quickly become a 600-pound gorilla or the publishers will walk away from you.

"The day I got my author copies of *Bird Dog*," adds Philip Reed, "I thought my job was finally done. I thought if the reviews were good I could sit back and the book would sell. But that was the very moment I needed to get my energy back up, to change gears and go out and promote. I realized if I didn't it might disappear without a trace."

Was the 6,500-mile trip worth it? Smith concludes, "We're earning a living doing what we love. Our books are being favorably featured in reviews, newspaper stories, radio broadcasts and TV interviews. If at this point we're unable to push *Shadow Image* and *Low Rider* onto best-seller lists—and in retrospect that seems a hopelessly naive goal—at least we were meeting hundreds of people who enjoyed our books and are looking forward to the next ones. ...We're doing everything we can to help our books succeed, and...that's a good thing to remember when you're headed for home but not quite there."[3]

The success of your book—and your career—is in your hands. Don't entrust your future to anyone else but *you*. Take your book to the airwaves, take it to the marketplace, and take it to the streets.

Next, let's polish up the crystal ball and see what the future of your writing career will look like...

THE FUTURE OF WRITING

The Internet is a wonderful medium for getting worldwide attention, but particularly attention of readers, to a book.

Donald S. Lamm, *chairman, W. W. Norton Publishing Co., interview with Harry Kreisler, February 5, 1998*

The writer will always be needed, to remind others who can't write what really happened and what it meant.

Writer Lukas Yoder in **James A. Michener***'s* The Novel

SYDNEY SMITH, THE ANGLICAN CLERGYMAN AND FOUNDER OF *The Edinburgh Review*, once said, "No furniture is so charming as books." True, there is something beautiful, rich, and refined about a home that is well-lined with books—books with spines, covers, and pages, books you can hold in your hand.

Today, however, the word "book" is being redefined to mean an organized collection of data in any form, print or electronic. Some experts are even predicting that the bound, printed, paper-page book will inevitably be replaced by such technologies as hypertext and e-publishing. Is that true? And if so, how will it affect the future of publishing?

The demise of paper-page books has long been predicted. In 1913, Thomas Edison claimed that his new invention, the motion picture, would replace books. And in 1945, physicist-engineer Vannevar Bush (1890–1974) announced that the development of the modern hypertext-manipulating computer (which he called a "memex") would render books obsolete. In *Man-Computer Symbiosis* (1960), computer engineer J. C. R. Licklieder predicted a bookless, paperless Brave New World by 1980. Two years later, Marshall McLuhan's *The Gutenberg Galaxy: The Making of Typographic Man* prophesied that electronic information systems would "reinvent" human society so that concepts such as "author" and "book" would disappear, along with the concept of "nation." Diversity and a return to tribalism, he said, would replace nations and corporations.

The twenty-first century has made monkeys of all those who prophesied the end of the printed page. In fact, the rise of computers and the Internet has only added another channel for popularizing and selling books. Electronic media have not replaced books; they have only taken their place alongside books in the marketplace. Despite competition from movies, audiobooks, software, and the Internet, the American publishing industry is churning out more books than at any other time in the history of civilization—135,000 new titles annually in America alone. So, I'm convinced that books are here to stay.

Is this the conclusion of a hidebound Luddite whose thinking is clogged with nostalgia? Nope. I've always been fascinated by the future, and quick to welcome each new technological wave. I wrote my first book on an Apple II Plus computer that I bought in 1978. I became a member of the CompuServe online community back in 1989, when a 1200-baud modem was state-of-the-art. I began surfing the 'Net with a primitive Mosaic web browser in the pre-Netscape, pre-Internet Explorer days of the early 1990s.

One thing I've learned over the years is that the rise of new media and new technologies doesn't always mean the end of old ones. The automobile and the airplane did not dismantle the railroad. Television did not put radio out of existence. And e-books are not likely to wipe out paper books anytime soon. From where I'm sitting, the future of books—and the people who write them—appears brighter than ever.

Of course, I could be wrong.

A cryptographer named Johannes Trithemius (1462–1516) once wrote a treatise called *In Praise of Scribes*, in which he observed, "Printed books will never be the equivalent of handwritten codices...The simple reason is that copying by hand involves more diligence and industry." Poor Trithemius could not have been more wrong. Check Amazon.com and see if you can order John Grisham's latest hand-calligraphied codex. Times change, and so do the technologies for producing books. Printed books may ultimately go the way of handwritten codices, but I strongly doubt it.

Still, I do have *one* worry regarding the future of books and the fate of writers. My worry is this: Kids today are being introduced to computers at the same age that my generation was being introduced to books. In many ways, and for a large number of kids, computers are actually *replacing* books as vehicles for stimulating the imagination. Computers interact, talk, play music, and display exciting, kinetic graphics. They do all the imagining for you and serve it up predigested so that the young, developing brain does not even need to chew on it. How, then, do kids develop an active, creative, imagination? And, how can they develop a love of books?

We know that children who develop a love of books from an early age will probably carry it with them throughout their lives. Those who don't, won't. Are we now raising a generation that will not have the same love for books and reading that you and I do? If so, then that, rather than direct competition from the Internet and electronic publishing, may ultimately spell the demise of the printed page.

PAPERLESS BOOKS

I remain militant about arrogant publishers. That's one reason for my ongoing survey of Internet Publishers, a market far more open to new writers. My advice to writers is to try the traditional print publishers, and when that fails, try the Internet publishers, and if that fails, go to one of the self-publishing companies.

Novelist **Piers Anthony**

Simon & Schuster's Children's Publishing Division planned to make history by publishing a biography of the forty-third president of the United States just one minute after election day. And no, the author's contract did *not* require her to write an entire book in sixty seconds flat.

The author, popular children's writer Beatrice Gormley, had already written the better part of two complete books by election day— thirteen chapters on the life of Al Gore and thirteen chapters on the life of George W. Bush. Those chapters covered the full span of each man's life, from childhood through the closing days of the 2000 campaign.

Election Day would determine which set of chapters would see the light of day.

Chapter 14 would include portions of the acceptance speech and a discussion of the future goals of the president-elect. The plan was for Ms. Gormley to finalize Chapter 14 from news accounts on election night, then e-mail it to Simon & Schuster. After a quick once-over by the editors, the book would be published as an instant electronic book (or "e-book") at precisely 12:01 A.M. on November 8, 2000. Book buyers could then download the book from the publisher's website. A trade paper edition would follow one week later.

Of course, we all know what happened on election night 2000. The TV networks first called the election for Gore, then for Bush, then for none-of-the-above. "My editor and I stayed up all night," Beatrice Gormley told me, "foolishly thinking we were going to finish the book that night!" Florida vote-tabulators spent days trying to divine the intentions of the electorate by holding punch cards up to the light and counting dimpled chads. Only after Al Gore conceded the election on December 15 could Beatrice Gormley's "instant" book, *President George W. Bush: Our Forty-Third President*, be released—a full five weeks behind schedule.

"The night of December 15," Gormley recalls, "my editor and I stayed up late (he in his office in New York and I in my home office) to write the last page. We had already spent the weeks between election night and December 15 rewriting and rewriting the last chapter. Simon & Schuster finally released the e-book the day after Gore's concession speech, and the paperback was published in early January."

Beatrice Gormley's experience demonstrates both the incredible speed of electronic publishing (or "e-publishing") and the power of Murphy's Law to upset publishing schedules. If Ms. Gormley chooses to accept a similar challenge in 2004, we all hope her book appears right on time.

E-publishing is a means of creating, storing, marketing, and distributing books in a completely electronic form. E-books may be published in a number of ways. They may be posted on a website for downloading, or transmitted via email, or stored on a magnetic or optical medium, such as a floppy disk or CD. E-books can be read on any computer with the appropriate software—desktop, laptop, or palmtop. Some e-books are available only in electronic formats; others, like Beatrice Gormley's book on George W. Bush, are available in both a print version and an e-version. There are essentially two kinds of e-books: 1) commercial e-books and 2) "vanity" (or subsidy or self-published) e-books.

A commercial e-publisher operates much like a commercial print publisher, the primary difference being that the e-publisher's "warehouse" is an Internet server instead of a building. Commercial e-publishers read and evaluate manuscripts and make an editorial decision to accept or reject them on the basis of their merit and marketability. Commercial e-books are edited in much the same way as commercial print books. They even have ISBNs, like paper books.

Although financial arrangements vary, authors of commercial e-books often receive no advance, but are paid a royalty on each download of their book—a download being the equivalent of a bookstore sale of a paper book. Commercial e-books are generally sold directly from the publisher's website, but many established booksellers (such as Barnes and Noble and Amazon.com) offer e-books from their websites right alongside their paper books. Because e-books do not enjoy the prestige of print books, they are less likely to be reviewed and to qualify for awards and membership in organizations such as the Authors Guild. Also, e-books are vulnerable to piracy, since there is no hack-proof means of copy-guarding e-book files.

One of the most promising uses of e-publishing is the so-called "back-in-print" service offered by many e-publishers. This service is for the working writer whose books are out-of-print but still commercially viable. Writers who have put their out-of-print books back in print via e-publishing include prolific children's authors Jane Curry (*Beneath the Hill, The Ice Ghosts Mystery*) and Maggie Twohill (*Bigmouth*), scientist-science fiction writer Robert L. Forward (*Starquake, Marooned on Eden*), novelist Christopher Davis (*Ishmael, Lost Summer*), action-aviation-war writer Hank Searls (*The Crowded Sky, Overboard*), *New York Times* best-selling novelist Cathy Cash Spellman (*An Excess of Love, Paint the Wind*), and many others. "Back-in-print" services have given a new lease on life to some very good books and have provided a modest but welcome source of income for some very good writers.

In contrast to commercial e-publishing there is vanity e-publishing—or what I would call "karaoke publishing." Vanity e-publishing is for people who say, "I'm not a real author, but I play one on the Internet." Vanity e-publishers will accept virtually any book for e-publication and will typically do no editing whatsoever. Most vanity e-publishers tell you up front that the author is 100-percent responsible for the content, form, accuracy, and editing of the manuscript—the electronic file you submit will be posted as is, word for word, character for character, error for error. The editorial standards most vanity e-publishers apply are minimal at best— no overt porn, no hate speech. Other than that, if you have the money, you can become an instant "author."

> "Vanity e-publishing is for people who say, 'I'm not a real author, but I play one on the Internet.'"

The advantage of vanity e-publishing over traditional vanity publishing (subsidy or self-published paper books) is cost: Vanity e-authors are generally charged $200 to $500 per e-book versus $5,000 to $20,000 to publish a vanity paper book. Vanity e-book authors receive a royalty similar to that paid by commercial e-publishers. E-publishers usually offer "print-on-demand" paper books in addition to downloadable e-books ("print-on-demand" is a new technology that allows books to be printed and bound one copy at a time, quickly and for about the same price as a mass-produced paper book).

E-publishing and print-on-demand publishing are not for every author or every book, but they do fill a need—and not just for "karaoke authors." E-publishing might be a good way to go if you have a book that is extremely time-sensitive (for example, if your book's appeal could expire during the nine to twelve months it normally takes to publish a paper book), if your book's target audience is simply too small (not enough people care about your topic to justify the expense of mass-market publishing), or if you simply *must* exercise autocratic control over the content ("I don't want any editors leaving their thumbprints all over my beautiful words").

But understand this: The reasons I have just listed for considering e-publishing are incompatible with the goals of a working writer. In order to make a decent living as a writer, you must write books that sell widely. A working writer can hardly make a habit of writing books that are so time sensitive that they have no shelf life at all, nor of writing books for tiny audiences, nor of ignoring and resisting editorial input. To be successful, you need to write books of timeless value and broad appeal, and you must be open to suggestions for improving the quality and marketability of your work.

Also be aware that, whatever kind or format book you write, you *must* be willing to promote like crazy. This is even more true of e-books than it is for paper books; people won't find your e-book unless you hustle and tell them where to find it. Promoting e-books is a much tougher sell than promoting print books—and for several reasons: First, e-publishing is new. Few book buyers are really keyed into the concept. For most people, the word "reading" means books and magazines, not electronic devices. Second, few people have warm-fuzzy feelings about curling up with a good e-book, because you just can't curl up with a computer screen, nor can you take your desktop computer into the tub or on the train for your morning commute. Third, while it might be possible to curl up comfortably with a palmtop reader, there are very few people who have invested in this new and relatively expensive technology. So if you are going to promote an e-book, you'll really have your work cut out for you.

After conducting an extensive study of the future of book publishing in America, the Forrester Research group in Cambridge, Massachusetts, forecast slow growth for the e-book industry through 2005, but projected rapidly increasing sales for print-on-demand trade books. Out of $7.8 billion in projected sales of digital and print-on-demand books from 2001 to 2005 (which would account for 17.5 percent of total publishing industry revenues), Forrester saw only $251 million in sales for e-books. "Publishers are expecting trade e-book sales that won't materialize," concluded Forrester senior analyst Daniel P. O'Brien. "The drawbacks of reading onscreen will discourage all but the most motivated readers."

The successful publishers, according to Forrester, will be those that manage all of a book's content within a single storehouse, and publish that content in a variety of forms—a "multichannel" publishing model involving mass-produced print formats, print-on-demand formats, electronic formats and so-called "modular content and structure" (making custom-tailored information available to consumers in custom-configured formats). Successful multichannel publishers will be those that adopt Internet-speed business practices and distribution technologies.[1]

As with any print publisher's contract, you should carefully examine the contract you get from an e-publisher. E-book contracts tend to be very different from those of print publishers, and they often require authors to surrender massive blocks of rights in perpetuity in exchange for piddling advances and minimal guarantees. Contracts often contain option clauses that lock your next work in (at slave-labor terms) as well as the one you submit. Keep in mind that if you are granting intellectual property rights to a publisher, the publisher should be expected to pay a reasonable advance—less, perhaps, than might be expected for a print work, but certainly more than the $00.00 to $25.00 that many e-publishers currently offer.

The net-net: Traditional books are here to stay, but new book formats and technologies will inevitably spring up alongside paper books, expanding the variety of ways that working writers can realize profits from their labors. But these technologies also present uncharted territory and new risks for writers. E-publishing contracts are minefields that should only be negotiated with extreme caution and expert legal help.

Just as publishers are adapting to a new multichannel model of publishing, we writers must also adapt to a multichannel model of writing. The key to success on the new writing frontier is to be aware of all publishing channels, particularly mass print, print-on-demand, and electronic channels. Our thinking and our writing must be shaped around all conceivable formats. Our contracts must be understood and negotiated in terms of all the various intellectual property rights that are inherent in a written work. A book is no longer just a book—it is a potential cascade of money-making formats, products, and media. The savvy working writer creates work that can be sold in as many formats as possible, and makes sure his or her property rights are protected in all formats.

E-ZINES

The future of publishing is electronic—there is no question of that. As the Internet and web publishing continue to grow, writers increasingly will be in demand. Traditional submissions by authors by regular mail are time-consuming and expensive—that will change in the future. In the meantime, more and more publications are accepting submissions by e-mail, a much more efficient process for both the author and the publisher.

Greg A. Knollenberg, president of Writers Write, Inc.

Online magazines ("e-zines") offer a wealth of opportunities for writers, whether for original material or for reprinted, reshaped, or recycled material from one's print output. E-zines, like newsstand magazines, are collections of articles that are updated on a regular cycle, usually weekly or monthly; also like their newsstand counterparts, e-zines are generally supported by advertising and sometimes by subscribers as well. Unlike newsstand magazines, e-zines are made entirely of pixels, no paper. E-zines are "published" either in the form of websites that readers can visit, or in the form of e-mails sent out to subscriber lists.

A brief sampling of some of the biggest e-zines on the World Wide Web: *Slate* (http://slate.msn.com/), published by Microsoft Network, is edited by former CNN personality Michael Kinsley. It's an eclectic, content-rich e-zine designed to look like a print magazine. *Salon* (www.salon.com) is a hip, brash e-zine

> ". . . whatever kind or format book you write, you *must* be willing to promote like crazy."

that covers politics, art, books, music, and media with an airy layout and breezy personality; it adroitly capitalizes on the e-zine format by offering a public message board (something a print magazine can't do). Then there's *Feed* (www.feed.com), a postmodern news e-zine that gathers articles from a range of online sources and brings readers together in a message-board community; subjects range from politics to business to science to religion.

Many e-zines are devoted primarily to entertainment and pop-culture. There's *Addicted to Noise* (www.addictedtonoise.com) for people who like loud music and loud graphics. There are cartoonish pop-culture e-zines like *Hotwired* (http://hotwired.lycos.com) and *Suck* (www.suck.com). There are e-zines devoted to women and girls (or grrls or gurls), such as *Chickclick* (www.chickclick.com) and *gURL* (www.gurl.com). Typical sections of girlzines include "Sucky Emotions," "Mizbehavior," and "Paperdoll Psychology."

There are literary e-zines like New York's *Literal Latté* (www.literal latte.com), *The Mississippi Review Online* (http://www.mississippi review.com), and *The Blue Moon Review* (www.thebluemoon.com). And there's *ParaScope* (www.parascope.com) for those who can't get enough of alien abductions, Area 51, and the Illuminati. If *ParaScope* doesn't give you all the weirdness you crave, click on *Viewzone* (www.viewzone.com).

The biggest e-zines are paying markets—and the most prestigious pay quite well. For updated information, check the Paying Markets page at the Writers Write website (http://www.writerswrite.com/paying/). Another indispensable resource for e-writers: *Online Markets for Writers: How to Make Money by Selling Your Writing on the Internet* by Anthony Tedesco and Paul Tedesco (Owl Books, 2000). And, of course, the latest edition of *Writer's Market* (Writer's Digest Books) also contains market reports and tips for exploiting online markets.

What about prestige? Don't e-zines lack the cachet of their tree-killing counterparts? Don't print editors turn up their noses at a writer with online credits? Increasingly, this is no longer true. Many editors, including print editors, will view your e-zine clippings with favor if they are from recognized, well-paying markets. A credit from *Slate* or *Salon*, for example, would be considered as prestigious as a credit from any print magazine.

One of the most attractive features of e-zines is *speed*. E-zine editors operate at Internet speed, accepting email queries, and responding quickly—usually within two or three days. (To know what you should expect of any e-zine, check the writers guidelines at its website.)

Many corporations and organizations are also looking for people to write copy for their websites and email newsletters. Writing for the web has turned into a regular, well-paying part-time gig for many working writers. Because the online medium is still relatively new and unknown, the writing community as a whole has been slow to recognize the opportunities and make the transition to e-writing. As a result, competition in online writing is generally less stiff than it is on the print side, and there are many opportunities for good writers to at least supplement their income on the Web.

PUB YOURSELF

You can go out there and spend $1,000 or $1,500 on Christmas gifts without thinking, and everybody hates the gift you get them. Instead, why not publish a book and give that?

Laurence Leichman, *author-publisher of* Self-Publish Your Own Best-Seller!

Thinking of self-publishing?

In the past, my advice was always: "Don't—unless you have a basement you're planning to decorate with books." And, in general, that's still my advice. But the new technologies—e-publishing and print-on-demand—have forced me to rethink that advice, though ever so slightly.

If you have a book that truly deserves to be published, then I still say that you should be persistent, follow the established pathway to publication, submit, submit, and keep on submitting—and eventually your book will get published. And that's experience talking. A couple of my book proposals have been snatched up by a publisher the first time I sent them out. One proposal I wrote was turned down a dozen times and circulated for five years before it was finally bought and published. Most of my projects fall somewhere in between.

Personally, I would never self-publish. *Never*. But at the same time, I would not tell another writer, "Never self-publish." Though I think self-pubbing is generally a bad idea, there are a few scattered success stories that prevent me from taking an absolute position.

> "Many editors, including print editors, will view your e-zine clippings with favor if they are from recognized, well-paying markets."

Take the story of advertising executive Richard Paul Evans and his book, *The Christmas Box*. In the early 1990s, Evans was inspired to write a Christmas story as a gift to his two daughters. It was a sentimental story of a widow and the young family who moves in with her at Christmastime, and how they learn together the real meaning of Christmas. Evans wrote the short book in less than six weeks, and had twenty copies printed to give as Christmas presents to family and friends. Those twenty copies were shared from household to household around the Salt Lake City area.

People began asking Evans to reprint the book, so he self-published an eighty-seven-page paperback edition, which sold briskly in stores around the area. When a literary agent heard how this little self-pubbed book was spreading like wildfire in the state of Utah, he contacted Evans and offered to auction the book to the New York publishing trade. Simon and Schuster won the bidding war—and Richard Paul Evans won a $4.2 million advance. Simon & Schuster brought the book out in 1995 as a lavish hardcover gift book, and *The Christmas Box* continues to be a best-seller today.

Out of all the self-published books that roll off the presses every year (some estimate as many as 100,000 self-pubbed titles annually), how many success stories are there? Few enough, I would say, to count on one hand. Let's see—there's James Redfield's *The Celestine Prophecy*, a lightweight piece of pseudospiritual fluff about enlightenment and destiny. And in a similar vein, there's Marlo Morgan's *Mutant Message Down Under*, an American doctor's semi-fictional, semi-spiritual account of a walkabout in the Australian outback. Both were later picked up by major publishers (HarperCollins and Warner Books, respectively).

Several business megabestsellers started out as self-pubbed titles, before being acquired (for big advances) by major New York publishing houses: *Leadership Secrets of Attila the Hun* by Wess Roberts, *What Color is Your Parachute?* by Richard Bolles, *In Search of Excellence* by Tom Peters, and *The One-Minute Manager* by Kenneth Blanchard and Spencer Johnson were all originally self-published. Ironically, even *How to Get Happily Published* by Judith Applebaum—a book on how to write and submit books so that publishers will buy them—was originally self-published!

So it can happen—you can get rich and famous by publishing your own book. If you've got the money and the desire, and particularly if you have a willingness to promote your brains out, then by all means, have at it. Who am I to stomp on your entrepreneurial spirit?

Just keep in mind that self-published books have next to no chance at all of being placed in libraries or the superchain bookstores. You must either have good design sense, or you must hire a designer to create an attractive cover. You must also do all the other things publishers usually do: plan a marketing strategy, line up media and promotional events, keep track of sales and tax records, and so forth.

If you have a great idea, an attention-getting title, and tons of gumption, then go for it—with my blessing.

To sum up this look at the future of books, an observation: It is becoming clear that our cultural idea of what constitutes a "book" is changing. It is an elastic and evolving concept. It is a concept that differs from one person to another. Whatever a "book" may be to you, I think the term can be defined very simply as "the thoughts and ideas of an author or authors, in the form of a theme or topic or storyline (fictional or non-fictional), contained in a structure that gives those thoughts a meaningful framework." Notice that this definition makes no mention of paper, ink, pages, binding, covers, or any other component we traditionally think of as comprising a "book." We now know that a "book" can exist in a format consisting entirely of magnetic traces, electrons, and pixels.

Personally, I like a book that I can highlight, write in the margins, and bookmark with Post-It Notes. Of course, there is no reason why e-book software can't enable all of this to be done even more easily and effectively than in print books (imagine if all your handwritten margin notes were computer-searchable!). Printed books are fine home furnishings and a pleasing tactile experience, as well as an enriching intellectual experience. E-books are software, and are highly functional and efficient to operate.

I think both kinds of "books" are going to be around for a long, long time.

SOUL SURVIVAL

> It's a rare month that goes by without my wondering that I have the
> temerity to go on writing for a living.
> **_Lawrence Block_**, Telling Lies for Fun and Profit

> Fundamentally, all writing is about the same thing; it's about dying, about
> the brief flicker of time we have here, and the frustration that it creates.
> _Novelist_ **_Mordecai Richler_** (The Apprenticeship of Duddy Kravitz _and_
> Barney's Version)

W<small>HY WOULD ANYONE WRITE JUST ONE BOOK</small>—then stop?
One of the most celebrated authors of our time is J. D. Salinger. His
entire oeuvre consists of one novel and a handful of short stories. That
1951 novel—the classic coming-of-age story _Catcher in the Rye_— is con
sidered one of the best examples of rich, fully realized characterization
ever penned. Its release was greeted by enthusiastic critical acclaim and
thunderous commercial success. Yet Jerome David Salinger, who is still
living, has never published another novel.

And there is Harper Lee. Her novel, _To Kill a Mockingbird_, combined a stinging indictment of racism with a poignant portrayal of childhood innocence. The book won a Pulitzer Prize, was adapted for both the
stage and screen (the movie was nominated for ten Academy Awards),
and had a powerful impact on racial attitudes in America. Yet Harper Lee
never published another novel.

And then there's Margaret Mitchell (1900–1949), who wrote only
one novel, _Gone With the Wind_. (I don't count her short romantic novel,
Lost Laysen, written when she was a teenager; she obviously didn't

consider the book publishable, and it was released only after considerable posthumous reworking). *GWTW* was an instant success upon its release in 1936, it garnered the Pulitzer in 1937, and was made into one of the best-loved films of all time. Even today, the book sells over 200,000 copies a year. Yet Margaret Mitchell never wrote another book.

Will someone explain this madness to me? Will someone explain how a writer can produce one book and then *quit*? Nonwriters often ask me, "Where do you get your ideas?—as if getting ideas is the hard part. We writers know that getting ideas is the easy part! I have files and files of ideas, enough to last three lifetimes. I'm sure you have as many ideas as I do. The hard part of a writer's job is not finding ideas, but finding time, money, discipline, and motivation.

In short, the toughest part of writing for a living is ensuring the survival of the writer's *soul*. If you want to quit your day job and become a working writer, you *must* produce *many* books, stories, plays, or articles in your lifetime. You must write every day. You must be productive and motivated over the long haul. You can't afford to be distracted, deterred, or blocked.

As a writer, your soul is under assault. There are forces that seek to keep you from your goals. Some of those forces are within you, such as self-doubt and procrastination. Others are outside you, such as rejection and financial hardship. To succeed as a working writer, you must battle those forces day after day. That is why I believe that this final chapter may be the most important chapter of all. Here, as a final word of encouragement, I want to make sure you know how to recognize the four deadliest enemies of every writer—so you can battle them and conquer them. They are:

(1) Financial Stress
(2) Deadline Stress
(3) Self-Doubt
(4) Rejection

Let's take a closer look at the four enemies of the writer's soul.

ENEMY NO. 1: FINANCIAL STRESS

Writing is the only profession where no one considers you ridiculous if you earn no money.

*French playwright/novelist **Jules Renard*** (Poil de Carotte)

Who are you gonna believe? Samuel Johnson or Stephen King? It was Dr. Johnson who, in 1759, made the statement, "No man but a block-head ever wrote but for money." To which the King of Horror replies, "The act of writing is beyond currency. Money is great stuff to have, but when it comes to the act of creation, the best thing is not to think of money too much. It constipates the whole process."

Me? I agree with both. Dr. Johnson is right—and so is Mr. King. If you are going to write for a living, you have to make money. If not, you stop living—and when you stop living, it naturally follows that you stop writing. You must get paid—or you're a blockhead.

At the same time, writing truly is beyond currency. When writing, you must be totally focused on the act of creation, not cash-flow. The best way to avoid focusing on money is to have it. When you have money, you don't think about money. It's when you *don't* have money that money becomes your focus.

Financial pressure poisons the well of imagination. It kills motivation. It complicates and distorts your life. Money worries can turn the joy of writing into the drudgery of churning out the next book and collecting the next check. At its best, writing is lonely work. Writing under financial stress becomes solitary confinement.

There is only one solution to financial stress: financial success. You must make good money, real money, with your writing. You must think and write commercially, producing the kind of writing that sells. If your writing doesn't sell, you'll make no money, and you will always be saddled with financial stress. You may think, "But I don't want to think and write commercially! I'm an artist!" Fine, you're an artist. You know what most artists do? Well, a few of them live like leeches off government grants, but most of them starve. You want to starve? Fine, be an artist. But before you decide to starve, grok this:

When I suggest that you should think and write commercially, I'm not saying you should prostitute yourself. I'm simply saying that the things you write should please an editor and an audience. That is, you should write with the objective of making sales. Will that mean you have to compromise? Perhaps. But is compromise such a dirty word?

As I see it, I'm a very creative guy. I know I can find ways to write what I enjoy, say what I believe, trumpet causes I care about, and create beautiful, meaningful pieces of writing while still managing to please large masses of readers. I'm just so danged creative that I can do all of those things at once! Now, are you going to tell me that you aren't as creative as I am? Come on, you're thinking, "I'm twice as creative as Jim Denney—five times, ten times." Fine. Prove it. Show me you can be commercial and still be a great writer, making passionate, important statements about the nature of the world, the nature of reality.

Dickens was commercial. So was Mark Twain. Hemingway too. Kurt Vonnegut writes brilliantly and commercially, as do Ray Bradbury and Harlan Ellison. Not to mention Willa Cather, Tom Wolfe, V. S. Naipaul, Ursula LeGuin, John Updike, and Stephen King. That is very distinguished company—and not one of these great writers ever turned up his/her nose at the thought of writing for commercial success.

You want to do your muse a favor? You want to do something nice for the writer within? Then write to make money. Write to earn a good living. Write to become popular, successful, and financially independent. You may get lucky and create a best-seller right out of the blocks. Not likely, but it could happen.

But even if you aren't an overnight success, so what? You'll just have to pay your dues like the rest of us Grub Streeters. And I won't kid you—it's tough. But if you really have the calling, if you've got that fire in the belly, you'll make it. I'm sure of it.

ENEMY NO. 2: DEADLINE STRESS

I love deadlines. I like the whooshing sound they make as they fly by.
Novelist **Douglas Adams** (The Hitchhiker's Guide to the Galaxy *and*
The Restaurant at the End of the Universe)

Everyone knows that a deadline is a time limit for completion of an assignment. But why is it called a "deadline"? Hmmm. Dead. Line. Deadline. Curious about the origin of the term, I looked it up. I was surprised to find that the term comes from prison slang. There used to be boundary lines drawn on the ground of the prison yard, and these boundaries were called "deadlines" because a prisoner daring to cross that line risked getting shot.

In recent years, some publishers have begun taking the same deadly serious approach toward contractual deadlines. I recently saw a contract with a *hundred-dollar-a-day penalty* for going past deadline. To tell you the honest truth, I don't like the idea of writing a book with a gun pointed at my wallet. I am *intrinsically motivated* to keep my word, meet my deadlines, and deliver on time. I don't need the *extrinsic* motivation of a threat to my bank account. In fact, I think such contractual threats can be counterproductive, interfering with a writer's creativity and motivation.

> "You want to do your muse a favor? You want to do something nice for the writer within? Then write to make money."

Deadlines can be a blessing or a curse, depending on the personality of the writer. Those writers who have a problem with authority may find that deadlines actually keep them from completing their work. They see the publisher with his big-stick contract and imposing deadline as symbolic of the critical, authoritarian parent. Such writers may actually rebel against the parent-publisher by procrastinating.

Other writers simply don't think that niggling little details like deadlines are all that important compared with The Work itself. Best-selling novelist Diana Gabaldon (*The Fiery Cross, Outlander, Dragonfly in Amber*) explained her view in an interview with Susan K. Perry, Ph.D.: "Let's put it this way: We have deadlines in my contracts because there's a space for them. I've never met one. They get the book when I'm finished with it. They scream and tear their hair a lot. ...But I have a much higher loyalty to my book than I do to any of them." Okay, Diana Gabaldon has the clout to get away with it—but you can count on this: If you or I were to take that position with a publisher, our next deadline would likely be our last.[1]

At the other end of this spectrum is Ros Jay. "I always think my discipline is dreadful," she told me, "but since I always deliver on time it must be better than I think. My saving grace is that when things are going well, I can write fast. I generally won't take on more than 50,000 words a month, but when I'm really on a roll, I can produce 5,000 to 10,000 words a day. This means I can afford quite a few off days and still meet my deadlines.

"Even when things are going badly, my ultimate discipline is that I won't miss a deadline. I know deep down whether I can afford to indulge poor discipline for a day or two or not; in the end I find the motivation I need by knowing that I've got, say, two days to write eight thousand words or I'm technically in breach of contract. That always does it for me. Having said that, things don't generally get quite that bad, I'm glad to say."

Deadlines impose pressure on writers. Some people thrive on pressure. They pride themselves on the fact that, if it weren't for the last minute, they'd never get anything done. To me, that seems an unhealthy way to approach the creative process. I believe pressure works against creativity. It robs you of the joy of writing—that feeling of being "in the zone" where creative magic takes place and brilliant books and stories get written. Pressure performs a reverse alchemy, transforming the golden act of creation into the leaden drudgery of a chore.

Writing is something you should *want* to do, not something you are *forced* to do under pressure. While you are in that near-hypnotic moment of being absorbed by your writing, your soul should be completely preoccupied by the pure act of creation. Meeting your deadline should be an overall goal, but should not intrude on your thoughts while you are writing.

Here, then, are some ways you can meet your deadlines and produce great writing without feeling stressed by deadlines:

(1) *Accept only reasonable deadlines*. You don't have to beg for work, and you don't have to accept unreasonable working conditions in order to find employment. An unreasonable deadline is an unacceptable working condition. You are not doing yourself or the publisher any favors by agreeing to a deadline you are not confident you can meet

(2) *Cultivate a reputation for reliability*. Market yourself as a writer who meets deadlines. Editors love writers who deliver on time (or early!). If you deliver quality work when promised, you'll never lack assignments and contracts.

(3) *View each deadline as an achievement to be celebrated—not a doomsday to be dreaded*. Negative thinking about deadlines produces fear—and fear induces paralysis. Stop negative thinking in its tracks. Instead of picturing the dire consequences of missing a deadline, think of the reward that is yours when you meet that deadline: You will have

finished another project and collected another check. So celebrate, buy yourself a present, take a night on the town.

(4) *Make sure that family and friends respect your deadlines*. Many people think that, because writers work at home, they have tons of time to spare. People will try to get writers to volunteer time and get involved in activities because, "After all, it's not like you work in an office!" Many writers find that they have to educate the people around them to understand that writers work under deadlines, and deadlines mean that writers have no time to waste.

(5) *Have fun*. When writing is fun, deadlines are not a problem. Instead of procrastinating, you *can't wait* to begin writing because writing is so much *fun*. Novelist and technology writer Michael A. Banks, author of *The Internet Unplugged* and *Web Psychos, Stalkers, and Pranksters: How to Protect Yourself in Cyberspace* (website at http://w3.one.net/~banks/) observes:

> The Japanese have an interesting word for deadline: *shimekiri*. Loosely and literally translated, the word means "cut-chop," which is what a lot of us do (or feel like we're having done to us) when up against a deadline. ...Oddly enough, although I have a few more deadlines looming (and past) than usual this month, I don't feel the stress. This is probably because virtually all the pending articles and books are works I *want* to write, as opposed to article assignments or book contracts taken on in order to belay mindless "When can we expect the payment?" queries from creditors. And I must say it's a nice feeling. All of which implies quite a bit about deadlines, and inspires me to pass along a bit of advice:...Stick with writing what you *want* to write. ...Keep it *fun*![2]

Novelist Piers Anthony agrees. "I hardly need to generate the motivation to write," he says, "because I *love* to write and I do it all I can." And, Robert Darden says, "My most exciting moments as a writer occur when I'm working on my fiction. This is the only time in my life that *I'm* in control. It's like a drug—I crave it. Writing fiction is the greatest joy in this business. Getting books published and getting interviewed is nice— but only as a means to get more fiction published. Writing fiction is *fun*—and when writing is fun, you can't keep from writing."

ENEMY NO. 3: SELF-DOUBT

The worst enemy of creativity is self-doubt.
*Novelist-poet **Sylvia Plath*** (The Bell Jar, Ariel)

While writing *The Grapes of Wrath*, John Steinbeck struggled against deep insecurities and self-doubt. "My many weaknesses are beginning to show their heads," he wrote in his journal. "'I'm not a writer. I've been fooling myself and other people.'...I'll try to go on with work now. Just a stint every day does it." Despite those doubts, the book he was writing at the time went on to win the Pulitzer, and ultimately the Nobel Prize for literature.

Self-doubt is the most common to all writers' afflictions—more common than writer's block and carpal tunnel syndrome combined. Self-doubt is really a form of *fear*. We are afraid of what we might find out about ourselves—that we are not as talented or brilliant or creative as we thought we were. We are afraid of rejection—that editors and readers will see our work and condemn it (and us with it). We are afraid of failure—that we will put our work out into the marketplace, and it will be a resounding flop. Most paradoxical of all, we are afraid of success.

Why would we fear success? Because success is the great unknown. We wonder: Will it change my life? Will I have to do media interviews? Am I up to the task of being treated as an authority or an entertainer or a storyteller? If I succeed, my life will be different and more difficult. It's easier to cower here behind my computer, pretending to be a writer, than to actually succeed.

To be a working writer, you must overcome those fears. A working writer willingly accepts the burdens of success and chooses to live courageously. Understand, courage is not the absence of fear. It is doing what you have to do *despite* your fears. And that means that you persevere, you press ahead, you *write*, disregarding your fears and self-doubt.

Novelist Ayn Rand urged writers to adopt an attitude of ruthless, relentless professionalism, regardless of self-doubts. She said, "You can be professional before you publish anything—*if* you approach writing as a job and apply to writing the same standards and methods that people regularly apply to other professions." She said that she herself approached writing as if she were an employee of Hank Rearden—the ruthless, steely-eyed industrialist in her novel *Atlas Shrugged*. Rearden, she said, "would not tolerate it if I told him, 'I can't work today because I have self-doubt' or 'I have a self-esteem crisis.' Yet that is what most people do, in effect, when it comes to writing."

James Scott Bell is an award-winning novelist (*Blind Justice* and *Deadlock*; his website is www.jamesscottbell.com). "I was an attorney before I turned to writing full-time," he recently told me. "Having worn a suit and tie each day for a couple of years, I now go into Starbucks in jeans and tee shirt. I often encounter a car salesman who knows me (he's dressed in a suit and tie) and he looks at my attire and says, 'Oh, I see you're dressed for work—again.'"

Before James Scott Bell could trade his attorney suit for his writing togs, he had to conquer every writer's common enemy: self-doubt. He told me how he did it. "There's a point that most novelists reach," he said. "I call it The Wall. For me, it's usually about 30,000 words into the writing process. The Wall is a form of writer's block. It's your nasty little internal editor telling you, 'This is all garbage. This book is no good. You're wasting your time.'

"The only way to break The Wall is to keep writing. You have to trust yourself and keep going. You have to give yourself permission to write badly in first draft, fully confident that your final draft will be brilliant. The saying is, 'Don't get it right, just get it written.' Stephen King calls it 'writing fast enough to stay ahead of the doubts.'

"Oddly, on the two books I'm working on right now, I haven't hit The Wall yet. I'm at 70,000 words on one and 60,000 on the other, and still going strong. This means that either I've learned to ignore that mischievous little editor-in-the-brain, or I'm completely deluded about my own abilities. We'll see. Maybe I'll get to the end of the process, read what I've written, and *then* panic.

"If you learn the art of pushing past The Wall, ignoring your internal editor, and tuning out your self-doubt, you will become something called an Author. You will have earned the privilege of writing for a living. It's a great feeling. I experience that feeling every day when I get up and think, 'Hey, they actually *pay* me to sit at home and write stories.'"

It's easy to see why self-doubt is such a huge issue for writers. We work in solitude, spending months to produce a novel, play, or nonfiction book that may be greeted by jeers and rejection. Our feelings rise and fall: "This is a masterpiece!" "This is garbage!" "I'll be acclaimed!" "I'll be laughed at!" In our solitude, working for months without paychecks, affirmation, or reinforcement, we have plenty of time to wonder if we are just pounding meaningless words into our keyboards, wasting our lives.

In my own experience, I have found that the best solution to the problem of self-doubt is a *spiritual* solution. After all, when I am plagued by self-doubt, it is usually because I am running low on two essential spiritual forces: *enthusiasm* and *inspiration*. You may think, "What's so spiritual about enthusiasm and inspiration?"

The word *enthusiasm* comes from the Greek adjective *entheos*, meaning "having God within" (from *en*, "within," and *theos*, "god"). The first recorded use of the word *enthusiasm* in the English language was in 1603, where it was used to refer to being possessed or indwelt by a god. I have found that I *must* have enthusiasm, I *must* have a sense of God living and operating within me, in order to achieve a creative act such as writing a book. As Ralph Waldo Emerson said, "Nothing great was ever achieved without enthusiasm."

The word *inspiration* is also a word with powerful spiritual implications. It comes from the Latin *inspirare*, meaning "to breathe into or fill with breath or spirit" (from *in*, "in," and *spirare*, "to breathe"). We get our English word *spirit* (or *Spirit*, as a proper name referring to the Holy Spirit of God) from the Latin *spirare*, because the ancients believed that the breath was the spirit of a person, and when the breath departed at death, the living spirit departed. To be inspired, then, is to be fully alive. As inspirational novelist Carol Gift Page once put it (paraphrasing athlete Eric Liddel), "When I write, I feel God's pleasure."

My solution to self-doubt, then, is *faith*—trusting God to restore my *en-theos* and my *in-spirare*, my enthusiasm and inspiration. When I approach a challenging writing task and think, "I can't do this," I simply pray, "God, do this through me"—then I wade right into the thick of it, and it miraculously gets done.

If you are not a person who relates to God in that way, this may not seem to be a very practical solution. Well, you'll have to find something that works for you. All I can say is that, in my own experience, God-faith invariably replaces self-doubt and enables me to punch through the doldrums of a difficult or intensive writing project. So I offer this insight for what it's worth.

At the same time, I would hasten to add that self-doubt—in appropriate small doses—actually serves a valuable function in our lives. It keeps us humble, it keeps our egos in check. It forces us to continually seek self-improvement. It makes us strive to constantly improve our craft, and to make our work stronger, more powerful, and more accessible to a broader audience. Writing is not just about reaching for success. It is also about taking risks—the risk of spectacular failure, the risk of rejection, the risk of withering criticism—in order to achieve something noble and good.

To us, as writers, the risk is worth it. We dare to spend long hours creating reams of words that no one may ever read because we *believe* in those words. We know that if our words can find their audience—if we can move our fellow human beings with our passion, our stories, our characters, our poetry—the rewards will be great. The risk will have paid off.

Novelist David Brin offers advice for those who sometimes doubt themselves and their work: "The arts are pyramidal, hierarchical, like medieval societies," he told me. "No matter how high you rise, there's always a narrowing tip above you. It can daunt and intimidate. Don't let it. Enjoy who you are and what you do. Do good work and do some good."

We must believe in ourselves, our stories, our characters, our words. If we doubt ourselves, how can we persuade others to believe in us? But if we *believe*, we will *achieve*.

ENEMY NO. 4: REJECTION

This manuscript of yours that has just come back from another editor is a precious package. Don't consider it rejected. Consider that you've addressed it "To the editor who can appreciate my work," and it has simply come back stamped "Not at this address." Just keep looking for the right address.

Novelist and humorist **Barbara Kingsolver** (The Bean Trees *and* Pigs in Heaven)

Does the name Theodor Geisel ring a bell? Probably not, but I'm almost certain you've read one of his books. Early in his career, Geisel found it extremely hard to get published. He sent his first manuscript to a publisher in New York, and promptly received it back with a curt rejection notice. He sent it to another publisher—and was rejected again. He submitted it to another publisher, and another, and another. In all, his manuscript was rejected by *twenty-three publishers*. But the twenty-fourth publisher bought it, published it—and the book sold six million copies.

The title of that book was *And To Think That I Saw It On Mulberry Street*, a children's book published in 1937. Of course, the book wasn't published under Geisel's own name, but under his now famous pen name: Dr. Seuss. That first book was soon followed by many more million-plus-sellers, including *The Cat in the Hat*, *Green Eggs and Ham*, and *Horton Hears a Who*.

Madeleine L'Engle has written more than fifty books. Her most famous was her first, the science-fantasy novel *A Wrinkle in Time*, published in 1961. Though it won the prestigious Newbery Medal and has remained in print since it was published, the manuscript for *A Wrinkle in Time* received more than thirty rejections before it sold.

Richard Hooker spent seven years writing his Korean War comedy *M*A*S*H*. The novel was rejected twenty-one times before it sold to Morrow. The much-rejected book quickly became a best-seller, and spun off a hugely successful movie and TV series.

Richard Bach's spiritual allegory *Jonathan Livingston Seagull* was turned down by eighteen publishers before it sold to Macmillan in 1970. It took a couple of years to find its audience—and then it began to soar. By 1975, the book had racked up sales of over 7 million copies in the United States.

Frank Herbert's science fiction epic *Dune* was rejected by thirteen publishers before it was published. The rejection letters called the book "too long," "too slow," and "confusing and irritating." But Herbert refused to let rejection stop him. In the end, he found a publisher—and a huge audience. The novel sold over 10 million copies, won the coveted Hugo and Nebula awards, and spawned two screen adaptations.

Lisa Alther wrote for twelve years and collected 250 rejection slips before she finally made a sale. Her first book, *Kinflicks*, was praised by critics who compared her to Mark Twain and J. D. Salinger. *Kinflicks* and Alther's later books, such as *Original Sins* and *Other Women*, have been enormously successful—but first she had to persevere through twelve lean years of rejection.

Mystery writer Donald Westlake (*Bad News*, *Don't Ask*, and *The Ax*) used to paper the walls of his apartment with rejection slips. The day he sold his first story to a magazine, he celebrated by ripping those rejection slips off the wall—all 204 of them! Today, with over seventy novels to his credit, he is one of the most successful writers in America.

Another mystery writer, Lawrence Sanders, claimed to have a trunkful of rejection slips from his early days. But with the publication of his first novel, *The Anderson Tapes*, in 1970, Sanders launched a thirty-year career as a novelist, producing thirty-eight titles with combined sales of over 57 million.

Other best-sellers that were rejected by publishers twenty or more times include *Dubliners* by James Joyce, *Heaven Knows, Mr. Allison* by Charles Shaw, *Kon-Tiki* by Thor Heyerdahl, *The Postman Always Rings Twice* by James M. Cain, and *The Peter Principle* by Laurence Peter.

Science fiction writer Isaac Asimov put it well when he observed, "Rejection slips, or form letters, however tactfully phrased, are lacerations of the soul, if not quite inventions of the devil—but there is no way around them." And another science fiction writer, Brian

> "Richard Hooker spent seven years writing his Korean War comedy *M*A*S*H*. The novel was rejected twenty-one times before it sold to Morrow."

Stableford, has this perspective on rejection: "The vital point to remember is that the swine who just sent your pearl of a story back with nothing but a coffee-stain and a printed rejection slip can be wrong. You cannot take it for granted that he is wrong, but you have an all-important margin of hope that might be enough to keep you going."

British mystery writer Alex Keegan is the author of five novels featuring the crime-solving exploits of private investigator Catherine "Caz" Flood: *Cuckoo* (Anthony Award nominee, best first novel, 1995), *Vulture*, *Kingfisher*, *Razorbill*, and *A Wild Justice*. His short fiction has appeared in print and online magazines, and has been adapted by BBC Radio. Keegan has made a careful study of rejection, and he has arrived at a startling statistical conclusion: If you make a persistent attack of the markets, you can develop a highly consistent and predictable ratio of sales versus rejections.

"It's a fact," says Keegan, "that the more you submit, the more you will be rejected, but...you cannot fail if you work at your art, if you read, read, read, write, write, write, submit, submit, submit."

A great antidote to the discouragement of rejection is the encouragement of a writer's group. In January 1997, Keegan started a "Boot Camp" of committed but mostly unpublished fiction writers—eleven founding members, only three with any publishing credits. It was a hard-nosed, tough-minded, no-excuses writing group. The demands: Each member must produce one short story every two weeks. The story must be submitted to the group for critique, then rewritten and submitted on the open market for publication. Though all eleven members professed a desire to write professionally, few had produced much output during the preceding twelve months, and even fewer had submitted any stories for publication.

But the rigorous demands of the Boot Camp changed that in a hurry. During the first year, 1997, the eleven Boot Campers racked up an astonishing number of sales—eighty-five stories sold for publication either in print, online, or on the radio. One Boot Camper won the BBC World Service's Short Story of the Year award. Keegan sold his fifth novel that year—and he sold forty short pieces. The following year, 1998, Keegan and his fellow Boot Campers racked up over 200 hits. In 1999, over 350 hits.

It stands to reason that more submissions means more sales—but more submissions also means more rejections. "In 1997," he said, "I had more rejections than in the previous forty-nine years of my life. But rejections are side effects, meaningless." What mattered was that Keegan was writing an enormous volume of stories, and he was submitting them. If they came back, he instantly resubmitted them. Keegan made 168 submissions in 1998, which returned 107 rejections—but also returned forty-three hits (with eighteen submissions not yet reported on by year's end).

Keegan kept a spreadsheet of his submissions, and was able to calculate a "hit rate"—a ratio of sales per submissions. He found that he was consistently selling one time out of every 3.5 submissions (which was a bit higher than the "hit rate" of his fellow Boot Campers, one sale for every 4.5 submissions—and much better than his average at the beginning of his writing career, when he averaged a sale for every *thirty* submissions).

Many writers view rejections as bad news, or even as a personal insult. Not Alex Keegan. He views rejections as feedback. If an editor appended a handwritten note to a form rejection slip, that was great! Often, rejections gave Keegan insight into ways to make his work stronger and more saleable the next time around. Most important of all, he knew he had a consistent batting average, and every rejection just brought him one step closer to his goal. "I can count," says Alex Keegan. "I know that three rejections mean a sale. I welcome rejections. ... I eat rejections like Popeye eats spinach."[3]

A good writer's group not only helps to steel you against the discouragement of rejection, but can help raise the quality of your work and increase your "batting average." My friend Deborah Raney is the author of such award-winning inspirational novels as *Beneath a Southern Sky*, *After the Rains*, *A Scarlet Cord*, and *A Vow to Cherish* (which was made into a film starring Barbara Babcock and Ken Howard). "I'm a great believer in writer's groups," she told me. "You never become so successful that you don't need a writer's group. In fact, the longer I write, the more I appreciate the friendship and encouragement of other writers.

"I recently got together with a group of writers in the Midwest for a weekend retreat. We met at an Italian restaurant on Friday night and talked shop. Then we gathered at the home of Nancy Moser on Saturday morning for coffee. Nancy is a fabulous writer and the author of such novels as *Time Lottery*, *A Steadfast Surrender*, and *The Seat Beside Me*.

> "A good writer's group not only helps to steel you against the discouragement of rejection, but can help raise the quality of your work and increase your 'batting average.'"

"We sat down in Nancy's living room at around nine and got right down to business. We had six books to brainstorm, and we went in alphabetical order, three books before lunch, and three after lunch. We set a timer for forty-five minutes and gave the author five minutes to present a brief synopsis of his or her book. Then for the next forty minutes everyone in the group suggested ideas for scenes, themes, plot twists, characters, and so forth. The author, meanwhile, would furiously take notes on his or her laptop computer.

"It was incredible to see how one idea spurred another and how our collective creativity triggered more and more ideas. Everyone in the group is a serious, disciplined professional writer, so we did a good job of staying on task. We all came away with tons of ideas, plus a lot of priceless encouragement and enthusiasm. Following the afternoon brainstorming session, we cooked dinner together. Over dinner, we talked about ideas and suggestions we'd thought of in the meantime. Even after the weekend was over, I kept getting e-mails with new ideas and suggestions. Now, how cool is that?"

DO YOU HAVE THE FIRE?

> All day I had been driven by the fire in the belly, as I call it—that won-
> derful heating-up of creative energy that lets me know I'm on the right track,
> that leads me directly to the volcano's epicenter where the words spew out
> effortlessly, flowing hot and pure and transforming everything. My body tem-
> perature actually rises. I sweat. I love this feeling.
>
> **Lauren B. Davis**, *author of* The Stubborn Season

In *Telling Lies for Fun and Profit*, Lawrence Block retells an old
story. A young musician approaches a world-renowned violinist. "Master," the young man says, "I want to pursue a life in music. I know that I
play well, but I don't know if I have the talent to become great. Please
listen to me play. If you give me encouragement, then I will devote my
life to music. But if you tell me I lack the talent for greatness—well, I
would rather know now and avoid wasting my life."

"Play," said the master.

The young man poured his heart out through his violin. He played
with feeling and intensity. He played every note flawlessly. His inflection
and intonation were the finest he had ever achieved. When he finished
playing, he knew he had done his best. He waited expectantly to hear the
verdict from the lips of the master.

The master violinist was silent for several seconds, then he frowned
and shook his head. "No," he said. "You lack the fire."

The young violinist was shattered. The best performance of his life
had been condemned from the lips of the master. He turned and walked
away, depressed and despondent.

Years passed.

The young violinist set aside his violin and became a prosperous
businessman. One day, he heard that the master violinist was in town to
give a concert, so the businessman went to the master's hotel room to call
on him. When the master came to the door, the businessman introduced
himself, and said, "Years ago, I played my violin for you and asked if you
thought I had talent."

"I think I recall you," the master said uncertainly. "But then, I meet
so many promising young musicians."

"That's all right," said the businessman. "I just wanted to tell you
that you changed my life. You said to me, 'You lack the fire.' I was bit-

terly disappointed at having to give up my dream of becoming a great musician, but I had to be realistic and accept your judgment. So I chose a career in the business world, and I've become very successful. But throughout the years, one question has nagged at me: How could you tell, after only hearing me play one time, that I lacked the fire?"

"Oh, I can't tell anything from hearing you play one time," said the master. "Whenever a young musician plays for me, I always say the same thing: 'You lack the fire.'"

The businessman gasped, his face turning purple with outrage. "How dare you!" he sputtered. "How could you do such a horrible thing to a young musician! I played my heart out for you! I looked to you for encouragement, and you broke my spirit! You shattered my dreams! You altered the course of my life! I could have been another Itzhak Perlman, another Isaac Stern! How could you do that to me?"

The master was unmoved by the businessman's rage. "I said you lacked the fire," he said, "and I was right. If you had the fire, you would have paid no attention to me. No one could have kept you from your dream—if you had the fire."

And so it is with you and me.

In this book, I have given you a road map to the life of a working writer. You'll notice I haven't sugarcoated anything. I've given it to you straight. I want you to know from the very outset that the life of a working writer is good, but it isn't easy. It is my life because for me there is no other way to live. If it is the life for you, then nothing will stand in your way—no amount of rejection, self-doubt, criticism, or hardship will stop you.

If you lack the fire, nothing can help you. If the fire burns within you, nothing can stop you.

If you are a writer, you *will* write. And I fully expect that, someday soon, I will hear your name and I will read your work.

And so will the world.

JIM DENNEY'S QUICK START GUIDE TO WRITING FOR A LIVING

Think you're ready to quit your day job and write for a living? Great! I hope you sell a ton of books, make a ton of money, and make a real difference in the world with your sparkling ideas! Here, then, are a few quick tips I've assembled that will greatly improve your chances for success:

1. Make sure you are ready before you leap. Before you take the plunge into full-time writing, ask yourself:

• Do I have a financial safety net? That is, do I have sufficient savings or other sources of income to carry me through the lean times?
• Can I handle the stress and financial insecurity of being self-employed?
• Do I write *at least* an hour a day, every day?
• Am I aggressively submitting what I write on a consistent, regular basis?
• Do I have at least two different editors or publishers who regularly assign work to me or buy my submissions?
• Have I built a reputation for delivering quality and meeting deadlines?
• Am I making serious money as a writer?
• Have I built the habits, attitudes, and professionalism that a working writer must have to succeed?
• Does my mate support my plan to quit my day job and write for a living?
• Do I have the emotional temperament to handle the frustrations and annoyances that are a normal part of being a writer?

2. Focus on writing that builds equity. When you write, you create intellectual property. You generate wealth when you retain the rights to that intellectual property—not only the right to receive royalties on future sales, but adaptation rights, reprint rights, and so forth. When you focus on building equity in your intellectual property, not just getting the next assignment or paycheck, you build long-term net worth.

3. Set your price and stick to it. Know how long it takes you to produce a given piece of writing, know how much money you need to live, and base your price on that. Build in at least 20 percent extra for those aspects of the writing business that consume time but aren't strictly "billable"—conferencing with editors and clients, logging manuscripts, tracking payments, bookkeeping, and so forth. Make sure you are making a livable wage from your writing—and then some. Don't sell yourself short.

4. Nurture contacts and professional relationships. Get to know as many people who buy writing as you possibly can: book editors, magazine editors, editors for in-house publications, webpage editors, and so forth. Cultivate contacts in big markets, small markets, niche markets, any market that will buy your work.

5. Diversify. Selling to a variety of markets enables you to maintain diversified sources of income. Diversified income sources help to stabilize your cash flow. If you get all your work from one editor, you could be financially ruined if that editor were to move, retire, or decide to use other writers. Never rely on a single publisher or editor for all your work—diversify.

6. Tell *everyone* that you are a writer. Not just editors—everyone. You never know where your next assignment or big break is coming from. Who knows? Your banker or butcher may have gone to school with an acquisition editor at Simon & Schuster—and that could be your big break. The more word gets around that you are a writer, the better your chances of landing a plum assignment or cracking a high-paying market.

7. Connect with other writers. Go to writer's conferences. Join or start a writer's group. Find an Internet forum for writers such as

Orson Scott Card's forum at www.hatrack.com/writers/ or the Writers.Net forum at www.writers.net/forum/ or the Silver Quill at members.nbci.com/ tsqforum/ and join the online community. Meet other writers who share your goals and struggles. It's a great way to gain practical insight and advice, and to share information.

8. Study both the craft and business of writing. Read books on writing. Learn everything you can about the artistic side. Learn everything you can about the business side. Write daily and get feedback and critiques on a regular basis. No one ever masters writing. We are all learning as we go—and the learning process never ends.

9. Deliver excellence. Surprise editors and clients by doing more than is expected of you. For example, when I turn in a book manuscript, I often include some suggested jacket copy (I have done that on several occasions, expecting nothing in return—and have sometimes gotten an extra check for $200 for the jacket copy). Build a reputation for excellence, for attention to detail, for writing text that does not need to be rewritten or salvaged. Make the editor's job as easy as possible—and you will make yourself indispensable. Best of all, you will never lack for well-paid assignments.

10. Deliver on time. Writers sometimes fail to understand the cycles of the publishing business. We think, "So my book's going to be a month late. It'll just come out a month later, no big deal." But that's not how it works. When a manuscript is delivered late, it creates a ripple effect that upsets publishing schedules, causes people in the production department to work late and not see their families, throws the sales department into disarray, causes books not to be in the warehouse when the catalog promised, and on and on. Ultimately, all of these ripple effects really do hurt the sales of your book. You signed a contract and promised to deliver by a date certain; make sure you keep that promise.

11. Watch out for the "can of worms." Avoid clients, collaborators, and editors who don't know or can't articulate what they want. Avoid taking on writing projects that seem amorphous and ill-defined. Take projects that are clean, clear-cut, and are a good fit for your abilities and strengths. The "can of worms" projects that are difficult to grasp, organize, and execute will block you, frustrate you, take too long to complete, and drain both your bank account and your soul.

12. Use your website to promote your writing business. Websites are cheap to acquire and easy to maintain. You can use your website to sell your books (either direct to the customer, or through a partnership with Amazon.com or Barnes & Noble's BN.com). You can also use your website as a tool for impressing editors. Post reviews, magazine clippings, and book chapters on your site. Then when an editor is considering you for an assignment, just say, "You can read some of my published work at my website," and give her your web address. It makes an impression.

(By the way, you're cordially invited to stop by my website at www.denneybooks.com.)

A GLOSSARY OF WRITING AND PUBLISHING TERMS

Acquisition Editor—The editor who reviews incoming submissions (manuscripts, synopses, and proposals) for potential publication. Acquisition editors also develop original ideas for books and series, then seek out authors to write them. Many acquisition editors also remain involved throughout the development of the book from acceptance to publication.

Advance—Money paid to the author of a book in anticipation of future sales and earnings. An advance is typically divided into two parts. The first half is paid on signing of the contract; the second half is normally paid on acceptance of the completed manuscript.

Appendix—Supplemental text appended after the body of the text of a book.

Audience—The demographic group comprising the most likely interested readers for a given book.

Backlist—Books from previous seasons that are still in print.

Back Matter—Any text that follows the main body of the text, such as the appendix, endnotes, addenda, index, bibliography, author biography, and advertisements.

Bar Code— The pattern of lines printed on the back cover or book jacket. The code is computer-scanned at the register and contains the book's ISBN and retail price. It is used to automate both checkout and inventory control.

Binding—The cover that holds the pages of a book together; or, the process of fastening pages into a cover to form a bound book.

Blueline—The printer's final proof of a book or magazine before the project goes to press; this is the very last chance to catch and fix any errors, and is usually inspected only by production people in the publishing house. Authors sometimes (but rarely) get to inspect bluelines. Normally, an author's last opportunity to make changes or corrections to a book is in the page proofs.

Blurb—A brief endorsement of a book or author that often appears on the back cover, jacket flaps, or with the front matter of a book.

Boldface—A font that is a heavier version of a roman font.

Book Doctor—A person hired by a publishing house or author to fix a manuscript that is in need of improvement.

Books In Print—The R. R. Bowker Company database of published and soon-to-be published books.

Breakout—Term describing a trade book that reaches a high level of public attention and bookstore sales (usually 100,000 copies or more). A breakout novel or nonfiction book generally has an attention-getting concept ("hook") or an appealing, high-profile author who can promote the book in the national media.

Camera-Ready—Typesetting and graphics that are finished and prepared for reproduction and printing.

Cast-Off—The process of calculating how long a book will run, based on the length of the manuscript, the typeset specifications, and the page format.

C.I.P.—Cataloging in Publication. Bibliographic information supplied by the Library of Congress and printed on the copyright page. This information (which includes author and title, the Dewey Decimal classification number, subject headings, and ISBN number) is used to categorize a book for library use.

Collaborative Writer—A writer who works with another writer or a nonwriter (who is considered the "author" of record) to help that person produce a book. Generally, the collaborative writer interviews the author, then structures the author's words and ideas into book form. If the collaborative writer receives no credit for this work, he or she is called a "ghostwriter." Normally, a collaborative writer receives a small credit, such as "with" or "as told to."

Content Editing—To work with an author in helping him or her to revise and improve a manuscript in terms of its overall organization, flow, content, and continuity.

Copy—Text that is set in type.

Copyeditor—An editor who focuses on mechanics, spelling, punctuation, and grammar (as opposed to style and content). Copyeditors also mark up text for typesetting according to the style of the publishing house.

Copyfitting—The process of calculating how much typeset copy is needed to fill a given space in a publication, or the process of determining how many pages will be required to accommodate the length of a given manuscript.

Copyright—The legal protection of ownership inherent in the creation of a literary, musical, dramatic, or artistic work, as specified by the Copyright Act, Title 17 of the United States Code, beginning at Section 101. Though a copyright technically exists at the moment the work is created, it is difficult to protect that right unless the work has been registered with the Library of Congress. A copyright protects the author's unique mode of expression in that work, but titles, character names, brief phrases, ideas, and methods cannot be copyrighted. Rights granted to a copyright holder include the right to reproduce the work, distribute copies of the work, create derivative works (adaptations), and the right to perform or display the work in public.

Copyright Infringement—Unauthorized use of the exclusive rights of a copyright holder (such as unauthorized reproduction or distribution of a book).

Cover Stock—Paper that is heavier and sturdier than book paper, used for covers of trade and mass-market paperbacks.

Critique—To summarize the strengths and weaknesses of a written work so that the author can improve the manuscript.

Crop—To trim an illustration or photograph in such a way as to fit it into a given space and/or remove unwanted portions of the image. Cropping is performed by marking or masking the original illustration or photograph as a guide to the printer's camera operator.

Distributor—A company that represents publishers by warehousing and shipping books to bookstores, libraries, and wholesalers. Distributors commonly require an exclusive relationship with the publishers they represent.

Earn Out—In book publishing, to sell enough copies to recoup the advance. Once your book "earns out," you begin accruing additional royalties.

E-book or Electronic Book—A book published as an electronic data file that can be downloaded to computers or handheld devices.

E-zine—A magazine that is published online.

Editing—The process of shaping and correcting a manuscript in order to improve the text, conform to house style, and fit a given format.

Epilogue—A short concluding section at the end of a literary work; also called an "afterword."

Fair Use—The quoting of a limited selection from a copyright-protected work in such a way that it is not considered copyright infringement. Criteria for fair use include: Is the use commercial (are you profiting from another person's copyrighted work) or is it nonprofit and educational? Does the purpose of this use involve research, teaching, news reporting, review, comment, or parody? How much of the copyrighted work are you quoting in relation to the whole (hence, you can quote far fewer words from a song or poem than you can from a book)? Will your use diminish the market value of the copyrighted work?

First North American Serial Rights—The right of a periodical to publish a previously unpublished story or article one time on the North American continent. These are the only rights an author should grant to a periodical when a new story or article is sold. All other rights (such as electronic rights) should be retained by the author or purchased separately by the publisher.

Flat Fee—A one-time lump sum that a writer receives for a work. A writer who receives a flat fee is said to be producing the book on a "work-for-hire" basis. The writer does not own the copyright or any other interest in the book, and will receive no royalties.

Folio—A page number placed at the outside end of the running head atop the page (i.e., in the upper left corner of a left-hand page and the upper right corner of a right-hand page). A page number at the bottom of the page is a "drop folio." A folio that is counted but not printed (such as a copyright page or title page) is a "blind folio."

Font—A typeface. A roman font, such as Times Roman, contains capitals, lowercase, small capitals, figures, punctuation marks, signs, and accents. Italic and boldface weights are often commonly thought of as part of a roman font, although these are technically separate fonts (i.e., Times Italic and Times Roman Bold).

Foreign Rights—Rights that are granted to publishers in other countries to produce editions of a book.

Foreword—A preface or an introduction, usually written by someone other than the author.

Format—The size, shape, style, and appearance of a book.

Freelance Writer—A self-employed writer who contracts on a case-by-case basis to write for a variety of publishers.

Frontlist—Books prominently featured in the publisher's current-season catalog.

Front Matter—Any text that precedes the main body of the text, such as the title page, copyright page, dedication, epigraph, table of contents, and so forth.

Galleys—Typeset proofs of a book, usually long and unpaginated. Galleys are rare anymore, since computerized technology permits publishers to produce paginated page proofs.

Genre—A specific market category of literature, such as romance, horror, science fiction, fantasy, detective, western, military, and so forth.

Ghostwriter—Strictly, an anonymous collaborative writer (that is, a writer who receives no credit for producing a work that is credited to another person). Loosely, a collaborative writer who may receive no credit or may receive such credit as "with" or "as told to."

Halftone—An image, such as a photograph, that has been converted from a continuous-tone image into a pattern of tiny dots, suitable for reproduction with a printing plate. The dots, which are visible under magnification, give the illusion of continuous-tone shades to the naked eye.

Hardcover—A book that is bound in a cloth-covered cardboard binding.

House Style—A set of rules defining various preferred style choices in such areas as grammar, punctuation, and spelling so that consistency is maintained throughout all the publications of a publishing house. House style is generally set forth in a manual called a "style guide."

Independent Publisher—A small press publishing house, not affiliated with the publishing megacartels, such as the Bantam Dell Doubleday Publishing Group. Independent publishers often fill niches in the market that the megapublishers overlook.

Index—An alphabetized list of names and subjects at the end of a printed work, listing the page or pages on which each subject can be found.

Institutional Sales—Books sold to schools and libraries.

ISBN or International Standard Book Number—A unique identification number assigned to a book. An ISBN is obtained from the R. R. Bowker Company, publisher of *Books In Print*.

Justify—To space out a line or column of type to the full width of the measure. Compare with ragged right, ragged left, and centered.

Lead Time—The interval of time between the editing process and the publication of a book or magazine. It is especially important to consider lead time in regard to seasonal stories, articles, and books. If a magazine's lead time is, say, six months, then an article with a Christmas theme should be submitted well in advance of that lead time (around March) in order to be considered for a Christmastime issue.

Leading—Pronounced "ledding," a term that dates back to the time when type was cast in hot lead. Leading is the amount of space between lines of copy. For example, 10-point type is often set with an 11-point or 12-point leading (one or two points of extra leading) to make the type look more open and readable.

Line Editing—This term is often used differently in different publishing houses. Commonly, line editing is roughly the same as copyediting. It involves editing text for clarity, grammar, punctuation, usage, tense agreement, logical transition, redundancy, conciseness, active versus passive voice, quality of expression, vocabulary, sentence and paragraph progression, and other technical issues.

Manuscript—An unpublished book in the form of loose 8 1/2" x 11" pages, or in the form of an electronic data file.

Marketing Plan—A written strategy for promoting and selling a book. A marketing plan typically includes a synopsis of the book, target audience, marketing budget, distribution plans, promotion ideas, timeline, and suggestions for author participation in the marketing of the book.

Mass Market Paperback—Inexpensive small-format (usually 4 x 7 inches) paper-cover book with a glued binding.

Media Kit—See Press Kit.

Midlist—An author or book that does not become a best-seller.

On Acceptance—In book publishing, payment of an advance soon after the manuscript has been read and approved by the publisher. In magazine publishing, payment for a story or article when the submission is approved (as opposed to payment on publication, when the story or article actually appears in print).

On Publication—This is rare in book publishing, but some publishers do offer contracts in which some portion of the advance (the second half or the final third) is paid at the time the book is published. In magazine publishing, it is a more common (but still undesirable) practice to pay on publication, which could be many months after the piece has been written and accepted.

On Spec or On Speculation—A work that has been completely written without having a contract, offer, or assignment by an editor. A first-time novelist typically spends months or years writing a novel "on spec" in the hope that it will someday sell to a publisher. A work that has been so written is sometimes called a "spec piece." The process of writing "on spec" is sometimes called "spec work."

Over the Transom— The submission of unsolicited material to an editor without the benefit of a personal relationship or introduction by a mutual acquaintance. The term originated in the days when editors' offices often had transoms (small hinged windows over the door) for ventilation. The phrase suggests that a writer who was not allowed through the door might submit his work by tossing it over the transom.

Out of Print—A book that is no longer reprinted or maintained in the publisher's inventory.

Page Proofs— Trial pages of a typeset publication, paginated and ready to be checked and corrected. In book publishing, page proofs are usually inspected by one or more proofreaders as well as the author. Long, unpaginated proofs are called "galleys."

Plagiarism—Presenting the writing or specific mode of expression of another writer as one's own. If copyrighted material is plagiarized, the act of plagiarism also constitutes copyright infringement.

Preface—A brief introduction to a book explaining the purpose and intent of the book.

Press Kit—A package of information that provides reporters and reviewers with information on a book. It typically includes a press release, information on the author, a reproduction of the book cover, testimonials, and other information. Also called a "media kit."

Primary Rights—Primary rights are one of two main categories of rights in a book publishing contract (the other is "subsidiary rights" or "secondary rights"). Primary rights are those rights that would be specifically exercised by the publisher (as opposed to "subsidiary rights," which would generally be licensed to third parties). Primary rights include the right to produce and distribute a book in various editions.

Proofreader—A person who reads typeset manuscripts to check for errors.

Proposal—A summary of a book idea, typically including a brief synopsis, chapter-by-chapter outline, author information, marketing ideas, one to three sample chapters, and any other relevant information.

Public Domain—Work that is not protected by copyright.

Publication Date—The announced date at which a book is officially available for sale to the public. Also called "pub date."

Query—A proposal letter for a prospective magazine article.

Ragged Left—Text that is set with the left margin unjustified. Also called "rag left."

Ragged Right—Text that is set with the right margin unjustified. Also called "rag right."

Recto—The front side of a leaf; the right-hand page of a book. The back side is called the "verso." The instruction "start recto" means to begin a section (such as a chapter, preface, or index) on the recto page.

Remainder—To reduce inventory by selling excess stock at deeply discounted prices, usually because of sluggish sales or outdated material.

Rewrite—To create a new and revised version of an existing manuscript.

Roman—Normal book-style type with serifs. The word roman is usually written in lower case.

Rule—A printed straight line. This is a rule: _____

Royalties—A percentage of the sales price earned by an author on books that are sold.

Saddle-Stitched—Printed sheets that are folded in half then stapled through the fold, as most magazines are.

Sans Serif—A typeface without serifs, such as Helvetica or Arial.

SASE— Self-Addressed Stamped Envelope.

Sell-Through—In book publishing, the number of copies that are actually sold to the public.

Serif—The fine line that finishes the main strokes of a letter on a roman or italic font. On a capital T, for example, serifs project downward from the ends of the crossbar and project to the left and right of the base of the upright stroke. Typefaces such as Helvetica or Arial are called "sans serif" fonts because they do not have serifs.

Signature—A group of pages that are printed together on a single large press sheet, then folded down and trimmed to form sections of a book or magazine. Signatures are typically groups of 16 or 32 pages. Also called a "sig."

Smyth-Sewn—A sturdy method of binding books by sewing signatures through the fold before binding the signatures together. Smyth-sewn books lie flat when open, unlike a side-sewn books.

Spine—The "backbone" of the book; the section of the cover that is visible when a book is on a shelf; the part of the book where the pages are bound to the cover.

Stet—Literally, "let it stand." When authors read proofs and find that an editor or proofreader has made an incorrect change or deletion, they mark the passage "stet" to indicate, "Let this passage stand as I originally wrote it." The word "stet" is also used when an author makes a change on a proof, then decides to cancel that change and restore the original text. The term comes from the Latin third person singular form of *stare*, which means to stand or remain.

Subsidiary Rights—Also called "secondary rights" or "sub rights." Subsidiary rights are those rights which reside in the work, but which are normally sold or licensed to a third party rather than being directly exercised by the publisher. Subsidiary rights may include electronic rights, motion picture and TV rights, dramatic and public performance rights, audio book rights, audiovisual rights, merchandizing rights, and so forth.

Subsidy Publishers—Publishing companies that charge authors to print their books. Subsidy publishers generally do little to edit, package, and promote the books they publish, and tend to make their money from fees paid by authors, not from book sales. Also called "vanity press."

Synopsis—A brief description of a completed novel accompanying the first two or three chapters of the book. A synopsis serves the same function for a novel that a proposal serves for a nonfiction book.

Trade Paperback—Large-format paperbacks, often published as a less expensive edition of hardcover books.

Trade Publisher—A publisher of books for consumption by the general public.

Trim Size—The dimensions of a finished book. The trim size of this book, for example, is 6" x 9".

Typeface—A lettering design that is produced as a complete font and known by a distinct name, such as Times Roman or Helvetica.

Typo—Typographical error, such as transposed letters or miss-spelled words.

Vanity Press—see Subsidy Publishers.

Verso—The back side of a leaf; the left-hand page of a book. The front side is called the "recto."

Wholesaler—A company that buys large quantities of books from distributors and publishers, then resells them to booksellers. Wholesalers, such as Ingram and Baker & Taylor, are viewed as representing booksellers, whereas distributors represent publishers.

Work-For-Hire—See Flat Fee.

Word of Mouth—Advertising generated when one satisfied reader tells other people about a book; the most effective and desirable form of advertising to have, and the most difficult to obtain.

NOTES

Chapter 1: A Holy Calling

1. Natalie Goldberg, *Writing Down the Bones* (Boston: Shambhala, 1998), p. 170.

2. Ray Bradbury, quoted in "People," *The Dallas Morning News*, 3 October 1997, p. 2A.

3. Harlan Ellison, interviewed by *The Onion*, electronically retrieved at http://avclub.theonion.com/avclub3407/avfeature3407.html.

4. C. S. Lewis, *God in the Dock* in *The Collected Works of C.S. Lewis* (New York: Inspirational Press, 1996), p. 258.

Chapter 2: Taking the Leap

1. Lawrence Block, *Telling Lies for Fun and Profit* (New York: Quill, 1981), p. 78.

2. Robert J. Sawyer, "On Writing: Heinlein's Rules," electronically retrieved at http:www.sfwriter.com/ow05.htm.

3. Stephen King, *On Writing: A Memoir of the Craft* (New York: Scribner, 2000), pp. 73–74.

Chapter 3: It's a Living

1. F. Paul Wilson, quoted by W. C. Stroby, "Five Questions Every First Novelist Must Answer," from *The Writer's Digest Handbook of Novel Writing* by the editors of *Writer's Digest* (Cincinnati: Writer's Digest Books, 1992), p. 12.

2. Anne Lamott, *Bird by Bird: Some Instructions on Writing and Life* (New York: Anchor Books, 1995), p. 112.

3. Source: Lynn Wasnak, "How Much Should I Charge?," electronically retrieved at http://www.writersmarket.com/content/charge.asp.

Chapter 4: What Have I Signed?

1. Marian Betancourt, Michael Capobianco, and Pat Potter, "Author's Bill of Rights," electronically retrieved at http://www.sfwa.org/contracts/bor1.htm.

2. Source: Debby Mayer, "From Royalties to Options: Five Thorns in the Book Contract," *Coda* (later called *Poets and Writers*), June/July 1983, electronically retrieved at http://www.pw.org/mag/articles/a8306-2.htm.

3. Sources: Debby Mayer, "From Royalties to Options: Five Thorns in the Book Contract," *Coda* (later called *Poets and Writers*), June/July 1983, electronically retrieved at http://www.pw.org/mag/articles/a8306-2.htm; and WritersMarket.com Encyclopedia, electronically retrieved at http://www.writersmarket.com/encyc/1.asp and www.writersmarket.com/encyc/f.asp.

4. Max Gunther, *The Luck Factor* (New York: Macmillan Publishing Co., 1977), pp. 88–93.

Chapter 5: The Seven Essential Habits of a Working Writer

1. Joseph Campbell, *The Power of Myth* (New York: Doubleday, 1988), p. 92.

2. Andrea Dworkin, "A Woman Writer and Pornography," first published in *San Francisco Review of Books*, Vol. VI, No. 5, March–April 1981, electronically retrieved at http://www.igc.org/Womensnet/dworkin/WarZoneChaptIIB.html.

3. Quotation by Isaac Asimov, electronically retrieved at http://ftp.chaven.com/pub/Literature/Asimov_Editorials/DISTRACTION.

4. James A. Michener, *The Novel* (New York: Random House, 1991), p. 123.

5. Melissa James, "Emotional Depth Workshop Number One," electronically accessed at http://www.melissajames.com/edworkshop1.html.

6. Sharon Ihle, "Goal-Setting for the Serious Writer," electronically retrieved at http://romance-central.com/Workshops/goalsetting.htm.

7. Andrea Dupree, "A New Kind of Resolve: Interview with Vineeta Vijayaraghavan," electronically retrieved at http://www.lighthousewriters.com/newslett/resolve.htm.

8. Levangie Grazer, "Conversations with a First Success Author," Writer's Digest Newsletter Archive, 2 August 2000, electronically retrieved at http://www.writersdigest.com/newsarchive/viewbydate.asp?date=8%2F2%2F2000.

Chapter 6: The Need for Speed: Writing in Overdrive

1. From an interview with Harlan Ellison, posted at http://harlanellison.com/text/chataol.txt.

2. Natalie Goldberg, *Writing Down the Bones* (Boston: Shambhala, 1998), p. 91.

3. Lawrence Block, *Telling Lies for Fun and Profit* (New York: Quill, 1981), p. 102.

4. Andrea Dupree, "A New Kind of Resolve: Interview with Vineeta Vijayaraghavan," electronically retrieved at http://www.lighthousewriters.com/newslett/resolve.htm.

5. Sean Stewart, "*Clouds End*: Author's Notes," electronically retrieved at http://www.seanstewart.org/ceNotes.php3.

Chapter 7: Professional Relationships

1. Jerry Gross, "What a Good Editor Will Do for You," interview with Beena Kamlani, *Fiction Writer*, July 1999, electronically retrieved at http://www.writersdigest.com/newsletter/editor_text.html.

2. First published in *Extro 1*, February/March 1982, electronically retrieved at http://www.ansible.demon.co.uk/writing/iwatson.html.

3. Patricia Nell Warren, "Secrets of Getting an Agent—and Doing Without One," electronically retrieved at http://www.wildcatpress.com/pat_se25.html.

4. Dean Koontz, "When Should You Put Yourself in an Agent's Hands?" from *The Writer's Digest Handbook of Novel Writing* by the editors of *Writer's Digest* (Cincinnati: Writer's Digest Books, 1992), pp. 221–222.

5. Stephen King, "Everything You Need to Know About Writing Successfully—in Ten Minutes," in *The Writer's Handbook*, ed. by Sylvia K. Burack, 1988 Edition (Boston: The Writer, Inc., 1988), p. 9.

6. Lewis A. Coser, Charles Kadushin, and Walter W. Powell, *Books: The Culture and Commerce of Publishing* (Chicago: University of Chicago Press, 1982), p. 362.

7. Lynne McNeill, "Book on Mothers and Sons Judged By Its Cover," University Wire, 5 May 1998.

8. Carol Brightman, "Bookend: Sweet Chaos, Fat Trip," *The New York Times*, 7 March 1999, electronically retrieved at http://www.nytimes.com/books/99/03/07/bookend/bookend.html.

Chapter 8: Generate Your Own Success

1. Robert J. Sawyer, "On Writing: Self-Promotion," electronically retrieved at http://www.sfwriter.com/ow11.htm.

2. James A. Michener, *The Novel* (New York: Random House, 1991), p. 107.

3. Martin J. Smith, "Are We There Yet?" electronically retrieved at http://www.writerswrite.com/journal/jan99/smith.htm.

Chapter 9: The Future of Writing

1. Forrester Research, Inc., press release, December 22, 2000, electronically retrieved at http://www.forrester.com/ER/Press/Release/0,1769,470,FF.html.

Chapter 10: Soul Survival

1. Susan K. Perry, Ph.D., "You Gotta Love Those Deadlines (Or Hate 'Em)," electronically retrieved at http://www.authormania.com/article1081.html.

2. Michael A. Banks, "Can Deadlines Ruin Your Writing?" electronically retrieved at http://w3.one.net/~banks/deadline.htm.

3. Alex Keegan, "Dealing With Rejection," *Writer's Write, the Internet Writing Journal*, October 1998, electronically retrieved at http://www.writerswrite.com/journal/oct98/keegan12.htm.

INDEX

ABOUT JIM DENNEY

Jim Denney is a freelance writer with more than sixty published books to his credit. He has been writing full time since 1989, and his written for adults and young readers, both fiction and nonfiction. Jim lives in California.

"The most important book I've ever done," he says, "is *Answers to Satisfy the Soul*, a nonfiction book that deals with twenty of life's most perplexing questions, from 'What is love?' to 'Does God exist?' It's not a book of fuzzy opinions and feel-good platitudes. These are real answers to the questions we all ask about life, and these answers are backed up by solid evidence. Writing that book was a life-altering experience for me."

Jim is also the author of the Timebenders series, a new science-fiction and fantasy series for readers ages 9 to 12. The first four books in the Timebenders series are *Battle Before Time*, *Doorway to Doom*, *Invasion of the Time Troopers*, and *Lost in Cydonia*.

Jim has also collaborated with numerous celebrities on their autobiographies, including supermodel Kim Alexis, *Star Trek* actress Grace Lee Whitney, and two Super Bowl champions, Reggie White and Bob Griese.

Visit Jim's website at http://www.denneybooks.com/. There you can learn about his latest books and download free articles on writing and other subjects. You can also e-mail Jim from his website. He would enjoy hearing from you.

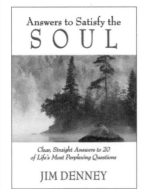

. . . *other great Quill Driver books on writing & publishing!*

$27.95 ($43.50 *Canada*)
• ISBN 1-884956-19-X.
(Replaces 2nd Edition, ISBN 1-884956-08-4)

The American Directory of
Writer's Guidelines, 3rd Edition
A Compilation of Information for Freelancers from More than 1,400 Magazine Editors and Book Publishers

— *Compiled and Edited by Brigitte M. Phillips, Susan D. Klassen   and Doris Hall*

Perhaps the best-kept secret in the publishing industry is that many publishers—both periodical publishers and book publishers—make available writer's guidelines to assist would-be contributors. Written by the staff at each publishing house, these guidelines help writers target their submissions to the exact needs of the individual publisher. *The American Directory of Writer's Guidelines* is a compilation of the actual writer's guidelines for more than 1,400 publishers.

❝ Unlike the entries in Writer's Market (Writer's Digest, annual), which edits the information supplied by publishers and prints it in a standard entry format, this new resource contains unedited self-descriptions of publications and publishing houses. ❞   —*Booklist*

$12.95 ($19.95 *Canada*)
• ISBN 1-884956-22-X

The Fast-Track Course
Nonfiction Book Proposal
— *by Stephen Blake Mettee*

Mettee, a seasoned book editor and publisher, cuts to the chase and provides simple, detailed instruction that allows anyone to write a professional book proposal and hear an editor say "Yes!"

❝ ...essential, succinct guideline. This is a must have reference book for writers ...sets the industry standard. ❞
—Bob Spear, *Heartland Reviews*

$14.95 ($22.50 *Canada*)
• ISBN 1-884956-17-3

Damn!
Why Didn't I Write That?
A
Book-of-the-Month Club,
Quality Paperback Book Club,
and
Writer's Digest Book Club
Selection!

How Ordinary People are Raking in $100,000.00... Or More Writing Nonfiction Books & How You Can Too!
— *by Marc McCutcheon*

More nonfiction books are breaking the 100,000-copy sales barrier than ever before. Amateur writers, housewives, and even high school dropouts have cashed in with astonishingly simple best-sellers. This guide, by best-selling author Marc McCutcheon, shows the reader how to get in on the action.

❝Comprehensive and engaging this book will save you time, energy, and frustration.❞
—Michael Larsen, literary agent, author

Available at better brick and mortar bookstores, online bookstores, at
QuillDriverBooks.com or by calling toll-free 1-800-497-4909

. . . other great Quill Driver books on writing & publishing!

The ABCs of
Writing for Children
114 Children's Authors and Illustrators Talk About the Art, the Business, the Craft & the Life of Writing Children's Literature
— *by Elizabeth Koehler-Pentacoff*

In *The ABCs of Writing for Children* you'll learn the many 'do's and don'ts' for creating children's books. You'll see that what works for one author may not work for the next.

$14.95 ($22.95 *Canada*)
• ISBN 1-884956-28-9

66 ...a thorough, complete, entertaining guide to writing for children—more alpha to omega than *ABCs*. I wish there was such a volume for every aspect of my life! 99
—Karen Cushman, author of *Catherine, Called Birdy*

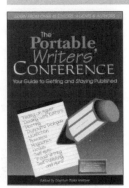

The Portable Writers' Conference
Your Guide to Getting and *Staying* Published
— *Edited by Stephen Blake Mettee*

Over 45 editors, authors, and agents advise writers on the art and business of writing and getting published. Chapters range from how to write a dynamite love scene to how to find an agent.

❝ Here is the perfect way to attend a writers' conference... ❞
— *Library Journal*

$19.95 ($29.95 *Canada*) • ISBN 1-884956-23-8

Feminine Wiles
Creative Techniques for Writing Women's Feature Stories That *Sell*
— *by Donna Elizabeth Boetig*

From *Feminine Wiles*: ...commit yourself. You are going to write stories of women's struggles and joys. You are going to discover information that changes the lives of readers. You are going to predict trends and you may even create a few of your own. You are going to look out into the world to see what's happening and take what you find deep within yourself to figure out what it all means—for you, and your readers.

$14.95 ($21.95 *Canada*)
• ISBN 1-884956-02-5

66 More valuable than a dozen writer's workshops or journalism courses. If you're interested in developing a successful career as a freelance writer for women's magazines, read *Feminine Wiles*—and get to work. 99
— Jane Farrell, Senior Editor *McCall's*